CONTEMPORARY CANADIAN ISSUES

Contemporary Canadian Issues is a partnership between the Bill Graham Centre for Contemporary International History and Dundurn Press to bring together the latest scholarship, from inside and outside academe, on current issues of concern to an informed Canadian general readership. General Editors for the series are John English and Jack Cunningham.

CONTEMPORARY CANADIAN ISSUES

Australia and Canada in Afghanistan

AUSTRALIA, CANADA, and IRAQ

AUSTRALIA, CANADA, and IRAQ

Perspectives on an Invasion

EDITED BY

RAMESH THAKUR | JACK CUNNINGHAM

bill graham centre | CONTEMPORARY INTERNATIONAL HISTORY

DUNDURN

A J. PATRICK BOYER BOOK

TORONTO

Project editor: Dominic Farrell
Copy editor: Natalie Meditsky
Interior design: Laura Boyle
Cover design: Laura Boyle
Cover image: © adrenalinapura/ 123RF.com
Printer: Webcom

Library and Archives Canada Cataloguing in Publication

Australia, Canada, and Iraq : perspectives on an invasion / edited by Ramesh Thakur and Jack Cunningham.

(Contemporary Canadian issues)
Includes index.
Issued in print and electronic formats.
ISBN 978-1-4597-3151-6 (pbk.).--ISBN 978-1-4597-3152-3 (pdf).--
ISBN 978-1-4597-3153-0 (epub)

1. Iraq War, 2003-2011. 2. Iraq War, 2003-2011--Diplomatic history. 3. Iraq War, 2003-2011--Participation, Australian. 4. Australia--Foreign relations--United States. 5. United States--Foreign relations--Australia. 6. Canada--Foreign relations--United States. 7. United States--Foreign relations--Canada. I. Thakur, Ramesh Chandra, 1948-, editor II. Cunningham, Jack (Historian), editor III. Series: Contemporary Canadian issues

DS79.76.A98 20155   956.7044'3   C2015-900545-0
                                                C2015-900546-9

1 2 3 4 5   19 18 17 16 15

  Canada

We acknowledge the support of the **Canada Council for the Arts** and the **Ontario Arts Council** for our publishing program. We also acknowledge the financial support of the **Government of Canada** through the **Canada Book Fund** and **Livres Canada Books**, and the **Government of Ontario** through the **Ontario Book Publishing Tax Credit** and the **Ontario Media Development Corporation**.

Care has been taken to trace the ownership of copyright material used in this book. The author and the publisher welcome any information enabling them to rectify any references or credits in subsequent editions.

— *J. Kirk Howard, President*

The publisher is not responsible for websites or their content unless they are owned by the publisher.

Printed and bound in Canada.

VISIT US AT
Dundurn.com | @dundurnpress | Facebook.com/dundurnpress | Pinterest.com/dundurnpress

Dundurn
3 Church Street, Suite 500
Toronto, Ontario, Canada
M5E 1M2

In memory of Malcolm Fraser

TABLE OF CONTENTS

INTRODUCTION

Jack Cunningham and Ramesh Thakur

The two long wars in Afghanistan and Iraq have now come to an end, at least insofar as the involvement of Western troops is concerned. Most Americans regarded Afghanistan as a war of necessity, forced upon the United States by an armed attack in the form of terrorist attacks in New York and Washington on September 11, 2001. By contrast, many Americans and most international observers viewed Iraq as a war of choice, whose justification, conduct, and consequences remain matters of intense controversy. Between them, the two wars shaped many of the contours of twenty-first-century international relations to date. They helped to define the nature of contemporary warfare and armed conflict; accelerated the shift of power, wealth, and influence away from the U.S.-led Western bloc; brought an end to the post–Cold War era of unchallengeable U.S. dominance of world affairs; and shook the foundations of the post-1945 multilateral order centred on the United Nations (U.N.). In addition, Iraq — much more than Afghanistan — inflicted considerable reputational damage on the United States with respect to its commitment to prevailing human rights standards and its competence at administering and rebuilding a defeated, occupied, and war-torn country. Not the least because of these lasting consequences, the two conflicts also compelled many long-standing U.S. allies to re-examine the bases of their relationships with the United States.

This volume originated in a conversation at the bar in Toronto's InterContinental Hotel, at the close of a 2012 conference assessing the Canadian and Australian experiences in the recent conflict in Afghanistan. The conference was a joint endeavour of the Centre for Contemporary International History (since renamed the Bill Graham Centre for Contemporary International History) at the University of Toronto's Trinity College and Munk School of Global Affairs, the Asia-Pacific College of Diplomacy at the Australian National University, and the Canadian Forces College. Looking back at the day's events, Jack Cunningham, John English, Bill Graham, Ramesh Thakur, and William Maley agreed to arrange a follow-up conference on the Australian and Canadian decisions to respectively take part in and stand aside from the 2003 invasion of Iraq. They also agreed to proceed with two volumes of conference papers as part of the current series, with Maley and Cunningham to edit the volume on Afghanistan, and Thakur and Cunningham the one on Iraq. A year later, in Canberra for the conference on Iraq, they nailed down the details for this compilation.

These volumes are rooted in a shared interest in the similarities and differences between Australia and Canada in their policies toward recent international conflicts and their foreign and security policies more broadly. Both countries are parliamentary democracies along the Westminster model, with obvious cultural ties to and affinities with Great Britain as well as each other. Both are "middle" powers. And both have complicated relationships with their American ally. In the Australian case this is defined above all by distance, in the Canadian one by intimate proximity and profound economic interdependence. The two volumes of conference papers in this series can be seen as complementary, one dealing with a case where the two governments made essentially the same decision, and the other with an instance where they clearly did not.

In trying to make sense of the Australian and Canadian decisions regarding Iraq, and indeed of the invasion itself, we are inevitably constrained by the limited vistas of our historical moment. After all, a decade's distance is very little in the historian's schema, and affords us relatively limited perspectives. That said, it is not too soon to draw some provisional conclusions and to pose questions that can be answered more confidently once the relevant documentary record is more comprehensive than it now is. And for that, we do have some material with which to work.

The Chilcot and Hutton inquiries in Britain have provided some documentary evidence regarding British, and to some degree American, perceptions and decisions.[1] The invasion and its aftermath have been chronicled in a number of solid journalistic accounts.[2] Other books have made some use of interviews to treat the American and British decision-making processes.[3] Some have examined the impact of the war on the international normative order,[4] and on the state of nuclear arms control.[5] And a growing body of memoir literature provides grist for the scholar's mill. Among major American participants, George W. Bush, Donald Rumsfeld, Dick Cheney, and Condoleezza Rice have given us their versions of events, as has Tony Blair on the British side.[6] As for the Australian and Canadian experiences, we now have the recollections of John Howard and Jean Chrétien.[7] There have been occasional articles and book chapters assessing the Canadian or Australian decision, but not, we believe, much by way of comparison, and no volume like this.

Most of the chapters here are reworkings of papers presented at the 2013 Canberra conference, though there are exceptions. As noted below, the chapters by Howard and Chrétien are reprints of addresses delivered in Sydney and Toronto respectively. In addition, Kim Nossal was slated to take part in the Canberra conference, although circumstances prevented it. We have, however, included a chapter that is based on what he would have said had he been present.

We have also attempted to incorporate the perspectives of Australian and Canadian policy-makers. John Howard is represented by a speech to the Lowy Institute for International Policy, and Jean Chrétien by remarks at a Graham Centre conference marking the fiftieth anniversary of the election of Lester Pearson's government. In these selections, they defend their respective decisions. Howard situates his actions in the context of the 9/11 attacks and the sense of vulnerability to terrorist attack they engendered. He concedes errors on the part of the coalition powers regarding intelligence on weapons of mass destruction (WMDs) and a failure to plan for the aftermath of the invasion, but is quick to point out there was widespread agreement across the Australian political spectrum that Saddam Hussein possessed WMDs. In response to critics of military action without U.N. approval, he points to the precedent of NATO's intervention in Kosovo and draws a contrast between those who, in his view, make a fetish of multilateralism and those who believe the nation-state must reserve the right to act independently *in extremis*. Chrétien stresses what he views as the patent inadequacy, even at the time, of evidence for Saddam's possession of WMDs, and the dangers of a global order in which regime change without U.N. approval became permissible practice.

To the reflections of these decision-makers, we have added excerpts from a round table on "Parliamentary Democracies at War" held at the Canberra conference. Here, the Honourable Bill Graham (Canadian foreign minister at the time of the invasion, and subsequently defence minister); the Right Honourable Malcolm Fraser, former Australian prime minister; and Paul Barratt, Australia's former secretary of defence, reflect on the Australian and Canadian decisions, the processes by which they were made, and potential lessons for the future.

As for the scholarly contributions to this book, they are unapologetically eclectic in approach and viewpoint. There is considerable variation among our authors in methodology and focus, although it is fair to say that all are, broadly speaking, empiricists, steering clear of the wider shores of theory. The contributors differ among themselves over the legality, morality, and prudence of invading Iraq, although none can bring themselves to defend the manner in which Saddam's overthrow and the reconstruction of Iraq were actually conducted, and the judgment of almost all is negative in varying degrees.

Several of them take a broad view of the invasion, not confined to the Canadian and Australian experiences. Ramesh Thakur's verdict on the invasion is unsparing. He depicts it as rooted in deliberate misrepresentation of the salient facts and as a catastrophe by every measure, including its own terms. He argues that the invasion and its aftermath served only to inflame jihadist sentiments and benefit Iran regionally and China globally, while dividing the United States from its European allies. He concludes that George W. Bush and his coalition partners gravely undermined the international norm against aggressive war and damaged the U.N. system to boot. But the United Nations, he writes, would have been discredited completely had it been coerced into bestowing its imprimatur on the invasion, and has been largely vindicated by subsequent developments.

Like Thakur's contribution, Roger Coate's piece about the invasion's impact on the U.S.-U.N. relationship is critical of the aggressive American exceptionalism and unilateralism associated with the second Bush administration. He contends that the Bush administration not only undermined the authority and effectiveness of the United Nations, but hampered the pursuit of its own goals in the process. U.S. and U.N. interests are more complementary than Bush administration officials knew, he continues, and the deliberate marginalization of the United Nations impaired the reconstruction of Iraq, the stabilization of the region, and the post-invasion containment of terrorism. In Coate's account, the United Nations emerges as perhaps the archetypal creation of modern American liberalism, and its discrediting as an instrument of global governance a self-inflicted blow of the first order.

Since the Australian and Canadian responses to the Anglo-American call for support diverged, it is that divergence that must be the focus of any comparative assessment. And here our authors differ in emphasis, and sometimes substance. Some emphasize deeply rooted variations in national experience and different positions on the globe and in the international system, or the dynamics of the respective Australian and Canadian alliances with the United States. Others give more weight to contingencies such as the immediate domestic political climate, the predilections of the individual leader, or the details of how the Bush administration went about the task of coalition building.

For example, Hugh White situates John Howard's decision within Australia's long history of involvement in the wars of its imperial or quasi-imperial patrons. Given the territory it must defend, the proximity of potentially threatening powers, and distance from its powerful protectors (first Britain and then America), Australia, he argues, has joined "other people's wars" from the Boer War onward, wanting to demonstrate its reliability as an ally in order to ensure that its allies remember and offer assistance in its own times of peril. Even after Richard Nixon moved to wind down the Cold War in Asia, White continues, Australia strove to assist the United States further afield, including in the Persian Gulf. He presents Australia as fearful of abandonment by its imperial protector, with Canada fearful of entrapment instead. Not having had to worry about the defence of its own neighbourhood since the United States asserted its responsibility for the security of the western hemisphere, Canada has tended instead to worry about being dragged into ill-judged military adventures, remote from its own interests, by its far more powerful neighbour.

Charles Sampford's analysis is similar in some ways. He notes that Australia and Canada have both historically sought to maintain independence from the United States and Britain. But over time it has emerged that Australia is more preoccupied with demonstrating independence from Britain, and Canada from the United States, largely as a function of geography. Region, Sampford argues, has been important in shaping Canadian decisions about military interventions abroad. A North Atlantic Treaty Organization (NATO) member, Canada took part in NATO's action in Kosovo but felt free to say no to Iraq; indeed, it did so under the same prime minister. Australia's leaders, on the other hand, feel compelled to demonstrate solidarity with the United States wherever the opportunity and obligation arise, geography notwithstanding.

William Maley considers Australia's combination of distance from and dependence upon the United States, and concludes that it would have been a surprise had John Howard not agreed to send troops to Iraq. In an asymmetrical alliance, he writes, the less-dependent power necessarily enjoys much more latitude in deciding when and where to come to the aid of its more dependent ally. Moreover, the latter cannot bank goodwill for past services; in honouring the perceived obligations of alliance, the salient question is always, "What have you done for me lately?" As a result, it is necessarily hard for Australia to pass up any opportunity to demonstrate its solidarity with America (harder, certainly, than it is for Canada). Maley does not look at alliance dynamics in isolation from historical context, however. He draws our attention to the 1999 East Timor crisis, when Timorese civilians and Australian peacekeepers were attacked by militias working hand in glove with the Indonesian military. Only after a period of apparent wavering, and indications by some American officials that the matter was not of direct concern to Washington, did the Clinton administration offer assistance. From this point forward, Maley speculates, Australia decided to yoke itself militarily more closely to the United States rather than risk isolation.

In assessing the divergent Australian and Canadian decisions, it can be tempting to move from a healthy awareness of their different histories and political cultures to a glib and reductive essentialism that attributes explanatory power to unchanging national character. This would be defined in terms of Australian "warriors" versus Canadian "peacekeepers," the former having more of an affinity for the hawks in the Bush administration, without whom there would have been no invasion at all. John Blaxland's contribution provides a healthy corrective against following such reasoning too far. He assesses the responses to 9/11 and the policies toward Iraq of both Republicans and Democrats, concluding that had the 2000 presidential election ended differently, Al Gore would have acted much as George W. Bush did in substance, although in a more emollient and consensual manner that would have raised fewer Canadian hackles and elicited at least a token contribution. The Canadian and Australian decisions did, he points out, reflect the preponderance of opinion within the governing party and its electoral coalition. But this was shaped by immediate contingencies and was hardly the same as deeply rooted national character, insofar as in both cases the governing party changed within a few years (though in neither case was Iraq a major electoral issue).

Taking a somewhat different view, John English argues that, at least in the Canadian case, national and even partisan traditions do matter. He situates the Chrétien government's situation within the longer history of Liberal governments' contending with issues of war and peace, with the sentiments of their own natural political coalition tending to make involvement in military adventures electorally problematic.

As our inclusion of statements by Howard and Chrétien indicates, we are mindful of the importance of the personalities and proclivities of the individual leaders, and that is reflected in the scholarly contributions. While there is not complete unanimity on the statecraft of either Chrétien or Howard, the former fares somewhat better in the eyes of most of our authors.

Hugh White sees Howard's own personal response to 9/11 as crucial to his actions regarding Iraq, and tends to agree with him that his mistaken assumptions about WMDs and the likely course of the invasion were widely shared across the spectrum. On the other hand, Charles Sampford takes Howard to task for claiming that there was and is widespread disagreement about the legality of invasion without a further U.N. Security Council resolution expressly authorizing the use of force. Sampford discerns a clear consensus on its illegality among serious students of international law and the laws of war, though he notes the existence of dissenting voices in Australian public life. He also chastises Howard and his colleagues for taking at face value the unqualified British and American intelligence estimates that argued Saddam had WMDs, rather than pressing for sustained and critical evaluation of the pertinent evidence.

Jean Chrétien was widely taken to task by the press and his political opponents in the run-up to the invasion for failing to stake out a consistent and coherent position. Timothy Sayle contends that not only did this hold Chrétien to a standard few leaders could meet in the face of rapidly changing events and uncertain information, but it was part of a deliberate strategy on Chrétien's part. By adopting an ambiguous stance in the months prior to the invasion, he writes, Chrétien maintained his freedom of manoeuvre in the event that the international consensus for military action that he considered a *sine qua non* for Canadian participation ever materialized. At the same time, he paved the way for an ultimate refusal by indicating to Bush and others that without U.N. approval, Canada would not take part in an invasion. The ambiguity of Chrétien's position, concludes Sayle, allowed him to remain a participant in the international debate over the merits of military action as opposed to continued inspections, and in the effort to reach a compromise on a further resolution in the United Nations.

Jack Cunningham's broadly similar analysis adds that Canadian diplomacy was initially directed toward supporting Secretary of State Colin Powell's efforts to make maximum use of multilateral instruments, and took hope from Powell's statement that full compliance by Saddam Hussein with the relevant U.N. disarmament resolutions would in itself constitute regime change. Cunningham also reminds us that the last-ditch Canadian effort at the United Nations (intended to be more discreet than it turned out to be) was a genuine attempt to forge a compromise between two sides seen as equally intransigent, and that Canadian statements made it quite plain that the onus of compliance was on Saddam, whose failure to disarm had triggered the crisis in the first instance.

Kim Nossal compares Chrétien's actions not to Howard's but to those of a previous Canadian prime minister, Brian Mulroney, when he declined Ronald Reagan's invitation to official participation in the Strategic Defense Initiative. In the process, Nossal compels reassessment of one of the truisms of Canadian-American relations — that the tone and manner in which Canadians reject an American overture is crucial to maintaining cordial relations. As he observes, Mulroney was tactful and polite in his refusal. Chrétien was markedly less so in his, and indeed announced it to a televised session of the House of Commons, to the exuberant braying of his own members of Parliament in a distinctly raucous atmosphere and to the evident discomfort of the Cabinet minister charged with ensuring Canadian-American amity (though how much of this Chrétien anticipated and might have been expected to control is unclear). There was a short-term difference, Nossal writes, with relations between Mulroney and Reagan remaining friendly while those between the Chrétien government and the Bush White House deteriorated markedly in the short run. Over time, however, the logic of institutionalized interdependence trumped personal pique, and relations resumed a businesslike tenor, if not a particularly affectionate one.

Of course leaders do not lead as they choose, but are inevitably constrained by the electoral climate of the day and what public opinion is prepared to tolerate. The papers here take this into consideration in assessing both the Australian and Canadian domestic contexts. In the Australian case, Ian McAllister sees public opinion as having been reasonable and pragmatic, judging actions in terms of their success or lack thereof. In his analysis, the Australian public was inclined to support Howard's decision to participate in the invasion out of a concern over the dangers of terrorism involving WMDs, with support for maintenance of the American alliance a strong secondary motivation. Once the claims about WMDs proved ill-founded, the secondary rationale proved too weak a reed to sustain public support, and it gradually eroded, not least because of effective attacks by the opposition Labor Party.

Indeed, as William Maley points out, in the short term Howard's position proved sound domestic politics. Labor leader Mark Latham's vehement attacks on President Bush were widely viewed as undignified and over the top, and backfired quite conspicuously in the 2004 election, during which the electorate seems to have been broadly supportive of Howard's position. Howard prevailed in 2004 but was defeated in the next election, in 2007. While the situation in Iraq had indeed deteriorated between the two elections, Howard's defeat rested on other causes.

As for the Canadian situation, Sayle notes that polling data showed widespread public opposition to Canadian participation, particularly in Chrétien's home province of Quebec, but also notes that public sentiment was in line with what the government already proposed to do, and in that sense was not a determinant of policy.

Jack Cunningham cautions that Canadian public opinion was perhaps less hostile to war than it might have seemed, and might well have moved in a different direction given a clear lead by the government. It also seems to have distinguished between the merits of overthrowing Saddam and those of bowing to American pressure to take part, after a somewhat clumsy intervention by the American ambassador to Canada that allowed Chrétien to frame the issue as one of standing up for Canada's right to its own foreign policy.

In any event, the debate over the merits of the invasion may no longer be the stuff of headlines, but it has not fully died away in either Australia or Canada. As English points out, in Canada, Chrétien's refusal is now widely regarded as one of the defining moments of his premiership. And in Australia, Malcolm Fraser is one of a number of eminent Australians advocating a public inquiry into the war and Howard's decision. There is no reason for the debate to end in either country, and every reason for it to continue. Presumably the voices in this book will be heard as part of it.

NOTES

1. See www.iraqinquiry.org.uk and webarchive.nationalarchives.gov.uk/20090128221546/http://www.the-hutton-inquiry.org.uk/content/hearing_trans.htm (both accessed March 16, 2014).
2. See, for example, George Packer, *The Assassins' Gate: America in Iraq* (New York: Farrar, Strauss and Giroux, 2005); Thomas E. Ricks, *Fiasco: The American Military Adventure in Iraq* (New York: Penguin Press, 2006); Michael R. Gordon and Bernard E. Trainor, *Cobra II: The Inside Story of the Invasion and Occupation of Iraq* (New York: Pantheon, 2006); and Rajiv Chandrasekaran, *Imperial Life in the Emerald City: Inside Baghdad's Green Zone* (New York: Knopf, 2006).
3. See Bob Woodward, *Plan of Attack* (New York: Simon & Schuster, 2004); and Peter Stothard, *Thirty Days: Tony Blair and the Test of History* (London: HarperCollins, 2003).
4. See Ramesh Thakur and Waheguru Pal Singh Sidhu, eds., *The Iraq Crisis and World Order: Structural, Institutional and Normative Challenges* (Tokyo: United Nations University Press, 2006).
5. See Waheguru Pal Singh Sidhu and Ramesh Thakur, eds., *Arms Control After Iraq: Normative and Operational Challenges* (Tokyo: United Nations University Press, 2006).
6. See George W. Bush, *Decision Points* (New York: Crown Publishers, 2010); Donald Rumsfeld, *Known and Unknown: A Memoir* (New York: Sentinel, 2011);

Dick Cheney with Liz Cheney, *In My Time: A Personal and Political Memoir* (New York: Threshold Editions, 2011); Condoleezza Rice, *No Higher Honor: A Memoir of My Years in Washington* (New York: Crown Publishers, 2011); and Tony Blair, *A Journey: My Political Life* (London: Hutchinson, 2010).

7.   John Howard, *Lazarus Rising: A Personal and Political Autobiography* (Melbourne: Harper, 2010); and Jean Chrétien, *My Years as Prime Minister* (Toronto: Knopf Canada, 2007).

1

STAYING OUT OF IRAQ

Reflections by the Right
Honourable Jean Chrétien

These remarks by Jean Chrétien are excerpted from an appearance he made at an April 9, 2013, conference marking the fiftieth anniversary of the election of the government headed by Lester B. Pearson, sponsored by the Bill Graham Centre for Contemporary International History and held at the University of Toronto's Trinity College. Rather than delivering a prepared text, Chrétien chose to answer questions from the audience. The event was moderated by the Honourable Bill Graham, former Canadian foreign minister and minister of defence.

Question:

I wanted to ask you about deciding not to go into Iraq, and what happened at that particular time. You broke with the U.S. on that, and I thought that was a very important moment for Canadian history. I wanted to hear your reflections about how you came to that decision, what was going on in the back channels, and all the things that you couldn't say while you were in office. [*Audience laughter*] Maybe you can tell us a little bit more about what was going on in the background and the negotiations and the pressure.

Chrétien:

We had time to reflect because there were rumours that they were planning and thinking of invading Iraq. But first, after September 11th, one night I was watching TV and I saw old Senator Helms, who was the head of the

Foreign Affairs Committee of the Senate in the United States. It was one of those nights where you don't know what you're doing, you are a bit tired, and you flip from one channel to the other. And I saw a politician, so I stopped. When I saw him, he said, "Now we have a good reason to go to Iraq." Two days after September 11th. And I knew that Saddam had nothing to do with September 11th. It was religious radicals that he had fought against. When there was a war between Iran and Iraq, Saddam had fought the same mentality. So for me, I thought it was a bit strange. It opened up a red light for me. I became very suspicious of what was being debated. But there was debate.

And President Bush, at the summit we had in Kananaskis, mentioned that to me, and we agreed to discuss that at the meeting that we were supposed to have, that we had eventually in September [2002] in Detroit. We were to look at the problem of, you know, the border problem we had there and find a solution. And he asked to have a quite unusual meeting. It's not that it's not right, but I was very surprised that he had asked to see me alone. It went an hour and a half, and he wanted to discuss the possibility of a war in Iraq. I had read all sorts of documents, and I read them at night always. Rather than watch the news at night, I would read and discover. Watching the news at night is terrible. You don't sleep! [*Audience laughter*] So you just get informed in the morning. So at nine o'clock I close everything, I go up to my office, and I will read these things.

And, you know, I said to him at that moment, "It's very clear for me." If you reflect, I mentioned to you the problem I had with listening to Senator Helms. And I said to him, "My information is hard. I'm not confirming that — I would not be with you." I said, "The policy is not to be with you if you don't have the support of the U.N., so you need to go to the U.N." And he said yes.

Because the week after in South Africa I discussed it with Tony Blair, who had urged me to go. But it was amazing: Blair was using the argument that we had to get rid of Saddam Hussein; President Bush was talking about weapons of mass destruction, which is a different problem. And I had said to Tony Blair before the meeting I had in Detroit, you know, I went and he said to me, "Jean, you have to be with us. We have to get rid of Saddam Hussein. He's a terrible dictator."

So I said to Blair, "Tony, if we were in the business of replacing leaders we don't like, who is next? I hope it's not me!" [*Audience laughter*] No, no.

But I thought about it. And he argued. And I said, "If we're in the business of replacing people we don't like and we're in South Africa, why don't you come here in Zimbabwe next door and replace the leader Mugabe?"

And he said, "Oh, Jean. Saddam and Mugabe, it's not the same."

And I said, "Of course it's not the same. Mugabe has no oil!" [*Audience laughter*] And for a long time after that, we didn't have [*inaudible*]. But I said, "You go, and if you have the U.N., I might be able to go. You have to convince George to go to the U.N." He was planning not to go to the U.N.

And Tony went to Washington. He convinced the president to try to have the resolution of the U.N. So that was my contribution, I guess: to try to get the U.N.

When I was with George, about an hour and a half — it was very short — I said, "If you have the U.N., I would be probably with you. But to have the U.N., you need better proof of weapons of mass destruction."

And he said, "Oh, but it's clear."

"No, no, no," I said. "I read a lot. I read a lot of documentation coming from different departments." And I said, "I'm not convinced." I wrote about it that there was in my mind not enough proof to convince a judge at a municipal court in Shawinigan. And I knew the guy, you don't! [*Audience laughter*] So I said, "I'm not convinced."

And he said to me, "Okay, I will send my people to convince you."

And I said, "No, I don't like that. I cannot be briefed with information from your government. My people have to brief me on that. We have personnel and security and so on who are very competent, and I don't want it."

And so he said, "Fine, I will go to the U.N." because he had discussed that with Tony Blair. So after half an hour, we had nothing else to talk [*sic*]. We talked about baseball, football, which is a subject that we share a lot of interest, the two of us. It would always surprise him that I knew so much about football and baseball.

And I had talked in a speech I made in Chicago in the February just before. And that was a very important speech where I clearly stated the position that there was a need for the U.N., and you have to proceed the way they want it. And when the day came to go to war, I said no. It was forty-five seconds in the House of Commons. People complained that I did not make a long speech. Usually you don't need a long speech. You say no. [*Audience laughter*] I had to decide it very rapidly, because others were joining, and we were not there, but they were waiting for us. So that morning I received a phone call from — I know from the information I received, from Great Britain, and they wondered what we answered. And the way it was presented to me I found it a bit irritating, at two o'clock. We said no in a forty-five-second statement in the House of Commons.

I did not call the president to tell him. You know, he was extremely civilized about it. He made his pitch to me, but he was not insisting very much. I had more discussion with Tony Blair than I had with him.

Graham:

But you also had a lot of conversations with [Vicente] Fox, with the president of Chile [Ricardo Lagos Escobar]. And remember, people were coming to you as the leader. They were constantly coming to you. I was talking to foreign ministers; you were talking to the leaders.

Chrétien:

Yes. Well, we were on the Security Council going to December. We were repaid by Mexico and Chile joining the Security Council. But President Fox and the president of Chile were new, and they felt the pressure. I was the old man around, so they were consulting me. And in the draft, and we were still pushing after the first of January, we believed we were no more on the Security Council. [Paul]Heinbecker, our ambassador, who was very good, was still consulted by his colleagues there and he was coming here to us. So we got involved in trying to find solutions up to the time that it was called. And it is the only thing that President Bush said to me that was irritating a bit, for him.

He said, "Do whatever you want, but leave the others alone."

I said, "Yes, but I return my phone calls."

So we were talking. Not to be with the Americans at this time was a very unusual and, for some people, unpleasant situation.

Graham:

But I think it was fair — Tom Axworthy said prime ministers will be judged as to whether they were on the right side of the big questions in history — and I think it's fair to say Canadians today are grateful that you made that decision to be on the right side.

[*Applause*]

2

WE WERE RIGHT TO INVADE IRAQ

The Right Honourable John Howard[1]

I am grateful for the opportunity to revisit the most controversial foreign policy decision taken by my government in the almost twelve years it held office. Before tackling the substance of that issue, can I pay tribute to the bravery and professionalism of the men and women of the Australian Defence Force (ADF) who served in Iraq? Theirs was a dangerous mission; mercifully, Australia suffered no battle deaths, but I am mindful of the impact the operation had on their lives, most particularly those who suffered injuries.

I left the prime-ministership of this country with a lasting respect for our men and women in uniform. They are an ornament to Australia. Thankfully we did not repeat the shame of forty years ago, when many of our returning men from Vietnam were the target of some who disagreed with that involvement. Although the level of engagement was vastly different in Iraq, on this occasion dissent was solely directed toward those responsible — the political leaders of the time — and not the men and women who had carried out their orders.

CONTEXT: THE UNITED STATES AFTER 9/11

Context, they say, is everything. It certainly is in assessing the wisdom of Australia joining the "coalition of the willing" in Iraq ten years ago.

Early in 2003, the world still lived in the shadow of 11 September 2001; the United States had entered a new phase of profound vulnerability and remained preoccupied with when and where the next terrorist attack on its homeland would occur; the notion of an Arab Spring was unthinkable; and here in Australia we had just felt the full force of Islamic extremism in Bali almost as if it had been on our own soil, and we had begun to embrace tough new anti-terrorism laws designed to smother homegrown threats to our peaceful society.

The 9/11 attacks challenged our normal understanding of international threats and conflict. They had not inaugurated a conventional war, no ultimatum had been delivered, and no armies had rolled across borders, as they had done as recently as 1991 when Saddam Hussein invaded Kuwait. It was a world away from the Cold War, when mutually assured destruction spawned a nervous peace. This was new and different, because of its scale, impact, and sheer audacity. The stunning success of the attacks unnerved Americans and many others.

Reflecting that new dimension, an American president said, "The greatest threat to U.S. and global security is no longer a nuclear exchange between nations but nuclear terrorism by violent extremists." Another said, "Our greatest fear is that terrorists will find a shortcut to their mad ambitions when an outlaw regime supplies them with the technologies to kill on a massive scale." When uttering those words, the two presidents were expressing a common American dread, doubtless entertained by millions of their fellow countrymen and women. The first statement belonged to President Barack Obama, the second to former president George W. Bush. They spoke eight years apart, but their respective words could easily have been spoken by the other, and from the same platform, as they expressed a like fear.

The terrorist attacks of 11 September ["9/11" in the American dating convention] 2001 were a greater violation of the American homeland than even Pearl Harbor. They produced among Americans an unaccustomed sense of vulnerability, which would last years. Vulnerability is a counterintuitive concept when it comes to the United States. How can the most powerful nation the world has seen ever feel vulnerable? Yet it did after September 2001 — and also, importantly for Australia, commensurately grateful for friends. Only in the absence of further attacks on America at home has that vulnerability gradually dissipated.

Yet, central to a proper understanding of why the United States acted as she did over Iraq, and the implications that had for a close ally such as Australia, is to recognize that vulnerability. Americans thought their country would be attacked by terrorists again, and soon. Many in the United States asked, "Why wouldn't a rogue state like Iraq supply dangerous weapons to terrorist groups? Why wouldn't there be further plane hijackings? And the next time a hijacked plane headed for a tall building, might it contain a chemical, biological, or even nuclear weapon?" Such sentiments might seem exaggerated today, but they did not in the United States in the wake of 9/11.

That no further attacks took place either during the remaining seven years of the Bush presidency or the more than four years of President Obama's occupancy of the White House is greatly to the credit of both men. Little of that credit has been forthcoming. The anxiety of the early years has given way to a growing complacency that it will not happen again.

So much of the narrative about Iraq has focused on what has been depicted as an ill-founded obsession regarding that country by George Bush and those close to him. Certainly, Iraq was never far from their minds. Within hours of the 9/11 attacks, Australia's then ambassador to the United States, Michael Thawley, said to me that he thought Iraq would be back on the agenda for the Americans.

Yet to understand the American mindset about Iraq is to recognize that if there was an obsession about Iraq, it was a bipartisan one.

To the Clinton administration, removing Saddam was unfinished business. On Bill Clinton's watch, the Iraq Liberation Act was passed; it expressly called for regime change in Baghdad. In 1998, President Bill Clinton declared that "the world had to deal with the kind of threat Iraq poses, a rogue state with weapons of mass destruction, ready to use them or pass them to terrorists, who travel the world among us unnoticed." That could easily have been George Bush or his defense secretary, Donald Rumsfeld. The belief that Saddam was a threat to the region and beyond, and should be removed, crossed the aisle in American politics. It was little wonder, therefore, that senior figures in the Obama administration, such as Hillary Clinton and Joe Biden, voted in favour of military action against Saddam when they were senators.

AUSTRALIA JOINS THE COALITION OF THE WILLING

Australia's decision to join the coalition in Iraq was a product both of our belief at the time that Iraq had weapons of mass destruction (WMDs), and the nature of our relationship and alliance with the United States. I never believed that Saddam was involved in the 9/11 attacks, nor did President Bush — or, to my knowledge, U.K. prime minister Tony Blair. Such a claim never formed part of the public case put forward by the Howard government for our Iraqi involvement. Some sections of the U.S. administration may have had this conviction. It did not influence the Australian decision-making process.

He may not have been involved in 9/11, but Saddam had a grisly track record. He had used poison gas against the Iranians and the Kurds; gave $25,000 to the family of every Palestinian suicide bomber; was classified by the U.S. State Department as a state sponsor of terrorism; was responsible for up to one hundred thousand dead in the al-Anfal campaign of 1988 against the Kurds; his 1991 campaign of reprisals against the Shia claimed fifty thousand lives; and between six hundred thousand and one million died in the Iraq-Iran war (1980–88). His human rights record was unspeakable. The claims of some that life in Iraq was better under Saddam than it has been since defy belief.

The belief that Saddam had weapons of mass destruction was near universal. As the Flood Inquiry put it, "Prior to 19 March 2003, the only government in the world that claimed that Iraq was not working on, and did not have, biological and chemical weapons or prohibited missile systems was the government of Saddam Hussein."

The Australian Labor Party

Critics of what my government did, ranging from President Jacques Chirac of France to Kevin Rudd of the Australian Labor Party (ALP), all averred that Saddam had WMDs. The latter famously told the State Zionist Council of Victoria, late in 2002, that it was "an empirical fact" that the Iraqis possessed WMDs. To drive the point home he even said this was based on a report of the Federation of American Scientists, a group which grew out of the Manhattan Project — that is, work on the first atomic bomb.

Hard though it is now for many to accept, the party political division in Australia in the lead-up to the military operation in Iraq was not over the existence of WMDs. Rather, it was whether or not a further resolution of the United Nations, explicitly authorizing the use of force, should be obtained as a precondition to Australia committing forces. Several times Simon Crean, Labor's then leader, said that if such a resolution were passed by the Security Council, he would support Australian involvement. Given the dynamics of the Security Council then, this meant that if France and Russia changed their positions, then Labor in Australia would change. Those two countries were the permanent members really standing in the way of a further resolution — for their own political reasons, not because they did not believe Saddam had WMDs.

I was convinced, after a discussion late in 2002 with the influential former Chinese premier Li Peng, that it was not a deal breaker for the Chinese, and if the Russians and the French shifted, Beijing would allow the resolution through.

On 15 January 2003, Simon Crean even hinted that there might be circumstances in which he would support military action being taken absent a further Security Council resolution, saying, "The United Nations could find itself in circumstances in which there is very strong support, based on the evidence that Saddam Hussein still has weapons, but a U.N. Security Council resolution can't be passed because one of the permanent members vetoes it. In those circumstances, I'm saying we should consider those facts at the time."

The debate in Australia about Iraq brought into sharp focus attitudes toward the United Nations. There were, on the one hand, the supreme multi-lateralists who abided, absolutely, by the U.N. book; if the Security Council said yes, then all was in order; if the Security Council refused to, or had not endorsed something, then it must not occur. On the other hand, there were those who believed that nations had the right to exercise a value judgment independently of the world body, when the circumstances warranted.

There have been recent cases of member states sidestepping U.N. deliberations in apprehension of the veto being used to frustrate their intentions. Kosovo was a clear example. NATO [North Atlantic Treaty Organization] countries never put this to the test before the Security Council, knowing that a Russian veto would emerge because of Moscow's traditional friendship with Belgrade. They simply began their anti-Serbian bombing campaign. It succeeded; Serbia's president, Slobodan Milošević, fell; the Balkans were a markedly better place; and the world was largely happy. Yet it was not endorsed by the United Nations.

U.S. REALISTS

Not all of those who opposed Operation Iraqi Freedom did so because they thought there was insufficient United Nations authority for the action to be taken, or because they did not believe Iraq had WMDs. One such group were the so-called realists, who included some senior Republican figures identified with ... George H.W. Bush, and in particular Brent Scowcroft, national security adviser to the forty-first president and a mentor to Condoleezza Rice. The realists were probably untroubled by the U.N. issue, likely believed Saddam had WMDs, and regarded him as a loathsome dictator. Despite this, they saw merit in continuing a policy of containing him and eschewing resort to military action. To them the world was too dangerous a place to become involved in such action except in the most compelling circumstances, which they did not think existed in Iraq in 2003. In other words, they largely shared the Bush administration's assessment of the threat, but differed as to the most appropriate response.

In the light of what happened after the invasion they, of all groups, might feel entitled to point the finger and say, "I told you so." Yet their attitude was open to criticism on two counts. To start with, Saddam was not being contained. Until George Bush wound up the pressure on the United Nations to return weapons inspectors to Iraq in 2002, Saddam had been thumbing his nose at the world body and its WMD strictures on him. The U.N. sanctions regime and the accompanying no-fly zones over Iraq were coming under increasing strain and were most likely unsustainable in the long term. The other flaw was that the realist approach did not in any way accommodate the huge psychological shift in American attitudes following 9/11. A policy of relaxed containment might have worked prior to the terrorist attacks; in the changed atmosphere of vulnerability, when Americans genuinely thought another attack on their homeland was only a matter of time and action should be taken to pre-empt it, containment must have seemed to many oddly passive.

ANSWERING THE CRITICS

My government never saw the obtaining of a fresh Security Council resolution as a necessary legal prerequisite for the removal of Saddam. It was always our view that Security Council Resolution 678, dating back to 1990, provided sufficient legal grounds for the action ultimately taken. That was reflected in the formal legal advice tendered to the government and subsequently tabled in Parliament. By contrast, there was great political value, especially for the British government, fighting much internal British Labour Party resistance, if an explicit authorization for military action were obtained. To have tried, albeit unsuccessfully, for a new resolution added weight to the moral and political case being built for a military operation.

The Clinton administration thought that Resolution 678 gave blanket legal coverage for all the military action it took to enforce the terms of that resolution. There was wide acceptance of that view, including in Australia. When Australia agreed, at President Clinton's request, to send special forces to the Gulf in 1998 to support "Operation Desert Thunder" by the Americans and the British against Saddam's WMD capacity as well as other strategic assets of the regime, because of another round of defiance by Iraq of U.N. resolutions, the Opposition readily concurred. Kim Beazley accompanied me to Campbell Barracks to farewell the men. We were as one on the correctness of their mission.

The late Jeane Kirkpatrick, addressing the American Enterprise Institute in June 2003, told of a conversation she had had with Richard Holbrooke (since deceased) when he said, "Three times Clinton did what many Democrats are now saying Bush can't do. He did it in Bosnia in '95, in Iraq with Desert Fox in December of '98, and in Kosovo in '99. In the Balkans case he had no Security Council authority."

A constant argument against our participation in the coalition of the willing was the claim that it would increase the likelihood of a terrorist attack on our country. My response then was that Australia had been a terrorist target for several years before Iraq. Osama bin Laden's first belligerent reference to us had been in the context of the liberation of East Timor, which was in 1999, something which had widespread support in the Australian community. I have never taken a cavalier approach to terrorist threats, and no credible guarantees can ever be given that Australia is immune from such attacks. However the evidence to date is that our security services, our strengthened laws, and an alert populace have combined to provide effective guardianship.

Another criticism was that joining the Americans and the British in Iraq would permanently damage us in the eyes of the Muslim world, and in particular Indonesia, the most populous Muslim country of all. I was sensitive to this issue, and that is why I paid a special visit to then-president Megawati Sukarnoputri in February 2003 to explain to her that if Australia did go into Iraq our actions should be seen as part of an international effort to disarm Iraq, and not anti-Islamic in character. She made it clear that she accepted this. There is no evidence that our involvement in Iraq damaged our relationship with Indonesia. Both through the close relationship I forged with [President] Susilo Bambang Yudhoyono, and in other ways, Australia and Indonesia grew closer in the years after 2003. It was legitimate of me to claim that when I left office in 2007 that our bilateral relationship had never been better.

The military operation against Iraq was speedy and effective, much more so than most had expected, including, for example, Ehud Barak, the former Israeli prime minister, and the most decorated soldier ever in the Israeli Defense Forces and until recently the Israeli defence minister. In Canberra on 26 March 2003 — a few days after the war had begun — he told me he expected the military operation then underway against Saddam would require tenacious hand-to-hand fighting in the streets of Baghdad. In that same discussion, he expressed little doubt that Iraq possessed WMDs.

FAILURES, NOT MANIPULATION, OF INTELLIGENCE

After the fall of Saddam, and when it became apparent that stockpiles of WMDs had — to me unexpectedly — not been found in Iraq, it was all too easy for certain people, who only months earlier had said Iraq had the weapons, to begin claiming that Australia had gone to war based on a "lie."

That claim is the most notorious one of all about the conduct of my government, and of others, and merits the most emphatic rejection. Not only does it impugn the integrity of the decision-making process at the highest level, but also the professionalism and integrity of intelligence agencies here and elsewhere. Some of their key assessments proved to be wrong, but that is a world away from those assessments being the product of deceit and/or political manipulation.

In Australia, there was a parliamentary inquiry, as well as the Flood Inquiry, which canvassed the pre-war intelligence. In its submission to the former, our Office of National Assessments (ONA) said, "ONA said in a report of 31 January 2003 that there is a wealth of intelligence on Saddam's WMD activities, but it paints a circumstantial picture that is conclusive overall rather than resting on a single piece of irrefutable evidence." The Defence Intelligence Organisation (DIO) said in its submission to the same inquiry, "Iraq probably retained a WMD capability — even if that capability had been degraded over time. DIO also assessed that Iraq maintained both an intent and capability to recommence a wider program should circumstances permit it to do so."

The Flood Inquiry found "no evidence of politicization of the assessments on Iraq either overt or perceived" or that "any analyst or manager was the subject of either direct or implied pressure to come to a particular judgment on Iraq for policy reasons or to bolster the case for war." Flood further said that "assessments reflected reasonably the available evidence and used intelligence sources with appropriate caution." Flood said the obverse conclusion that Iraq had no WMDs "would have been a much more difficult conclusion to substantiate."

Neither inquiry gave a skerrick of support to the proposition that members of my government had manufactured convenient intelligence or strong-armed the agencies into saying things they did not believe.

The National Intelligence Estimate [NIE] of October 2002, declassified in July 2003, gives some idea of the strength of the intelligence advice coming to the United States and her allies, such as Australia. A National Intelligence Estimate is a distillation of the views of all the American intelligence agencies, including the Central Intelligence Agency (CIA). Its key judgments were as follows:

We judge that Iraq has continued its weapons of mass destruction programs in defiance of U.N. resolutions and restrictions. Baghdad has chemical and biological weapons as well as missiles with ranges in excess of U.N. restrictions; if left unchecked, it probably will have a nuclear weapon during this decade.

We judge that we are only seeing a portion of Iraq's WMD efforts, owing to Baghdad's vigorous denial and deception efforts. Revelations after the Gulf War starkly demonstrate the extensive efforts undertaken by Iraq to deny information. We lack specific information on many key aspects of Iraq's WMDs programs.

Since inspections ended in 1998, Iraq has maintained its chemical weapons effort, energized its missile program, and invested more heavily in biological weapons; in the view of most agencies, Baghdad is reconstituting its nuclear weapons program.

The intelligence bureau of the U.S. State Department entered a reservation to this assessment, but limited to the claim in the NIE that Iraq had sought yellowcake from Niger. Using entirely different intelligence sources, Britain's MI6 had verified the claim disputed by the State Department.

The strength of this assessment is unmistakable. If that assessment had indeed been accurate, and Saddam had been left in place only to provide WMDs to a terrorist group for use against the United States, the administration would have failed in its most basic responsibility to protect the nation. Such a hypothesis underlines the eternal dilemma of intelligence. Intelligence assessments never produce evidence beyond a reasonable doubt. Almost always, the art of intelligence assessment involves assembling a mosaic from varying, incomplete, and sometimes contradictory sources. To insist on such a standard of proof in the future would certainly avoid an Iraq-style intelligence failure but could have other consequences. To illustrate, in his book *The Finish: The Killing of Osama bin Laden*, Mark Bowden quotes the deputy director of the CIA, Michael Morell, telling President Obama that he had spent a lot of time on both WMDs and the tracing of bin Laden to Abbottabad, "... and I am telling you the case for WMDs wasn't just stronger, it was much stronger."[2]

I had accepted the intelligence, as had all of the other senior members of my government who had sat through numerous meetings of the National Security Committee of Cabinet. The Iraq Survey Group found no stockpiles. The gist of its conclusions was that although no stockpiles existed, Saddam intended to reconstitute his WMDs once U.N. sanctions had been lifted, and that he had the programs and wherewithal to do so. Importantly, the Iraq Survey Group judged that Saddam's regime attached great significance to its WMD capability; it had been crucial in maintaining superiority over the Kurds, and vital in the war against Iran.

As well as the available intelligence, logic had suggested, strongly, that Iraq had WMDs. As the Flood report observed, "The fact that Saddam chose to resist inspections to the bitter end suggested strongly that he had WMDs to protect (and perhaps that he hoped to avoid defeat by using them). If he did not have WMDs, why did he not ultimately comply with the inspection regime, in order to ensure the survival of his regime?" But logic proved an imperfect tool.

FAULTY POST-INVASION PLANNING

We know now that planning for and implementation of the stabilization phase was much more problematic than the initial operation to overthrow Saddam. The decision of the Coalition Provisional Authority (CPA) under Paul "Jerry" Bremer to disband the Iraqi army was a mistake, and the de-Ba'athification process directed by the CPA went too far. As well as denying coalition forces a homegrown vehicle through which to help maintain order, disbanding the army put on the streets tens of thousands of unemployed and disgruntled Iraqis. Many of them became eager recruits for the insurgency, which raged until largely subdued by the surge in 2007–08. And, as the former president George W. Bush acknowledged in his book, it was a mistake for the Americans to cut their troop levels, in the ten months following the invasion, from 192,000 to 109,000.

The CPA held sway for too long, thus reinforcing the sense of an American occupation, anathema to all Iraqis, irrespective of their attitudes toward the removal of Saddam. The original disposition to cede quickly a large slice of genuine executive authority to a representative (although unelected) group of Iraqis in advance of elections being held should have been preserved.

The post-invasion conflict, especially between Sunnis and Shiites, which caused widespread bloodshed, did more damage in my judgment to the credibility of the coalition operation in Iraq than the failure to find stockpiles of WMDs. Persecution by the pro-Saddam Sunnis of the Shia majority had been a feature of Iraq for the previous twenty years. It was inevitable that after Saddam had been toppled, a degree of revenge would be exacted, but a stronger security presence would have constrained this.

The worsening security situation in Iraq, particularly the intense sectarian violence starting in 2006, which produced an alarming number of deaths, led to the adoption by the Bush administration of the surge strategy, under the leadership of General David Petraeus. Based on improved intelligence and a "clear, hold, and build" approach, which required committing thirty thousand additional American troops at a time when there was growing pressure at home to pull out, it was a gutsy political call and in the result, overwhelmingly successful.

President Bush was a somewhat lonely believer in the surge. Many of his generals did not want it, and plenty of his senior officials were lukewarm. Many in Washington advocated cutting America's losses and, in the case of the current vice-president, Joe Biden, partitioning the country. Coupled with the "Sunni awakening" in Al Anbar province and the intelligence-led special forces operations against terror networks, it turned the tide against al-Qaeda in Iraq, and gave hope that a relatively stable and peaceful nation was in prospect.

IRAQ TODAY

Iraq today is not a full democracy as we understand it — only Israel in the Middle East can lay claim to that description. Yet its citizens have on five occasions since 2003 voted either to elect people to govern them, or approved the rules under which they are to be governed, despite the violent intimidation they have faced in doing so. That says something for the thirst for freedom they have, and their willingness to participate in a democratic electoral process.

There are still major gaps in Iraqi infrastructure, with basic services still falling short. Yet the Iraqi economy enjoyed 10 percent growth in 2012; oil exports in 2012 hit a thirty-year high at 2.6 million barrels a day. Per capita GDP is now markedly higher than it was before Saddam was removed.

To what extent has democracy really taken root in Iraq, and to what degree, if at all, have events in Iraq had an impact on the rest of the Middle East? I hope I won't be accused of invoking the Zhou Enlai defence when I say that more time should be allowed to pass before attempting to fully answer those questions. When asked what he thought had been the impact of the French Revolution on world history, the Chinese Communist leader replied that it was too early to tell!

Unlike most of its region, Iraq's polity has not been roiled by the Arab Spring. That must surely have something to do with the democratic framework which has been established there in recent years. Shortly after the coalition operation in Iraq, Libya's leader Muammar Gaddafi renounced his WMDs and sought readmission to the international community. He and his regime are now gone. Also, it is hard not to agree with Nadim Shehadi of Chatham House when he said, "The idea that the Arab Spring was triggered by a self-immolating street trader in an obscure Tunisian town is just not credible." The ferment in the Middle East now is such that it is difficult to predict what the outcomes will be in five or ten years' time, and what influence, if any, events affecting Iraq have exerted.

In this context it is worth speculating that if Saddam had not been toppled in 2003, he very likely would still be in power. In response to a manifestation of the Arab Spring in Iraq, his suppression of any uprising would have been just as brutal as that of Bashar al-Assad in Syria.

The reality is that the Middle East remains an incredibly complex place, where linkages and causal connections between events are very hard for even the most learned analysts to unravel. To my mind, however, it is implausible that the events we now know as the Arab Spring bear no relationship of any kind to the overthrow of Saddam's regime in 2003.

THE AUSTRALIA-U.S. ALLIANCE

Although the legal justification for the action taken against Iraq was based on its cumulative non-compliance with U.N. Security Council resolutions and a properly grounded belief that Saddam possessed WMDs, a powerful element in our decision to join the Americans was, of course, the depth and character of our relationship with the United States. Australia had invoked ANZUS [Australia, New Zealand, United States Security Treaty] in the days following 9/11. We had readily joined the coalition in Afghanistan; Australia had suffered the brutality of Islamic terrorism in Bali. There was a sense then that a common way of life was under threat.

At that time, and in those circumstances, and given our shared history and values, I judged that, ultimately, it was in our national interest to stand beside the Americans.

There were many who argued that we should stay out; we should say no to the Americans for a change; that the true measure of a good friend was a willingness to disagree when the circumstances called for it; that in the case of Iraq we would hurt our country by backing the United States; and that in the long run, declining to participate in the coalition of the willing would be good for the alliance. The logic of that argument escaped me then, and it still does. In my view, the circumstances we recall tonight necessitated a 100-percent ally, not a 70- or 80-percent one, particularly as no compelling national interest beckoned us in the opposite direction.

For those who believe that destiny has condemned Australia to a fateful choice between the United States and China — not a belief that I share — it is worth noting that in the years that followed the Iraqi operation, Australia's relationship with China burgeoned, apparently unhindered by concerns in Beijing that we were too close to the United States. I have long held the view that the Chinese "get" our alliance with America. They understand its historical, political, and cultural provenance.

If anything, our actions in Iraq reinforced the reputation of Australia as a nation that stands by its friends, even in difficult circumstances. The recent strengthening of our strategic relationship with Japan, for example, is in part a result of the close co-operation between the ADF and the Japan Self-Defense Force in southern Iraq.

I acknowledge that my government's decision on Iraq polarized attitudes in Australia. It is unlikely that the passage of time has softened attitudes toward that decision. It remains my conviction, however, that it was right because it was in Australia's national interests, and the removal of Saddam's regime provided the Iraqi people with opportunities for freedom not otherwise in prospect.

NOTES

1. This is a lightly edited version of a speech by former prime minister John Howard, delivered to the Lowy Institute for National Policy in Sydney, Australia, on April 9, 2013. It is reprinted here with Mr. Howard's kind permission.
2. Mark Bowden, *The Finish: The Killing of Osama bin Laden* (New York: Atlantic Monthly Press, 2012).

3

PARLIAMENTARY DEMOCRACIES AT WAR: A PANEL DISCUSSION

Melissa Conley Tyler (moderator); Paul Barratt A.O.;
the Honourable Bill Graham P.C., Q.C.; and the Right
Honourable Malcolm Fraser A.C., C.H.

This is an original transcript and all quotations are as they originally appeared, with the exception of some speech traits being deleted.

Tyler:

Welcome, ladies and gentlemen and members of the diplomatic corps who've come to join us here today. It's a great pleasure to welcome you here. My name is Melissa Conley Tyler. I'm the national director of the Australian Institute of International Affairs [AIIA]. I know a number of you here are already aware of the AIIA. If you're not, I do urge you to look us up.

It's a real pleasure to be here as a friend of the Asia-Pacific College of Diplomacy and the ANU [Australian National University]. I really want to congratulate the Asia-Pacific College of Diplomacy and Professors Ramesh Thakur and Bill Maley, and their Canadian counterparts, for bringing together such a high-quality event.

Coming here together today, we're ten years since Australia, the U.S., and the U.K. forces invaded Iraq, and Canada did not. There are still many questions. As you've seen from the flyer for this event, how did Australia come to be part of the invasion? What was the decision-making? Are there ways that this decision-making can and should be improved for the future? These are all current questions with long-term consequences.

We're very lucky here today to have an absolutely extraordinary panel of people to help us answer those questions. We have first the Right Honourable Malcolm Fraser A.C., C.H., former [Australian] prime minister. During the Vietnam era, Mr. Fraser was minister for [the] army, then minister for defence; following that, minister for education, before becoming prime minister and serving this country from 1975 to 1983. We thank him very much for joining us tonight.

Secondly, we have a very admired former foreign minister and defence minister of Canada, the Honourable Bill Graham. He was foreign minister during the time of the invasion of Iraq. Previously he'd been a lawyer, teaching even at a university, which we can all admire, and served as chair of the House Standing Committee on Foreign Affairs and International Trade before coming to that position.

Finally, we have Mr. Paul Barratt A.O., who's the former secretary of the Department of Defence in Australia. Originally a graduate in physics, he started his career as a scientific intelligence analyst. He was deputy secretary of [the Department of Foreign Affairs and Trade], secretary of departmental resources ... and as I said, secretary of the Department of Defence.

TO JOIN OR NOT TO JOIN THE INVASION OF IRAQ: THAT WAS THE QUESTION

Tyler:

We have an extraordinary group of people who are able to take us through some of these issues. Now, what I'm proposing to do is ask them some questions, and then turn over to [the audience] to get questions from you on some of the things that you think are key on this topic. So, particularly for some of the younger members of the audience, to whom this might be somewhat ancient history, I'm going to lead off just by asking how did Australia come to be involved in the invasion of Iraq? And I might ask Paul to start us off.

Barratt:

Thanks, Melissa. To put it very briefly, we came to be involved in the invasion through a series of government malfeasances. First of all, we were lied to about when a decision was taken. The prime minister was telling the Australian public right up to the eve of the invasion that no decision had as yet been made. I believe that we had made a decision to participate in the invasion of Iraq not later than July 2002, when the prime minister visited Washington. From that time on, we had Australian planners embedded in the planning process in Tampa, Florida. You do not participate in the planning of American military operations on an on-spec basis, because, of course, you are planning your part of the military operation, and if you withdraw, you will be leaving a hole in it. So, we were absolutely committed before we were taken on board, there's no doubt about that.

We were deceived about the intelligence that was available and the quality of the intelligence that was available. In February 2003, the prime minister said that we know that Iraq has — Saddam Hussein has — chemical and biological weapons and wants to acquire nuclear weapons. And speaking as a former intelligence analyst, I have to say when I heard that magic word "know," I thought there is intelligence that makes this a rock-solid case, that this is knowledge, not assessment or belief. And when the prime minister uses language like "we know" to Parliament, we should not expect a subsequent inquiry to come to the conclusion that the intelligence was thin, ambiguous, and incomplete.

There was also the spurious connection to al-Qaeda drawn in the course of the case, such as it was, made to Parliament. That doesn't even pass the laugh test. Whatever Saddam Hussein was, he was not a jihadist. He was what you might call a secular modernizer. A very brutal and nasty one, but al-Qaeda was the last kind of organization he would want to align his interests with because they're utterly counter to his own.

When it all turned out not as planned, the government pulled a further stunt of having two inquiries into the performance of the intelligence agencies. What we saw in the three villain countries — United States, United Kingdom, and Australia — was that they either ignored the intelligence assessments of their own agencies, or they cherry-picked the intelligence assessments for their own purposes. And when everything became unpopular with their public, they set up an inquiry into the performance of the intelligence agencies. So, that was another stunt.

And, finally, on this "how did we get involved" [question], there was a gross misleading of Parliament and public about the legality of the war. The prime minister told Parliament that we have legal advice that we don't need another United Nations Security Council resolution. Government legal advisers don't settle matters of international law. Those matters are finally resolved before a court of competent jurisdiction. In the absence of a decision of a court of competent jurisdiction — and there are plenty of decisions that haven't yet been made — the best advice is that of senior international legal counsel. Forty-three international lawyers wrote to [Australian prime minister] John Howard to say, "This is not legal." And the job of government lawyers is not to frame the law; it is to advise the government on what a court of competent jurisdiction would be most likely to decide. So, there were deceptions at every level.

Tyler:

And malfeasances as well.

Barratt:

I think I should probably cease and desist. Malfeasances as well.

Tyler:

Mr. Fraser, you've been very critical about the decision-making process leading up to war. What do you see as the main problems? What should have been done differently?

Fraser:

Nearly everything. I'd just like to add one thing to the question of legal advice, because the person who had to give the decision for the British troops to invade, [Admiral] Michael Boyce, Chief of British Defence Staff, asked for a legal opinion that the war would be legal under British and international law or he would not give the order. On the seventh of March that year, [U.K. attorney general Lord Peter] Goldsmith, the British law officer, gave about a fourteen-page opinion: "On the one hand this, on the one hand that; it may be, it may not be; it will depend what jurisdiction you're in ..." Clearly not the kind of advice that Michael Boyce was wanting.

On the seventeenth of March of that same year, 334 words appeared over Goldsmith's name, which were the words given to the British Cabinet, which were the words that [Prime Minister Tony] Blair tabled in his parliament. And they said the war would be legal, those words. But later, Goldsmith said that was not a condensation of his legal opinion. He also later had a bit of dementia and said that he had changed his mind between the seventh and the seventeenth because of discussions he'd had in Washington. Well, the discussions he'd had in Washington with senior officials there happened in January, well before his first bit of advice. So, that was just not true. I think there's still a mystery of who wrote the 334 words. The British Cabinet was not given his full legal advice of fourteen pages, nor was the Australian government. That document was not tabled in the Australian Parliament. The 334 words were tabled in the Australian Parliament, and that, at the very best, has to be a fabrication.

What went wrong? You've got to, I think, ask what went wrong with America. Why did they suddenly want to go to war? Every one of the highly respected Bush I's senior advisers — James Baker, Lawrence Eagleburger, Brent Scowcroft,[1] and a couple of others — publicly said, "Don't go to war." I knew those people. I knew the first President [George H.W.] Bush quite well. He'd visited Australia when he was vice-president. And they would not have said that if the first Bush had not agreed. So, he also agreed that they should not go to war. So, why did they? Perhaps because neo-conservatives — perhaps because religious fanatics of a Jewish or a Christian kind, but not of an Islamic kind — had got hold of American policy-making, American beliefs. It's worth reading a statement of principles ... about America's role, America's God-given duty in the next century, which was this century. [The statement] was published in 1997 [and it said]: "America's only going to be secure when the whole world is a democracy in America's image, and they need to achieve that, if possible, by persuasion — if not, by force of arms." So, where to start? Obviously, they wanted to start somewhere. They chose Iraq.

Now, how people who some university has given probably first-class degrees or several of them, and doctorates perhaps — and I hope this university wouldn't — could be so fundamentally stupid as to think that you defeat Iraq and democracy will immediately flow, not only all over Iraq, but all over the Middle East [sic]. But that's what people like [Deputy Secretary of Defense Paul] Wolfowitz still, in fact, believe. It's what people who signed on to the statement of principles, published in 1997, believed. And was that the main motivating factor for the Americans? Perhaps. I think it was.

For us, we just wanted to cuddle up and earn brownie points. We should have learned long before this that no middle to small country — and in real terms, we're small — earns brownie points from a superpower or a greater power. I have known, in my own time, circumstances where not only America but also Britain, whom one might have trusted greatly, have only given us information that would help us to come to the decision they wanted us to come to, when they had additional information which they would not give us but which we discovered for ourselves from other sources. So, you don't earn brownie points.

And it might be worth recalling that as long ago as 1961, during something called Konfrontasi, *The Economist* wrote that the United States would never choose Australia over Indonesia, unless Indonesia were governed by a blatantly communist government. Now, why would they? Indonesia — that's two hundred million people. A very progressive, in many ways, Islamic country; a peaceful Islamic country. You could put twenty million Australians into the scales against that in terms of America's interest. And we find that government after government has said, "We've got a special relationship," which means nothing. But it was on that special relationship that John Howard would have single-handedly, without any questions from his Cabinet, without asking the advice of the Defence Committee ... As I am told — and Paul probably knows better than I would — but as I am told, the Defence Committee was told, "Tell us how to do this most quickly. We don't want you to tell us whether it's a good idea or not, because that decision's already been made." And whatever Paul said about the timing of our decision, we had special forces operating in Iraq even before the United States had declared war.

Tyler:

You've talked about the cuddling-up process. I might turn to Bill Graham to give us a different perspective. Can you tell us more about Canada's decision not to go to war and how that occurred?

Graham:

Well, we were already cuddled, whether we [wanted to be] or not, as someone once said. You know, I used to say to the Americans, the Americans are our best friends, whether we want it or not, or whether they want it or not. So, there was some ambiguity in the Canadian position — I must be, you know, honest with you. Now, it looks in retrospect, [Prime Minister] Mr. [Jean] Chrétien made his announcement on March 17 to great acclaim in the country and to his parliamentary colleagues — except the Opposition [the Conservative Party], who were strongly in favour of going to war with the United States — that we would not go without a Security Council resolution. And Mr. Chrétien had made that clear to [President] Mr. [George W.] Bush as early as September of the previous year at a private meeting he'd had with him. But at the same time, we live beside the United States. Our security is tied to the United States. Eighty percent of our trade is with the United States. We don't deliberately poke the United States in the eye just gratuitously.

Fraser:

Sometimes you give the impression of so doing. [*Audience laughter*]

Graham:

Well, I can assure you it's very good domestic politics to do it. There's a bit of a price to be paid sometimes, Prime Minister, and so usually the prime minister lets the lesser officials like the foreign ministers go and do it for him. We're allowed off our leashes occasionally!

But to shorten a long story, we were always very skeptical, to begin with, of the evidence. Others have spoken about the evidence. I personally spoke to [U.N. chief weapons inspector in Iraq] Hans Blix on many occasions. He said, "Be careful of what you listen to." Mr. Bush offered to come and brief Mr. Chrétien personally, and Mr. Chrétien said that would not be a good idea. One can say no easier on the phone than we can say no to his face. But throughout the piece, we started out saying, "Perhaps you will get a U.N. authorization." And we felt that if the United States were able to get a U.N. authorization, that would be a demonstration, in fact, that the world community was agreed that Saddam Hussein did have weapons of mass destruction and had the capability of delivering them, because there was some doubt of that in the early days.

But as time went on, through September and through the fall, we became more and more skeptical about the reality of the actual situation, and also whether, in fact, the United States and its British allies would ever get a

Security Council resolution. So, Mr. Chrétien made it his business to consult with Chile, with Mexico, with all our allies, with France. I myself was on the phone regularly with foreign ministers. And in the end, we ... were members of the planning committee that you mentioned, because we felt if we were going to get engaged, we had to be properly prepared. But then suddenly they decided to move the planning out of Tampa, Florida, over to the Gulf. Now, this was an indication to us that the trains were starting to leave the station and maybe if we didn't want to be on the train we'd better get off. And so we said, "No, we will not send our planning group."

That was a decision that was then made as early as the fall [and] made it very clear to the Americans we couldn't be counted on just to be an automatic yes. There were many Americans who thought even without a Security Council resolution, Canada would go along. And the American ambassador, Paul Cellucci, who was a very close friend of Bush, assured him that Canada would be there. "Don't worry, the rhetoric will be anti-war, but they'll be there. We can count on them." He was listening to people in the Canadian defence department and a lot of business people in Canada who felt we should go with the American allies regardless. Right or wrong, we should be with them.

That was a debate that played out in Canada. But in the end, for reasons that we believed ... this was a threat to the United Nations system, that it was dangerous adventurism, that it was not based on good law, and it certainly was not based on evidentiary facts that we independently analyzed, Mr. Chrétien rose in the House of Commons on the seventeenth of March and said there was no Security Council resolution, and that Canada would not be joining the troops to go to Iraq. In so doing, we made it very clear to our American colleagues, as part of the fact that we live in North America with them, that we would not be critical, particularly, of their decision. That [it] was their decision to go, but we were deciding we wouldn't go.

Was that problematic? To some extent. As I said, in the House of Commons of the day, that decision had the support of three of the four parties in the House. The Conservative Party, however, was vehemently of the opinion that we should have joined our American allies and, in fact, accused the prime minister of being [U.K. prime minister Neville] Chamberlain at Munich [1938]. There was a lot of talk in those days, if you remember the rhetoric, there were all sorts of analogies of Hitler, and "Remember if we hadn't stopped Hitler?" and "We're stopping Hitler and you're not." And there [were] a lot of false historical analogies being thrown around, and that was one that was thrown at us.

Tyler:

It's interesting. You were faced, in a way, with a second decision, with what to do with Canadians who [were] on exchange, who were already embedded with U.S. forces. And I've always found it interesting that they did serve, some in quite exalted positions. I think you had the deputy commander of U.S. forces in Iraq who was Canadian. You had destroyers and frigates. In fact, for a country that didn't go to war, you actually almost did as much as Australia did. But you gained some other benefits.

Graham:

Well, you can look at this as either highly duplicitous and embarrassing, or very clever, depending on which way you want to. [*Audience laughter*] I personally believe it to be — I believe it was necessary. I made the point that Canada is dependent upon the United States for our defence. As part of that dependency, we are integrated to some extent in various American operations.... And for us to have pulled out individuals from units that they were attached to, at the last minute, would have been so disruptive to their operations that it would have created an enmity with the United States that would have lasted far beyond, and I think we would have paid a political price in a way that was not necessary. What Paul Cellucci said to us [and] Mr. Bush made ... clear in meetings [was that] they really weren't interested in our troops. They wanted our troops to go to Afghanistan. That was a decision that had been made months before with [Secretary of Defense] Mr. [Donald] Rumsfeld. They knew that we had no troops to go to Iraq, in any significant number. They wanted the flag. They wanted the international credibility that came with yet another country that could say, "Yes, we have a global support for this mission." The flag was far more important.

But that said, we did leave those troops in. We left some ships in the Gulf of Hormuz [Gulf of Oman], but they were there as part of the Afghan mission. And I remind people when they're critical of Canada for doing that, the French, who were vociferously against the war, had a ship in the Gulf there as part of [Operation] Enduring Freedom, and they left their ship there too.

So, many of us were taking positions that maybe on their face were a little bit inconsistent, but in no way was that inconsistent with our principal decision that this was not a war that we should participate in, and that Canadians should not be part of.

THE CONSEQUENCES OF THE IRAQ WAR

Tyler:

Well, I'll get us to think ... ten years in hindsight. What are some of the consequences that you all see having come from the invasion of Iraq? Whether that's for Iraq itself, for Australia, for Canada. Why don't I start with you, Paul?

Barratt:

Well, our political leaders of that time, particularly John Howard and [Foreign Minister] Alexander Downer, although they said that regime change was not a justification for invading Iraq, have relied on that as the principal achievement of the invasion, that we've got rid of a very nasty dictator and given the Iraqi people the opportunity to build their own freedom and democracy. And my response to that is, there are several hundred thousand Iraqis who will never experience that opportunity because they're dead as a direct or indirect result of the invasion. There are millions of internally displaced Iraqis, and there are millions of Iraqis who are refugees and who are now trying to figure out whether it's more or less dangerous to be in Syria or Iraq. And I don't think that the situation in Syria is completely disconnected from the events in Iraq ten years ago with the disruption of some kind of Sunni-Shia modus vivendi. It maybe needed to be disrupted, but in the way it was disrupted it's produced a horrendous price in bloodshed right across that Shia majority tier in the Middle East. People now are enduring poor infrastructure, poor government services, vicious sectarian fighting. They're not sure whether they're safe anywhere. And as some Iraqi refugees or expats have said to me or to people I know, it wasn't good living under Saddam Hussein, but there were rules for survival. If you behaved in certain ways, you could just get on with your life, keep your head down, and when you switched the light on the electricity came on, et cetera, et cetera. The main privations were to do with sanctions. Now, no one is safe, no one knows where they're safe, and life is very difficult. So, I think of the humanitarian consequences.

And I must say on that subject, that was something else that governments ignored. Iraq had endured a decade of sanctions, and the economy was in a very rundown state. A very large proportion of the Iraqi community was dependent on U.N. food relief, which meant they were dependent on a distribution system that would fan food out from the ports throughout the country. And humanitarian NGOs [non-governmental organizations] and official agencies forecast before the invasion that there would be an enormous humanitarian price to be paid when you disrupted that U.N. relief operation.

Tyler:

What are some of the other long-term consequences you can see from the invasion?

Fraser:

Well, they're continuing. There may well be a civil war in Iraq. It will have been a direct consequence of the intervention. I haven't seen the figures, but I would love a comparison with the number of civilians killed by Saddam Hussein over ten years and the number who've died or been killed as a consequence of the invasion, including those killed by the invading armies, and the Americans would not count. I suspect that more have been killed in the last ten years. Iraq used to be the safest country in the world for [the humanitarian agency] CARE Australia to work in, part of CARE International. It became the most dangerous, and we had somebody killed, just by thugs, who are very common. We don't work there any longer, and I think a number of other agencies also don't work there.

So, the consequences for Iraq have not yet played themselves out. We forget also that Saddam Hussein prevented any sectarian violence between the different sects. They knew they would have a greater punishment if any of them stepped out of line, so they all behaved. And that, in a sense, was beneficial. Certainly beneficial compared to the circumstances today.

But there are consequences for Australia. We have now, unlike Canada, followed the United States into three totally mistaken wars. The first might have been the biggest mistake. The CIA analyst, by the way, had it right in relation to Vietnam. The military had it wrong. The American military in particular had it wrong. [President Lyndon B.] Johnson ignored the CIA, and we weren't even told what the CIA was saying at the time. That was one disaster we followed America in. The second was Iraq, and the third was Afghanistan.

I keep asking myself when there's going to be the next war in which we follow America. They are preparing for war in the Pacific, and if anyone suggests they're not, just look at the military buildup. Look at the American defense secretary visiting Vietnam and Cam Ranh Bay. If they want to, as I'm told, reopen Cam Ranh Bay as an American naval base, the main naval base during the Vietnam War, every American naval ship is nuclear-capable. Isn't that just as bad as [Soviet leader Nikita] Khrushchev wanting to put nuclear missiles in Cuba? It's hard to say it is not as bad, if that's the way it goes.

We have troops in Darwin, which, we are told, are just on rotation and training. I don't believe it. I think there is another lie which two countries are involved in, America and Australia [*sic*]. And I think it's a lie because [when] CSIS [Center for Strategic and International Studies], which many of you will know of, a Washington think tank, but a think tank that lives and breathes off the Pentagon … they publish major reports, it's generally a Pentagon contract, and what they recommend generally they know has already been approved by the Pentagon. So, extract from that what they say about Australia. Darwin becomes a fully rounded offensive marine base with an offensive air arm and an offensive naval arm attached to it. Now, is America going to come along and say, "Oh, Prime Minister, we want to use our forces based in Darwin to attack this or to attack that, or to bomb something or to do this?" We are going to be totally complicit in whatever the Americans do. And I happen to believe that that's notoriously dangerous. And we had a prime minister in the middle '50s who said to [U.S. president Dwight D.] Eisenhower, "If you have a war with China over Taiwan, we're not part of it. It's not our affair. It's yours."

We should not be following America into other ventures, or forced by circumstances to follow America into other ventures. And I fear that American policies are not necessarily … a direct consequence of an American action. We have a militarist government in Japan, and if anyone tells you this is a passing phase, it is a growing phase, and my liberal Japanese friends will say that to me very plainly and very openly. And they can provoke China. America would be on their side automatically, even though articles that have been published in the *New York Times* would say, in relation to the particular provocations — rocks in the East China Sea — China happens to be right and America wrong. And that's a well-documented article with [*New York Times* columnist] Nicholas Kristof's imprimatur behind it.

So I'm more concerned with the future than the past. I don't want us to be following America into more wars that are wrongly based and based on a lie, which are going to get Australia into grievous problems, into grievous difficulties. And I fear that's the way their current policies are leaning.

Tyler:

Maybe I can turn to Bill and ask what were the consequences for Canada taking a different approach?

Graham:

Well, I think my colleagues have pretty well summed up the disastrous consequences in the Middle East. I mean, I remember meeting with [U.S. Secretary of State] Colin Powell regularly about this and saying, "Well, you know, you think you're going to be met with flowers in their guns, but what happens if you're treated like an occupying power and get into a civil war?" Which is exactly what happened. And it was not that difficult to foresee that. I mean, you had to be pretty naive to accept this concept that it was all going to be peace and light immediately.

But I don't think anybody foresaw the degree to which the United States of America — George Bush, having said that the axis of evil consisted of Iraq, North Korea, and Iran, invades Iraq and delivers it to Iran. I mean, that has got to be one of the most colossal foreign policy blunders in the history of mankind. I mean, all the loss of life you described in Iraq itself, the devastation of a society, the loss of life of Americans — and I'll come to that in a moment, the cost to their treasury, which we'll come to and the consequences of that — but the cost, and from a foreign-policy perspective, was to enhance Iran. As somebody said, this is the first time since the eleventh century that the Shias are now in as strong a position as the

Sunnis. It's completely changed the balance of power throughout the whole of the Middle East — and Syria's a part of it — and the whole balance of what is happening there. So, from a Middle Eastern perspective, this has created seriously bad consequences.

From an American perspective, it weakened the United States in international affairs because it weakened its credibility. The prime minister has just talked about "Would Australia follow America again into another war?" And [President] Mr. [Barack] Obama's had to deal with that. He's had to deal with the fact that he had to change completely the atmosphere in which he was operating. The whole wonderful credibility the United States of America had, to some extent, was eroded by this action that other countries just said, "We can't take American leadership."

I sat in NATO, which used to be completely pro-American; it was an American-led alliance and everything else, and within NATO, you had NATO members saying, "We don't want to accept American leadership anymore." We had a complete divergence in the North Atlantic alliance. Never seen anything like this. So it destroyed, I would say, the United States' international reputation. Its human rights reputation is in tatters because it still hasn't dealt with the human rights issues in Guantánamo Bay and others, so that it remains problematic when it stands up and says that it is the defender of human rights around the world and others are violators. It doesn't have the credibility to criticize other violators, which it used to have, which I find very disappointing.

And thirdly, from a Canadian perspective, we look at the United States as an important part of the prosperity of our country. Our economies are inextricably linked. If the United States is weak, it is bad for Canada, and the United States is fiscally weak today. And my friend Barney Frank, who was a prominent congressman and head of the finance committee, said to me, "Bill, the fiscal crisis in the United States is directly due to the fact that George Bush decided to give a tax cut and run a war on a credit card." And future Americans are going to pay for it. You've got a trillion-dollar debt that's there, and you've got probably a two- or three-trillion-dollar damage bill for wounded soldiers and others that have come back that will be affected. For years, this bill will be being paid. The fiscal position of the United States was seriously damaged by this war, and that is a consequence. So, their international credibility and their fiscal status. And I'm not happy about that. I'm not happy to see that happen to the United States, but that's a fact. I think you have to look at that and say, "That's a fact."

And fourthly, I would say from a Canadian perspective, it reaffirmed that our position was that we can have an independent foreign policy. That we can be part of North America, but that the Americans — you don't get anything from a great power because you say you're going to go with them, necessarily. The Poles went to Iraq, and they got a promise from Mr. Bush that their visa problems would be removed. I saw the exchange with the president of Poland: "No problem. You come with us. All will be looked after." "Where's my visas?" said the president of Poland when it was all over. "Oh, that's Congress's problem. I'd love to do it for you, but Congress just can't — I'm so sorry." Well, we know that in Canada. We know that when you deal with the administration, there's also Congress. And we know that this is how the United States operates, and we know what we can expect and what we don't. So, we don't have unrealistic expectations that we're going to be punished, and we don't think we're going to get rewarded, because that's not the way the United States operates. And that was certainly reaffirmed by what the consequences of this particular [*inaudible*].

Barratt:

I think just before we leave this subject, there's just one other consequence that sort of follows on from what Bill's saying. By a very misguided use of American power, the United States has demonstrated the limits of American power. Theodore Roosevelt used to say, "Speak softly and carry a big stick." Well, what the United States demonstrated in Iraq is that the big stick doesn't work when you become an occupying power because you very quickly find yourself in a counter-insurgency operation. And on our ABC program *Four Corners* a few weeks ago, the Australian counter-insurgency expert David Kilcullen said that, "My advice to you about anything that might lead to a counter-insurgency operation is, 'Don't do it.'"

Now, he went on to say that the U.S. is not very good at that stuff, and echoes comments made by military historian Robert O'Neill in a submission on the private member's bill to shift the war powers to our parliament, where he was saying, basically, in these counter-insurgency situations there's no doubt about the capacity of the United States to deploy lethal force, but they do it in such a heavy-handed way that as an occupying power, to get the U.S. Army out of the armoured vehicles and the Kevlar jackets and actually having them mingle with the people is a big cultural change, and one that they're struggling with and likely to struggle with. So, when you think about going to war with the United States, you've also got to think about what are the prospects of success. And if the modern war is a war of choice, which means invading and occupying somebody, chances of success are pretty bleak. And I think that's one of the big lessons too.

WAR POWERS AND PARLIAMENTARY DEMOCRACIES

Tyler:

So I might turn then to the war powers, because Iraq has been used as an example of why parliamentary democracies should have some sort of institutional checks and balances to maybe prevent that momentum of going to war. Perhaps I can ask, Prime Minister, how does Australia currently decide to go to war?

Fraser:

Well, one man can take us to war. One man took us to war in relation to Iraq. There will be a Cabinet decision that says, "Yes, we go to war in Iraq." But a strong prime minister, and circumstances of a recent visit to the president, a prime minister who was in America when 9/11 happened, and with all the relationships that have been well-written about, who in that Australian Cabinet was going to get up and say, "Hey, what about a bit of evidence?" Nobody was. The prime minister wasn't. The defence minister wasn't. So now one man can take Australia to war, and I think that is an extraordinarily dangerous situation. And probably — you know, I don't believe China can go to war on the say-so of one man. Their system is not democratic; it is not our system, but they have a system, they have committees, they have consultation. And they've also got a great deal of intelligence. I mean intelligence between the ears, quite apart from SIGINT [signals intelligence] and all of that sort of stuff. So, I think we're in a thoroughly dangerous situation.

I would give war powers to Parliament. If you're going to war, which is about the most serious decision that you can make — and the most evil decision you can make is to go to war on the basis of a lie — what other options have we got? We're not going to change our system of government radically, dramatically. So, we've got a parliament, and I'd say you've got to have a resolution. I'd want to debate whether a simple majority is enough, or [whether] you need 60 percent or two-thirds. Personally, I would go for something over a 50-percent vote. Now, if you've got an evenly divided Senate, if a real issue of national security is involved — and this also involves sharing intelligence in a proper way, which the government would not have been able to do because they didn't have it. So, Parliament would have said no. But if you really have got the information, if you have got the intelligence, who in Parliament can you name that would not vote for it? I'm sure there will be some, but I think that would split across party lines, absolutely. I mean, you know, the Liberal Party would point to the Greens and say they would always vote against it. I just don't believe it. I know members of the Greens who would certainly be prepared to fight for Australia if they thought Australia was under threat. So that's nonsense.

With all the deficiencies, all the problems of needing a war powers resolution through both houses, it's the only other option we've got. We don't have another option. There are people in Parliament now who've spoken about it and who believe it, people like [Labor MP]Melissa Parke, who's accused of being too left. Well, she's about as left as I am, I guess. And I hope that comment won't do her any harm. But that's about where I was about twenty years ago or thirty years ago on this subject.

I think that's enormously important. But to give one man, any one man, that amount of power, is inviting the most terrible catastrophe.

Tyler:

So, I might turn to you, Paul, to just tell us more about the arguments for and against.

Barratt:

Yes, thanks, Melissa. I would first make the comment that the power of that one person to take us to war is the historical legacy of ancient times when the sovereign was the state, and everybody else was a subject of the sovereign. The sovereign decided that he wanted to enlarge his domain or needed to defend himself against somebody. There may be good or bad reasons for going to war, but the sovereign decided that and everybody else just fell into line. Now, if you think that power — as I'll imagine everyone in this room does — that power flows from the people to the state, rather than from the state to the people, having that ancient prerogative of the sovereign clung to by the executive is both an anachronism and an anomaly. I think the power has to be transferred to the people.

So, what are the arguments? There are three arguments that I commonly hear, and Mr. Fraser's just disposed of one of them, but I'll re-summarize. The first one is, what if the minor parties act up? What if you can't get it through Parliament? Is anyone seriously saying that if the nation were genuinely in peril that you would have a problem with the minor parties? The first reason you wouldn't have a problem with the minor parties is that the two major parties would be voting to save the nation, and the second reason is the minor parties would vote too. Do you think the Greens wouldn't vote to defend Australia? Do you think Tony Windsor wouldn't? Do you think Rob Oakeshott wouldn't? Do you think Bob Katter wouldn't?[2] That is just a nonsense argument.

The second argument: Oh, well, what if Parliament's not sitting and it might all take too long? Let me tell you, the Australian Defence Force is maintained in such a low ... material state and state of training and readiness, that Parliament can easily keep up with its capacity to go to war. [*Audience laughter*]

Well may you laugh, but let me tell you a concrete example. In February 1999, CDF [Chief of the Defence Force] Chris Barrie and I went to the National Security Committee of Cabinet and said that in the light of what I regard as a very ill-advised letter that Prime Minister Howard had written to the president of Indonesia, [B.J.] Habibie. This letter, I might say, was designed to construct a stunt in which East Timor would remain part of Indonesia. But John Howard stuffed up completely and precipitated a chain of events that led to East Timor's independence. I'll take you through that in detail any time you want. But anyway, having not been consulted about this letter but found out about it, Chris and I went to the National Security Committee of Cabinet, February 1999, and said, "We have reason to believe that by the time this year is out, you may well" — these are almost the words we used — "you might be glad if you had raised another brigade group to twenty-eight days' readiness." That means that given twenty-eight days' notice to move, they could be off and ready for war, which meant A$267 million, a great deal of the savings from the Defence Reform Program, getting people up to the readiness that — getting platoons fully trained, getting them used to operating as companies, getting them used to operating as a brigade. Getting armour and artillery and infantry exercising together. Just all the things that you do to get something polished and ready to go.

Now, when finally it was decided in about August that we had to send people, there was another twenty-eight days to put them into the field in Timor, and there was coalition building and all the rest of it. The doctrine of the 1990s really originated in [Labor Defence Minister] Kim Beazley's era; [it resulted in] all our major platforms [being] fitted for but not with. That means that you've just got a platform and it doesn't actually have all of the electronic warfare self-protection, the missiles, the weapons, et cetera, on it, because we'll have enough warning to kick this stuff out before we need to go to war. Now, in my time we added something to the electronic warfare self-protection of the Hornets, and that was about a two-year project.

So, the notion that we're all waiting there in a state of readiness and the government's just ready to go, getting parliamentary approval is not going to be a problem. And also, going to war is such an important business, you might even think about recalling Parliament. You know, it might just about be worthwhile recalling Parliament.

And the third one is equally false: "Oh, but the government might have information it can't share with the Opposition." Now, I'd be the first to say that there is intelligence that you cannot broadcast in Parliament. I'd also say that, doctrinally, if you're relying on intelligence assessments that aren't about 80 percent open-source material, you're starting to get into trouble. So, if the hard stuff's telling you what you really know, you can construct a story to Parliament based on the 80 percent that's open-source. But aside from that, the more important point is, the whole basis of the Westminster system of government is that today's opposition leader could quite literally be tomorrow's prime minister. The notion that there is anything that you can't share with the leadership of the Opposition is a statement fundamentally opposed to the notion of Westminster government. So, that one you're knocking to the members, then.

Tyler:

I might turn to Bill Graham. You're having some of the same debates in Canada. Tell us how that's progressing now.

Graham:

Well, having listened to yours, I'm not too sure that we'd be rushing off to war either with any degree of alacrity. I think there are a couple of issues here that are complicating matters now. There's no doubt about it, the tradition was established in Canada at the time of the Second World War. Because of the Statute of Westminster, originally, of course, it was thought if Britain was at war, we were all at war. That old saga. Well, that lasted till the First World War, and in the Second World War, the prime minister said, "No, no, we're going to have a debate in the House of Commons and we're going to have a motion in the House of Commons before we declare war on Germany." And that was done, and I think that's a firm precedent. But the trouble is today's military operations are seldom involving a declaration of war. The Americans didn't declare war on Vietnam; they just went. Our troops in Afghanistan are not the result of a declaration of war. They're there under authority of a Security Council resolution, which was the legal basis of their being there.

So it's really a question of the extent to which you want to have debates around the deployment of troops under certain operations, and that becomes — and I'm speaking with my defence minister's hat on, here — somewhat trickier. If Canada says, "We're called upon; we need 1,500 troops quickly in Haiti," because there's a catastrophe in Haiti, do we have a debate around that issue? Because deploying troops to Haiti, some people are going to be in favour, some people are going to be against. It's very hard to make a case. I totally subscribe to [the] case of war when the existence of the state is threatened. I don't think there is any problem; people would rally to that. But the operations ... which Canada's been involved in recently with the deployment of troops have been rather like Afghanistan. They've been like Haiti, and troop deployments of this nature.

My own argument, because of the nature of the complexity of those, is I've been arguing at home that we need a parliamentary control over this by government. But I would argue that the foreign affairs committee and the defence committee of the House, being knowledgeable about these issues, should be able to make that decision on behalf of the House. They are all-party committees; they're well briefed on these issues; they're experts in the area, and you would have an informed debate and an informed discussion and an informed vote around that, rather than members voting because they don't like the prime minister or they've got some issue.

So, I mean, this is a bit of a gloss on your argument. I accept the same principle: you need a control over the government, but I'd like to see it in a somewhat different form than just a straight up-and-down vote in Parliament itself.

Fraser:

Well, we didn't ratify the Statute of Westminster for a very, very long while, and we didn't do it because John Latham, who'd been foreign minister and other things,[3] argued that it would weaken Britain's obligation to defend us. Not a very noble reason for not wanting to stand up.

Canada, actually, in 1922, said that Parliament would have to have a vote when the British asked for troops in relation to another incident involving a possible war with Turkey. And we were asked, and I don't think we answered. But if it's Haiti, if it's a natural disaster, I don't think anyone's going to quibble about it. We forget that war under the U.N. Charter is outlawed unless there is a U.N. resolution or unless it's self-defence. So, Afghanistan, all right. You don't have to have — if there's been a Security Council resolution in favour because of a particular reason, well, then that's going to be legal, and the need for your own vote in the Parliament is probably very significantly diminished. But if it is a case of aggression against a country, where you are determined to change the regime, then I think the responsibility should be shared as widely and as broadly as possible.

Graham:

I would accept that on that condition. As I said, my own experience recently has been largely involved in these types of engagement, largely because Canadians have been involved in U.N. operations and peacekeeping operations on a fairly regular basis, where the government has taken its responsibility to send them. And we've always had the tradition, actually, in our parliament of having what we call "take note" debates, so that there would be a discussion in the House. And certainly when we extended the Afghan mission for the second time in 2006, at that point the prime minister said he wanted a vote on the issue. But it was in very controversial circumstances. He insisted we were only going to have four hours of debate, and he conducted the vote. His argument for having the vote was that it would strengthen the troops on the ground to know that Parliament was behind them. He managed to offend the official Opposition, or most of it, such that they didn't want to vote for him. He managed to offend the Bloc Québécois, which represented fifty seats in the House, and the NDP [New Democratic Party] had already said they weren't going to vote in favour. He managed to turn about almost half the House off, before he went to get a vote that he said was going to strengthen the troops. So, the whole thing was a little bit of a crazy exercise.

Fraser:

But what we've all forgotten is that President Bush changed the U.N. mission. The mission and the authorizing resolution was to hunt al-Qaeda. It was not "regime change and establish an American-style democracy in Vietnam." And from that moment, I think you could also argue — oh, in Afghanistan — I think, from that moment, you could also argue that Afghanistan became an illegal war, because America unilaterally, without statement, changed the mission. It wasn't a Security Council mission.

Graham:

Well, we took the position that our ISAF [International Security Assistance Force, in Afghanistan] troops were there under a Security Council resolution. We've always been of the position [that] the Canadian troops, and the Dutch and the British we were with, strongly argued that we were there … under a proper United Nations authorization.

Fraser:

Yeah, I know that. But the authorization was for a purpose. It was for a purpose, and the United States unilaterally changed the purpose. They did not consult with Canada or Britain or anyone else when they did that.

Tyler:

I might get Paul to make a final comment on this, and then I want to open it up to questions from the floor.

Barratt:

I just wanted to respond to Bill about … this scheme of the Australian legislation doesn't depend on a declaration of war or any kind of hostilities. This is the private member's bill that was introduced in 2009. The scheme is that the authority of Parliament is required to deploy elements of the Australian Defence Force into international armed conflict. And it explicitly says that does not have any bearing on people training overseas. To go to your situation about Iraq embedded with foreign forces. So, if someone mobilizes the RAAF [Royal Australian Air Force], and someone deploys that unit, that's outside the ambit of this bill. It's about the Australian government making a conscious decision to deploy force elements for armed conflict. So, it's not about peacekeeping, and it's not about disaster relief. And if, let's say, an Australian patrol boat is fired on by pirates on the [Indonesian] archipelago, it can return fire.

There's also a provision for emergency action. We have a ready reaction force in town, a small one which is ready to go. But it's for sort of police-type actions. Now, there was provision in the bill that you can use a ready reaction force, then you must, within seventy-two hours or some period, state in Parliament as to why it was necessary to just jump off. And if that's used in a responsible and sensible way, that is never going to be a problem either.

I think that the bill that we had in the House was a pretty robust starting point. Disappointingly, the major parties just didn't take it seriously and said, "Well, the … bill's like this, and this doesn't resolve any of the problems," which simply showed that they were not serious about it. Because if they were saying, "Well, I think it'd be perfectly reasonable. This is a damn good starting point, but there's this problem and this problem. Let's design our way around those problems," that would be a serious political debate.

Graham:

It sounds like you've thought this out thoroughly, as to exactly the circumstances in which it would apply and those in which it wouldn't.

Barratt:

There have been four go's at this. But you see everyone — this is one of the most important reasons we need to wrest this power out of the prime minister's sticky fingers. Every prime minister wants to have in his giving, when the president of the United States rings, he can go on prime-time television and say, "I've just had a conversation with the president of the United States and I said, 'We're with you all the way.'"

Fraser:

I never did. [*Audience laughter*]

Graham:

Yeah, well, I don't think Mr. Chrétien ever did that either. And neither did [former prime minister] Mr. [Pierre] Trudeau.

Barratt:

But the head of the ACT Civil Liberties Union wrote to [Prime Minister] Kevin Rudd saying this would be a good idea, and for an avowed republican, he got a very interesting reply saying, "I want to stick to the ancient privileges of the sovereign, thank you very much."

Graham:

I think Mr. Chrétien would have said, "I'll play golf, but I'm not going to play war."

QUESTION AND ANSWER

Tyler:

And on that note, now I'm going to turn over to the audience. We've got a great capacity crowd. I'm going to get a few people to make comments and then come back to our panellists. So, Ramesh, very fitting for you to be the first question.

Ramesh Thakur:

Ramesh Thakur from the ANU. Just a quick question to all the panellists: Everything you've said seems so sensible, so unobjectionable, so much of a no-brainer. One, why hasn't it been accepted? Two, how can we make sure it is accepted?

Question:

I'll just get a question in. To avoid us being lied into any more wars, and to concentrate the minds of our political leaders, that would also need some sort of sanction other than the ballot box. Perhaps the crime of "war of aggression" could be written into our domestic law, and perhaps even parliamentarians could be placed under threat of indictment. [*Audience laughter*]

Tyler:

You're using the big levers there, aren't you?

Comment:

I just feel that the sanctions against political leaders who clearly lie us into wars are very inadequate. Just to be voted out of office, that's really paltry, really.

Jack Cunningham:

All three of our panellists have spoken about the matters of parliamentary oversight and war powers within the legislature. I'd be curious to know what your thoughts are about the pros and cons of a strong, standing intelligence committee composed of members of all parties within your respective legislatures.

Tyler:

And I'll finish up with Bill. Thank you.

William Maley:

William Maley from the ANU. Just an observation: in certain circumstances, if one's being invited to become involved in a really stupid exercise, it might be liberating for a prime minister to be able to say, "I would love to be able to come to your help, but as I don't have the ability to do it on my own, I would have to have the approval of my parliament, and it might not be forthcoming." That could actually empower somebody under pressure in certain circumstances.

Fraser:

Only somebody who's really weak. [*Audience laughter*]

Tyler:

Who'd like to have a go?

Graham:

Well, yes, it's a little bit like negotiating and saying, "Well, I'll have to take it back to my board for approval," and then you'd know the whole thing starts to unravel at that point.

But I think, Jack, just to take your point up about a standing intelligence committee, I'd be interested to know what the debate has been here in Australia on that. Canada obviously looks at the United States regularly for this. They have very effective intelligence committees both in the House and in the Senate. And I've done a lot of work with various senators. Bob Graham was head of that committee. I knew him very well. We looked for years at establishing one in the Canadian House, and it has always come unravelled because we have elected at this particular time, in the Canadian House, members of a party called the Bloc Québécois, who are devoted to taking Quebec out of Confederation. So, in fact, you have members of Parliament whose avowed purpose is to destroy the state. And we never saw how we could establish an intelligence committee which would be an all-party committee, because you couldn't have an intelligence committee which wasn't all-party, but how could you invite into the all-party intelligence committee, which is going to open everything up to the very parties which are going to turn around and use it politically to help destroy Canada? In the American system, they're all Americans, in it together.

I personally felt there are reasonable people in the Bloc Québécois. When we stepped outside Canada with our foreign affairs committee, these people were proud Canadians. They were so proud. They were as proud about us saying no to Iraq as anybody else in Canada. So, I think you could have gotten over that issue, and I think it's a shame, in fact, that we haven't established one in Canada, because I think that's — having been the minister of defence responsible for our intelligence, this has to be one with — with cyber warfare taking place now and what's going on in cyberspace. It's incredible, the threats to every one of your bank accounts in this room, the threats to our communications, the threats to your water supplies. The knowledge that citizens should be having and what's happening about that, and an informed parliamentary committee that would be directly involved in what is happening in the intelligence community, I think, would be very helpful to a democracy. I'm strongly in favour of it.

On the sanction issue, I might just suggest on crime of aggression, at least in Canada — and I believe it's true in Australia; I believe you're signatories to the Rome Statute in the International Criminal Court [ICC]. And if you're like Canada, we've adopted that into our Criminal Code. So, in fact, a crime of aggression in Canada is not only a violation of international law, it's a violation of the law of Canada and a violation of the Criminal Code. It would be interesting to see who would choose to prosecute a sitting prime minister, or what attorney general would undertake that job. But technically, it would be a violation to conduct an illegal [war] — and war of aggression is illegal in the law of Canada. It's a violation of our own Criminal Code.

Question:

Is it the case in Australia, Mr. Barratt?

Barratt:

I'm not sure. I don't think it is. There is somebody trying to — there are people pursuing John Howard on a war-crimes basis, but I don't know what their legal basis is.

Fraser:

We've ratified the ICC and the Rome Statute and whatever, and Australian lawyers had quite a prominent part in helping to draft those statutes. But ratifying a convention does not mean something automatically becomes part of Australian law, and I don't believe that we have passed it into Australian law up to this point.

Barratt:

I don't think we have. And we changed our stance on it in 2002, which was probably not a coincidence.

Fraser:

Well, we ought to write it into Australian law. No, but we still apply the statute internationally. We're fully committed to it. But we should apply it to domestic Australian law.

I believe there ought to be sanctions, because I think going to war on a wrong basis or on a lie or whatever can be a crime. It can be a crime against humanity and whatever, and people should be sanctioned for it. But the prosecution, you'd have to understand, would be extraordinarily divisive. There are many cases in British practice where the chief law officer has not prosecuted because it would have too divided the body politic within Britain. And I think it might have been Lord Acton who said that a law officer who is the final determinant of what prosecution should take place or not take place, but a law officer who refuses to listen to the advice of his senior political colleagues is a bloody fool. And you might remember there were people who wanted my government to prosecute [former Labor prime minister] Gough Whitlam. There was no way I was going to allow that to happen. There was a private case, but it was not going to be taken over.

Comment:

He wasn't a war criminal, though.

Fraser:

No, no, I agree with that. But it was meant to be something against the Crimes Act, which was quite serious. I mean, in the end, there was nothing there. But it shouldn't have happened anyway. So, devising a sanction against a prime minister is not just a simple matter of law. There are other issues which a rational community will need to take into account. You could end up totally dividing your own country when nobody would listen to the truth. A parliamentary committee — there used to be in my time, and I'm out of date, a foreign affairs and defence committee. But compared to what's needed as an intelligence committee, who learns things that are important, it was trivial. I think it involved both houses. Each house would have its own committee, and it would be an important part of a much better fabric for making sure that these kinds of issues are handled sensibly and advisably in Australia, where now they are not.

Graham:

We do have an effective parliamentary foreign affairs committee and a defence committee, which are independent of one another and carry on.

But this would envisage, as you say, an intelligence committee, and in that case, probably everyone would have to be sworn in as a privy councillor and subject to the Privy Council oath for secrecy, because they'd have to be able to get access to highly secret information, and therefore be able to be sanctioned as a privy councillor if they misuse the information.

Barratt:

And to go to Ramesh's question, I think it hasn't happened partly because certainly the current political leaderships are very happy with the status quo, and I don't think we're going to get that changed by appealing to logic or reason to politicians. The only way to get it to happen is to persuade the general Australian public that we need to change this. So, the sort of campaign that I'm involved with, that you know about, is aimed at the —

Thakur:

What campaign is that?

Barratt:

The Campaign for an Iraq War Inquiry is aimed at the public, not primarily aimed at the political body. I agree with the comment about the crime of aggression. There is an International Criminal Court Act 2002, which in its Orwellian language is designed to facilitate our compliance with the International Criminal Court, and the way we facilitate it is by saying whenever the Australian authorities want to investigate the matter, we will have primary jurisdiction and the ICC can stay away, thank you very much.

Fraser:

But the ICC says that. It was quite deliberate. The ICC will not prosecute if the country concerned is going to prosecute. That's not unique to Australia.

Barratt:

Yeah.

Fraser:

Every country that signed on —

Graham:

Well, in fact, that's what we always say. When we're telling our American friends, "Listen," you know, they won't sign it. "Oh, 'cause we'll be dragged in."

I say, "You can't be dragged if you're going to prosecute in your own jurisdiction." There's no reason. Why would you assume an American wouldn't be prosecuted properly for war crimes? And they've done it. I find that one of the most important reasons why the Statute of Rome is so important is because individual countries, it's only if they fail to do their own job that the international court takes over.

Fraser:

Yeah, that's right.

Barratt:

So, it is there in our domestic law. I would also say that if you introduce — you know, this idea doesn't have wide currency, but if you introduced a deployment resolution into Parliament and can't get it through, I think we ought to proceed to an election. The government ought to fall if it fails on a war, as it does if it fails to get its budget to pass. If you want politicians to stop and think about whether we want to go off to war, that would be something for them to think about. "If I can't get this through both houses, we're off to an election."

I would be all in favour of a strong standing intelligence committee. I think one of the problems in our parliamentary system is that most parliamentarians have no interest in foreign policy whatsoever and not much knowledge of it. And I think having a good, solid group of people in Parliament who have been working through these issues as they go along would be a very healthy thing, not only for the Parliament but for our foreign ministry, our defence department, just to have an educated parliamentary base.

Graham:

Absolutely.

Tyler:

I'm sorry. Thank you.

Question:

My question is to the whole panel. You have been involved in some of the other ways in making these decisions, like, for the intervention for war. So, how much of these decisions were made to go into a war or not go into a war is about opposing international norms or moral obligations? Rather than sort of kind of [*inaudible*] space and cost space. I mean, in the discussion that you had within the parliaments [*inaudible*], so how much of these debates were like, "I'm not going to war because it's against the international norms" or because it's against the moral obligation that you had? And if it's about these international norms and moral obligations of not going into a war, then how do you balance this with the benefit of freeing, as an unintended sometimes-consequence of some of these wars, in case the way that the prime minister mentioned that it was only about al-Qaeda and not about a regime change in Afghanistan. Well, I think the consequence of that was that there are millions of people were free from a very fanatic rule of Taliban. There was no option — there was no opportunity for those millions of young men and women to be freed and to be given this opportunity. So, how are you going to balance it if you look at all these inventions as evil in hindsight? Thank you.

Audience member:

I was just going to say there is a statutory committee on intelligence of the Australian Parliament. It's not an all-party committee. It was up until very recently only the two major parties, and their members were appointed by the prime minister or the leader of the Opposition. They did not have to have a clearance, but the staff of the secretariat did have to have a clearance to the level of an ASIS [Australian Secret Intelligence Service] officer, so it was quite a high clearance. The parliamentary committee doesn't have a role in deciding upon going to war, and is certainly not asked beforehand about it. It was asked, as you know, afterwards, to assess the intelligence on Iraq's weapons of mass destruction, but that was a confined inquiry that dealt only with the intelligence and not with the broader questions of Australia going to war, and there's scope, I think, for a much broader inquiry into that process.

There is also in the Australian Parliament a very large committee, the Joint Committee on Foreign Affairs, Defence and Trade, which has thirty-two members, and it attempts to develop expertise amongst members of

Parliament about foreign affairs and defence matters. It's quite a long-standing committee. But no committees of the Australian Parliament, with the exception, perhaps, of things like the Public Works Committee, have a role to play in making decisions before a government acts on certain matters. So, I think that's something for the strengthening of the committee system, if we wanted committees to play that sort of part. And it could still be advisory to Parliament in a decision that Parliament needed to make about going to war.

Tyler:

I'll take a couple more, just to make sure that everyone's had a chance. At the back ...?

Question:

This question's for all panellists. When you were discussing before about misused intelligence in the case of the Iraq War, is there any possibility that this could repeat itself in the Syrian conflict? Particularly with recent news talk of chemical weapons being used?

Question:

My question is really for Bill Graham. I'd be interested in your view of why it was not in Canada's interests to be involved in the Iraq invasion. We've had lots of information about why it was originally in our interests and why it was in international interests, but what was the argument in Canada about it not being in the national interest to be a part of the coalition?

Fraser:

It wasn't in our interest either. [*Audience laughter*]

Tyler:

Would you like to respond to any of those?

Fraser:

International norms. I think you've got to take the international norm as being, if you're a serious member of the international community, that war is illegal, unless it's in relation to self-defence or unless it is sanctioned by the Security Council. Now, that is the norm to which we aspire. And it's interesting to ask which countries have ignored that norm and which have not. But if you're talking about international norms, that's the norm established when the United Nations was established.

I think our statutory intelligence committee needs infinitely stronger powers, and it needs to be able to go behind and underneath the intelligence that is offered to it. And I don't think it did that with anything like the due diligence which it should have, with all respect. And I've seen its report. Because it's not just long after the event you knew that it was wrong. There were people at the time who knew that it was wrong, who said it was wrong and why it was wrong. And the very fact that [Hans] Blix was not allowed to continue said very loudly [that] he's going to come up with a negative, and then we're not going to be able to go to war. So why our intelligence reported as it did, God knows.

Syria? I think [U.S.] President [Barack] Obama is trying desperately to be very cautious at the moment. He's coming in for a lot of criticism from people like [Republican senator John] McCain and others. "We got to do something, we got to do something." Well, at the moment, the evidence is not there. There are some photographs or whatever, and you know, maybe it's Republicans wanting to hunt somebody who's got no right to be president, A) because he's black; B) because he's a Democrat; and C) because he wasn't born in America. And I know people who were my Republican friends who have taken exactly that view and argued it with great seriousness over a long dinner. And, you know, these were people who've been to universities meant to be good — Yale and Harvard! [*Audience laughter*]

But he is being cautious, and I think that's encouraging. But what do you do in that situation, especially when you know that al-Qaeda are amongst the rebels? There are all sorts of radical fundamentalists. Who in the hell are the rebels? We helped rebels in Libya, but what sort of government is Libya going to have? And so, just helping rebels because they happen to be fighting against a wretched person is not necessarily a reason to go to war. It would be nice to know something about them.

And another cautionary thing, which I hope President Obama has learned: the last person to listen — which President Bush had not learned and America had not learned, [President John F.] Kennedy had not learned — the last person you listen to for intelligence about a particular country or situation is an expatriate from that country. He has a vested interest to try and advance his own interests. Think of [Iraq's Ahmed] Chalabi. Rumsfeld was saying, "What a wonderful person! He'll be the president!" Well, nobody in Iraq wanted to know anything about him. And that's how Kennedy got into the Bay of Pigs, through Cuban expatriates living in Miami. So, who you get your evidence from, who you get your advice from, is a question that democratic countries haven't really taken to heart.

Barratt:

And the second-last person you listen to is [Israeli prime minister] Mr. [Benjamin] Netanyahu, who has been telling us that an Iranian bomb is just around the corner since 1992.

Graham:

Well, I've had various awkward breakfasts with Mr. Netanyahu, but we'll let that pass.

Maybe I can pick up on the ambassador's question about international norms, and it fits into Peter's question about Canada's position about Iraq. I mean, the first position I take, of course, is in matters of war or all foreign policy: ultimately it's driven by domestic policy first. It has to represent the basic interests of the country and has to represent the domestic political concerns of the country. But as we are more and more integrated globally, there is a blurring between the lines of what's domestic and what's international, and everything that's domestic now tends to have a bit of an international dimension to it, and that's including a lot of things, which makes decisions here sometimes rather difficult.

But when we came to the question of whether we would go to Iraq or not, the issue of international norms was important, because my predecessor, Lloyd Axworthy, as foreign minister with Mr. Chrétien, had spent years along with our Australian colleagues working on the International Criminal Court system, working on beefing up the U.N. system. Countries like Australia, if I dare say, and certainly Canada, our position is that countries of our size, we want an international system that works and with enforceable rules. The big powers, they don't need them. We need the rules. And we, living beside one of the greatest powers, need them perhaps more than any. So it has been a long practice of Canada to strengthen the United States and the United Nations institutions, to strengthen its way of operating, and for us to have gone and said, "Oh, well, we're going to go to Iraq and ignore the United Nations" would have been totally against everything that we've been trying to achieve for the last five or six years. So it was precisely consistent with what we've been doing in our foreign policy in strengthening international norms, but also strengthening the institutions that apply those norms when we said we will only go if it has Security Council authorization. Because that was a recognition, as the prime minister has said, that that is the gold standard of global authority for going to war, apart from self-defence.

I think that those two things intersected and came together at the same time, when it came to making up our decision not to go to Iraq, because we really were very concerned about the effect that this was going to have on the United Nations. And quite frankly, we were concerned about the effect it was going to have on NATO, too, and we were borne out. This caused a lot of awkward years, subsequently, both at the United Nations and in NATO, the animosities that were created by those who did and those who didn't in this particular circumstance.

CONCLUSION

Tyler:

Well, we've come to the end of a fascinating discussion. I'd like to thank the Asia-Pacific College of Diplomacy for putting together such a wonderful event. And I'm going to ask our panellists to end with one final lesson you'd like us to take home that we should be keeping in mind in future cases, from the Iraq experience.

Graham:

War has got to be the last resort. Absolute last resort.

Barratt:

I'll just go back to something I said a little bit earlier. As the republican debate's warming up, what I want everyone in this room to take out of the room is, every time someone tells you they're a republican, say to them, "Do you believe the power to deploy the ADF [Australian Defence Force] should be removed to Parliament?" And if they say no, say to them, "You're not a real republican." [*Audience laughter*]

Tyler:

So, what lesson to take away?

Fraser:

Well, the most important one for us is to get out of bed with America. Not to make them an enemy. ANZUS is fine, but read it. What it says is fine. But get out of bed for going beyond it. Then to be independent and stand up. Canada's done a much better job of that than we have.

Tyler:

And I think this has been a great panel to show the wisdom of bringing together Australia and Canada to reflect on some of the similarities but also the differences in the way that we've approached these issues in international affairs. Can I get a nice thank you?

[Applause]

NOTES

1. James Baker and Lawrence Eagleburger served as secretary of state respectively, and Brent Scowcroft as national security adviser, in the administration of the first President Bush.
2. Independent members of Parliament in Australia, 2010–13.
3. Sir John Greig Latham GCMG (1877–1964) served as attorney general (1925–29, 1932–34), deputy prime minister, and minister for external affairs (1932–34), and was Australia's chief justice (1935–52).

4

THE SHOCK OF THE IRAQ WAR, AND AWE AT THE LINGERING EFFECTS OF THE FOLLY

Ramesh Thakur

Barbara Tuchman famously argued that historical figures made catastrophic decisions contrary to the self-interests of their countries, that were held to be damaging to those interests by contemporaries, and alternatives to which were available at the time.[1] The 2003 Iraq War is that rare mega-disaster that was richly foretold at the time.[2] The decade since has done little to soften the criticism and much to validate and deepen it. At the time of completing this chapter in early January 2014, Fallujah, the emblem city of resistance to "occupiers" and "oppressors," had fallen to al-Qaeda-linked militants, the Iraqi government was massing troops to retake it, and Washington expressed support for the government but insisted it would not be sending troops back. A new United Nations report concluded that 8,868 Iraqis died in 2013, of whom 7,818 were civilians. A report by the independent public data base Iraq Body Count estimated the year's death toll at 9,475 civilians. Both figures are comparable to the toll in 2008, and both sources predicted a worse year to come in 2014.[3]

How do we impress on U.S. neo-conservatives — and their Australian-British fellow travellers — the enormous disparity between the vision dreamed, the goals pursued, the means used, and the results obtained? Ten years after the event, conventional wisdom seems to have settled into the conclusion that the war was one of the gravest foreign policy blunders of modern times. To paraphrase Mark Antony in Shakespeare's *Julius Caesar* (act 3, scene 2), the good that the coalition may have done lies interred with the bones of the dead in Iraq; the evil they unleashed will live on in infamy.

This chapter looks back in wonder at the motives behind the invasion, to assess whether the war was a result of compound errors and badly implemented, or dishonestly conceived. It then describes the costs of the war under twelve headings.

MOTIVES

We're an empire now, and when we act we create our own reality.[4]

Was the 2003 Iraq War well-intentioned but based on flawed evidence and faulty intelligence, or was it rooted in intentional deceit? A decade after the fact, the balance of probabilities seems to suggest that it resulted from a campaign of deliberate falsehoods rather than honest mistakes. The gravity and immediacy of the threat from Iraq were deliberately exaggerated.[5] Washington reversed the usual sequence of trial, conviction, and punishment. The outcome was predetermined: a swift and heavy military defeat leading to regime change in Baghdad. The justification (weapons of mass destruction, or WMDs; involvement with international terrorism; humanitarian atrocities) came after the fact and was changed from WMDs to liberation when the former were conclusively proven not to exist.

Saddam Hussein was on the Bush administration's agenda when it came into office;[6] "9/11" provided the alibi, not the reason. General Wesley Clark, who commanded the NATO intervention in Kosovo in 1999, noted in a public speech in California in October 2007 that the neo-cons had shifted the role of the U.S. military from deterring conflicts and defending America against threats to invading other countries, overthrowing their governments, and installing U.S.-friendly regimes.[7]

Going by the writings of many of the neo-con warriors since their departure from power, they are like Philip II of Spain: "No experience of the failure of his policy could shake his belief in its essential excellence."[8]

"The belief that Saddam Hussein had weapons of mass destruction was near universal," former prime minister John Howard argued in his Lowy speech on April 9, 2013.[9] The self-exculpation is at variance with the facts, as this quote from February 2003 proves: "Little evidence links Hussein to al-Qaeda leader Osama bin Laden. Hussein has been successfully contained and does not pose a clear and present danger to regional, world or U.S. security. Washington has scarcely concealed its real agenda of regime change.... Iraq does not have usable nuclear weapons."[10]

According to fresh reports, British intelligence services informed Prime Minister Tony Blair in April 2002 (a year before the war) that Saddam had no nuclear weapons and any other WMDs would be "very, very small." The Chilcot Inquiry was told that Blair accepted this but converted to George W. Bush's way of thinking after a subsequent visit to the U.S. president's ranch in Crawford, Texas.[11] This is corroborated in the infamous Downing Street memorandum of July 23, 2002, which made it clear that the U.S. administration was determined to go to war and military action was inevitable. But British officials did not believe there was sufficient legal justification: there was no recent evidence of Iraqi complicity with international terrorism; Saddam's WMD capability was less than that of Libya, North Korea, or Iran; and he was not a threat to his neighbours. It was necessary to create the conditions that would make an invasion legal, hence "the intelligence and facts were being fixed around the policy" and the United States "had already begun 'spikes of activity' to put pressure on the regime."[12]

The more interesting question is why independent analysts from "the marketplace of ideas" — columnists, public intellectuals, university professors — failed to challenge the inflated threat assessment by the administration based on manipulated evidence, selective intelligence, and flawed analysis. Chaim Kaufmann provides a five-part answer: the administration engaged in a deliberate issue manipulation by reframing the threat posed by Iraq from regional aggression to direct attack on the U.S. mainland; government control of intelligence; exploiting White House authority on foreign policy; the failure of institutional checks (opposition, media, research institutions) to function with matching authority; and the atmosphere of crisis engendered by the shock of 9/11.[13]

COSTS

In his defence of the 2003 decision on the tenth anniversary of the occasion,[14] John Howard is as unshakably in denial about the reality of Iraq as his comrades-in-arms George W. Bush and Tony Blair. Is their collective and continuing complacency really proof against every evidence to the contrary of the most compelling kind? Blair in particular calls to mind a character in Dickens' *Bleak House*: "Sir Leicester is generally in a complacent mood.… When he has nothing else to do, he can always contemplate his own greatness. It is a considerable advantage to a man, to have so inexhaustible a subject."[15]

The balance sheet has to include the following "dirty dozen" costs as the lasting legacy of the war:

1. The human toll of those killed, wounded and displaced

2. The economic costs

3. The spread of jihads

4. The strategic retreat of the United States

5. Setbacks to the rule of international law

6. The damage to international criminal justice as a normative project

7. Soiled U.N.-U.S. relations

8. Fractured transatlantic relations

9. Domestic divisions in U.S. society and polity

10. The compromised project of democracy promotion

11. The damaged credibility of U.S. and Western media

12. Erosion of U.S. soft power

Human Toll

The invasion mutated into occupation, insurgency, and finally a full-fledged civil war. According to the Costs of War Project, the total deaths over the March 2003–March 2013 decade (Figure 4.1) break down as follows: U.S. military, 4,488; U.S. contractors, 3,418; Allied military and police, 10,819; other Allied, 318; opposition forces, 36,400; journalists, 231; and humanitarian workers, 62.[16]

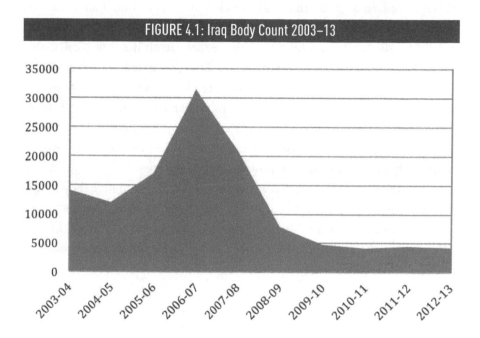

FIGURE 4.1: Iraq Body Count 2003–13

Source: Iraq Body Count, *www.iraqbodycount.org.*

But what of civilians dead? This is surely the key measure if we are going to evaluate the Iraq War primarily as a humanitarian misadventure. According to the Iraq Body Count project, by mid-March 2013 between 112,017 and 122,438 civilians had been killed in Iraq, with another 11,500 likely to be added to the total from the Iraq War Logs.[17] A U.S. medical team, collaborating with Iraqi specialists, calculated the civilian casualty toll based on a scientific household survey and came up with the stunning figure of 650,000 "excess deaths." (That was without counting Fallujah, which was categorized as an outlier because it was the scene of the fiercest and most prolonged fighting in 2004.)[18] Women and children made up more than half the total killed.[19] According to the Iraqi government, the death toll is almost a quarter million. The figure climbs to more than a million dead by August 2007 as estimated by the London-based polling organization Opinion Research Business.[20]

In October 2013, a new study by a team of scholars from the United States (Washington and Johns Hopkins universities), Canada (Simon

Fraser), and Iraq (Mustansiriya) concluded that around half a million people died in Iraq of "war-related causes" from the U.S. invasion in 2003 until mid-2011. Of the total figure, the "excess death" total was calculated to be 461,000, 60 percent of which was directly attributable to violence. The remaining 40 percent can be accounted for by such factors as people not being able to leave their homes under war conditions to seek medical help, hospitals being overwhelmed with people suffering from violent injuries, degraded medical-supply distribution networks causing scarcity of urgently needed medicines, power outages, et cetera.[21]

Unless commentators are lazy, incompetent, or intimidated, they should say "between 174,000 and one million Iraqis have been killed or have died as a result of the 2003 war." In addition, the war caused "the largest human displacement in the Middle East since 1948."[22] Two million fled abroad and another two million were displaced internally. Iraq's Christians in particular have left in large numbers.[23]

Economic Costs

Nobel Prize–winning economist Joseph Stiglitz and his colleagues have calculated the substantial and lasting costs of the Iraq War at US$3 trillion.[24] According to the Costs of War project based at Brown University's Watson Institute, the direct costs of the war — the U.S. federal government spending on it — is US$2.2 trillion through Fiscal Year 2013. Future health and disability payments for veterans will come to $590 billion, and interest accrued to pay for the war will add up to $3.9 trillion.[25] One can only speculate on the contribution of the treasure wasted in Iraq to the global financial crisis of 2008 that originated in the United States, on the one hand, and to degrading the capacity of the U.S. government to mitigate its effects and promote recovery, on the other.

FUELLING THE FIRE OF JIHADISM

In a memo on the war on terror on October 16, 2003, Defense Secretary Donald Rumsfeld memorably asked, "Are we capturing, killing or deterring and dissuading more terrorists every day than the madrassas and the radical clerics are recruiting, training and deploying against us?"[26] His wise question was ignored in Washington, not least by himself. Yet it received remarkable affirmation from the British ambassador to Italy, Sir Ivor Roberts, who explained to a private gathering of policy-makers in Rome in September 2004 that al-Qaeda would celebrate the re-election of President Bush, since he was their "best recruiting sergeant."[27]

Iraq was a distraction from the war on terror. The administration indulged its *idée fixe* on Saddam Hussein at the cost of letting many of the real culprits behind 9/11 get away. For months, with the focus sharply and almost solely on Saddam, Osama bin Laden, in effect, became Osama bin Forgotten, while Washington was drawn into fighting a war on the terrorists' terms.

It remains a mystery why Australia, Britain, and the United States believed they could achieve victory in the war on international terrorism against Western targets by inciting a still-deeper hatred of the West's foreign policy. Most informed observers predicted that the sight of American forces occupying Baghdad would spur more terrorism, not less. Iraq became a hotbed of terrorism as a result of the war. Diverse strands of evidence corroborate the thesis that the radicals were dispirited and at a loss in 2002 after the rapid defeat of the Taliban in Afghanistan, but became exuberant with the United States being tied down in Iraq from 2003. They were able to "expose" the real nature of the United States as a global enemy of Islam bent on stealing Arab oil. The inconsistency in U.S. policy was exploited by al-Qaeda recruiters as the perpetual and systematic hypocrisy of American foreign policy. Nor was the spur to terrorism confined to Iraq or the Middle East. U.S. officials in Southeast Asia conceded that recruitment and fundraising for the terrorist organization Jemaah Islamiyah had become easier because of the region's widespread opposition to the war on Iraq.[28] And the British public simply refused to accept the government's denial of any link between the Iraq War and the London bombings on July 7, 2005.[29] As Ian McAllister shows in his chapter, Australians were like the British on this point.

Strategic: Iran and China as the Regional and Global Victors

Paul Kennedy's thesis of imperial overstretch may yet prove correct.[30] The demonstration of the limits to U.S. and NATO power to impose American will on local populations willing to fight back in Iraq and Afghanistan left many less fearful of "superior" Western power. Abusive practices in the "war on terror" left them less respectful of Western values. The Iraq and Afghanistan wars hastened the military, financial, and moral decline of America. The U.S. economy was now characterized by mounting debt and deficit and declining levels of innovation. China exploited the United States's entrapment in Iraq and Afghanistan and the collapse of its reputation for moral and financial rectitude to extend the reach of its own soft power. In 2013, Russia exploited the decline of America's reputation and the war-weariness of its public to regain a strategic foothold in the Middle East by successfully playing the role of peacemonger against U.S. threats of military strikes against Syria.

The big strategic victor of the Iraq War was Iran, whose coffers were filled by the spike in oil prices, and whose local rivals in Baghdad and Kabul were toppled. U.S. and allied forces were entangled in Iraq and Afghanistan, support for overseas military entanglements fell steeply across the Western world, pro-Iranian Shias were in firm control of Iraq, and Western resolve to go to war yet again against another Islamic country was much reduced. In effect, President Bush helped Iran to win its 1980–88 war with Iraq after a two-decade pause.

The Rule of International Law

A preventive war is like committing suicide for fear of death.

— Bismarck

The fabric of orderly relations between nations, the health of the human rights norm, and the struggle for a better world are built on respect for international law. The legal issues in relation to going to war are canvassed briefly by Charles Sampford in his chapter in this volume. The belligerent countries insisted that the war was both legal and legitimate, based on a series of prior U.N. resolutions and the long and frustrating history of deceitful defiance of the United Nations by Saddam. Others conceded that it may have been illegal, but that it was nevertheless legitimate, as with the Kosovo War in 1999, in its largely humanitarian outcome. Yet a third group insisted that the war was both illegal and illegitimate.[31]

There are only two grounds for the lawful use of force against another country: individual and collective self-defence against armed attack, or under U.N. authorization. Iraq had not attacked any other country in its own region and it had no credible connection to those who planned and executed the terror attacks of September 11, 2001, on the United States. Washington did not help its cause by a continually shifting justification. Containment and deterrence worked against the far more formidable Soviet enemy during the Cold War; why did they have to be replaced by the destabilizing doctrine of prevention? In effect, Iraq became the testing ground for the doctrine and weapons of preventive war, for which there is no justification in international law. Washington was seen as being determined to wage war not because it had to, but because it wanted to and could; not because Iraq was strong and, as such, posed a threat, but because it was weak and could be attacked with ease.

Deputy Defense Secretary Paul Wolfowitz conceded subsequently that the WMD issue was chosen in the end for good "bureaucratic" reasons. *Vanity Fair*'s reporter did not tape the telephone interview, and quoted Wolfowitz as saying, "For bureaucratic reasons we settled on one issue, weapons of mass destruction, because it was the one reason everyone could agree on."[32] Responding to the burgeoning controversy as President Bush toured Europe, the Pentagon released its own transcript of the interview, in which Wolfowitz is quoted as saying that "there have always been three fundamental concerns. One is weapons of mass destruction, the second is support for terrorism, the third is the criminal treatment of the Iraqi people. But for reasons that have a lot to do with the U.S. government bureaucracy, we settled on the one issue that everyone could agree on, which was weapons of mass destruction as the core reason."[33] In other words, it was a marketing gimmick.

In October 2004, the CIA's Iraq Survey Group reported with finality that while Saddam had harboured ambitions to obtain WMDs, the Iraqi programs to build them had decayed completely. Iraq's arsenal of chemical and biological weapons was negligible, its nuclear weapons program was virtually non-existent, and it had little ability to revive the weapons programs.[34] U.N. sanctions had helped to dismantle them and U.N. inspections had given an accurate assessment of Saddam's WMD capability. Asked to comment about the reports that his office was bugged, U.N. chief weapons inspector at the time Hans Blix reportedly said, if so, his only regret was that those bugging him were not listening to what he was saying.[35] Subsequent studies have confirmed that U.S. intelligence analysts were internally questioning almost all pre-war claims about Iraq's WMDs: that Iraq tried to buy uranium in Africa for its nuclear program, that it was producing biological weapons in mobile labs, that it had an active chemical weapons program, and that it had acquired unmanned aircraft for delivery of WMDs.

The same was true in Australia. According to Margaret Swieringa, secretary to the Australian federal parliamentary intelligence committee from 2002 until 2007, the report of its inquiry established the following: that the scale of Iraq's WMD threat had declined from a decade earlier, that Iraq did not have nuclear weapons and had not obtained fissile material to make them, and that it lacked biological and chemical weapons production. In sum, under U.N. sanctions, "Iraq's military capability remained limited and the country's infrastructure was still in decline" and "no intelligence had accurately pointed to the location of weapons of mass destruction."[36]

Liberal democracy rests on the rule of law. U.K. attorney general Lord Goldsmith had serious reservations about the legality of war, based on six arguments: it was for the United Nations and not individual states to decide if Iraq was in breach of U.N. resolutions; Security Council Resolution 1441 was an unreliable basis for war because it did not use the key phrase "all necessary means" to enforce it, hence the need for a second U.N. resolution; earlier U.N. resolutions going back to the first Gulf War could not easily be revived to suit the exigencies of 2003; there were reports from Hans Blix that U.N. inspectors were still doing their job; he also reported that Iraq was being compliant; and the U.S. position on the legality of military action did not apply to Britain because Congress had granted special war-making powers to President Bush.[37] Goldsmith was persuaded to change his mind just before the war began.[38] In her resignation letter. submitted on the eve of the Iraq War, Elizabeth Wilmshurst, deputy legal adviser to the Foreign Office, described military action in Iraq as "an unlawful use of force" that "amounts to the crime of aggression."[39]

Victory in Iraq came at the price of re-legitimizing wars of choice as an instrument of unilateral state policy. It is not possible to promote the role of international law in world affairs by hollowing out the legal framework that restricts the right to go to war. U.S. senator Robert Byrd warned that "we may have sparked a new international arms race as countries move ahead to develop WMDs as a last ditch attempt to ward off a possible pre-emptive strike from a newly belligerent United States which claims the right to hit where it wants."[40] Few will accept the doctrine that the administration of the day in Washington can decide who is to be which country's leader, and who is to be toppled. Others will not politely accept the new U.S. imperial order. Instead, they will arm and align themselves so as not to become tomorrow's Iraq.

International Criminal Justice

Starting with the Nuremberg and Tokyo tribunals after the Second World War, and including ad hoc tribunals in Rwanda and the former Yugoslavia as way stations, the world has made revolutionary advances in the criminalization of domestic and international violence by states, and in holding individuals criminally accountable for those acts.[41] The statute of the International Criminal Court (ICC) was adopted in Rome in 1998 by a 120 to 7 vote and came into effect in 2002. The court's remit is to prosecute individuals for the crimes of genocide, war crimes, crimes against humanity, and from 2017, if approved, the crime of aggression. Danilo Zolo concludes that international tribunals are little more than victors' police and a tool of Western imperialism.[42] The African Union has issued several strongly worded communications to the ICC and the United Nations complaining that the court has singled out Africans for prosecution, and has advised member states not to co-operate with the ICC with respect to indictees from Sudan and Kenya.[43]

The effects of the Iraq War have been particularly pernicious in damaging the ICC as the institutional custodian of international criminal justice. I saw this repeatedly in my conversations on the ICC while I was with the United Nations. Blair and the U.K. defence and foreign ministers were accused of crimes against humanity by Greek lawyers who lodged a case with the ICC.[44] The doctrine of universal jurisdiction was employed also to threaten prosecution against President Bush and General Tommy Franks (commander of the U.S. forces in Iraq). Rumsfeld retaliated by warning that if U.S. officials could no longer travel to Brussels without fear of prosecution, NATO headquarters would have to be relocated to another country.[45] In July 2003, Belgium amended its law on universal jurisdiction and restricted trials in Belgian courts to crimes committed or suffered by its citizens or residents. In 2012, Nobel Peace laureate Desmond Tutu explained his refusal to share the stage with Blair by recalling the "immorality" of the U.S. and British invasion of Iraq in 2003: "In a consistent world, those responsible for this suffering and loss of life should be treading the same path as some of their African … peers who have been made to answer for their actions in the Hague."[46]

A Damaged U.N.-U.S. Relationship

The United Nations was doubly damaged. For some, it failed the test of standing up to a tyrant who had brutalized his own people, terrorized his neighbours, and thumbed his nose at the United Nations for twelve years. For most, it failed to stand up to a superpower in defence of a country that posed no threat to any other country. Lest we forget, protecting a small country from being attacked and invaded by a major power, like Czechoslovakia and Poland by Germany, was the primary reason for setting up the United Nations.

For Washington the issues could hardly have been more serious. One of the world's most brutal regimes could not be permitted to remain in power until it succeeded in acquiring the world's most destructive weapons. Bush famously declared that by refusing to support the war, the United Nations would become irrelevant. From a test of U.N. relevance, however, the agenda shifted to being a test of the legitimacy of U.S. action as the issue metamorphosed into that of whether we wish to live by rules and laws or by the force of arms.

Had the United Nations been bribed and bullied into sanctioning the war, the result would not have been to legitimize war but to cast the United Nations' own legitimacy into doubt. Because the rhetoric about WMDs was seen as a transparent ruse, the recourse to the United Nations was seen simply as an effort to harness U.N. legitimacy to a predetermined U.S. agenda: the United Nations is "now more than ever reduced to the servile function of after-sales service provider for the United States, on permanent call as the mop-up brigade."[47]

The United Nations is both a site of and an actor in global governance.[48] The relationship between the legitimacy-dispensing United Nations and the power-wielding United States is critical for the provision of both authoritative and effective international security to underpin world order.[49] Those who wish to degrade the United Nations should be careful of what they wish, for the organization is often useful in picking up the pieces after others have shattered the fragile edifice of world order. Its capacity to mobilize political will in reluctant governments and rally the faithful to the internationalist dream whose death has been prematurely predicted cannot be matched by any other institution. After the invasion, the United Nations had to tread the fine line between A) being seen as legitimizing an illegal and unjust war by collaborating with the occupiers "who wanted a U.N. presence in occupied Iraq as a legitimizing factor — not as a partner with a vast reservoir of post-conflict peace-building experience;"[50] and B) abandoning the people of Iraq who were the true victims thrice over (of Saddam's brutality, U.N. sanctions, and U.S. war).

U.S.-Europe Relations

Transatlantic relations were also damaged. When the major European nations objected that the case for war had not been proven beyond reasonable doubt, instead of dialogue they got bad-tempered insults. The neo-conservative ideologues "regard allies not as proof of diplomatic strength but as evidence of military weakness."[51] If friends and allies are to be useful, they must avoid both slavish obedience and instinctive opposition; be prepared to support the Americans when they are right despite intense international unpopularity; but be willing to say no to Washington when it is wrong, despite the risk of intense American irritation. As this volume demonstrates, Canada performed this role rather better in 2003 than Australia.

Moreover, Donald Rumsfeld's characterization of old and new Europe was, in fact, quite mistaken. In light of the past few centuries of European history, France and Germany standing together in resisting war represent the new Europe of secular democracies and welfare states, built on peaceful relations embedded in Continental institutions. The former Soviet satellites that sided with the United States represent continuity with the old Europe built on balance-of-power policies that had led to two world wars.

Domestic Divisions

The American people were domestically divided by Iraq, with an edge to their opinions that was quite disheartening for those who recognize that the American role in world affairs as a great and virtuous power has been historically unique and both vital and necessary. The deep internal frictions were especially troubling because of the impressive national unity shown in the aftermath of 9/11.[52]

Iraq was the first of three military missions that U.S. forces took part in across the Islamic crescent — the other two being Afghanistan and Libya — whose essential failures have drained support for any further foreign adventures. In a Reuters/Ipsos poll published on August 24, 2013, 60 percent of Americans opposed U.S. intervention in Syria's civil war, against just 9 percent saying President Barack Obama should act. In a subsequent Pew Research Center poll, Americans opposed U.S. military action 63 to 28 percent.[53] In another survey of active-duty U.S. service personnel, opposition to strikes stood at three to one.[54] Reflecting widespread and strong public unease, a *Washington Post* analysis of the likely congressional vote at the time that Russia rescued Obama from the trap of his own making showed 253 to 26 opposition in the House (with 154 undecided) and 40 to 23 opposition in the Senate (37 undecided) to granting Obama authority to launch military strikes on Syria.[55]

The story in Britain was the same. Prime Minister David Cameron tabled a motion in Parliament on August 29 that would have paved the way for British participation in the impending air strikes. The ghost of Iraq 2003 hovered unmistakably in the ensuing seven-hour debate, with coded — "We must not let the spectre of previous mistakes paralyze our ability to stand up for what is right"[56] — and explicit — "The well of public opinion has been well and truly poisoned by the Iraq episode"[57] — references from Cameron and his opponents. Parliament rejected the motion by a vote of 285 to 272.

In 2013, Australia proved to be out of step with its U.S. and U.K. allies in not being prepared to take the case to Parliament. The ghosts of Iraq in 2003 will continue to haunt and hobble the response to future acts of WMD barbarity. This is why parliamentary democracies, including Australia and Canada, need urgently to modernize their procedures and structures for going to war with full parliamentary debate and sanction, instead of by government fiat based on the instincts of a strong-willed prime minister or through subterfuge.

Democracy Promotion

One of the professed goals of the war was to establish democracy in Iraq and use it as a beacon to promote political freedoms across the Arab world.

How does one impose democracy by bombers, helicopter gunships, and tanks? Many other regimes with equally questionable democratic credentials remained solid U.S. allies. The global expansion of democracy has not been a pillar of American foreign policy; the rhetoric of democracy is an expedient justification in support of other, more traditional goals. As the United States retreated after wars in Iraq, Afghanistan, and Libya, it left dysfunctional and autocratic governments in each country as proof of the failure of nation-building and democracy-promotion efforts. At the St. Petersburg G8 summit in 2006, responding to U.S. president Bush's suggestion that Russia should be more democratic, President Vladimir Putin pointedly retorted, "We certainly would not want to have the same kind of democracy as they have in Iraq."[58] Yet another perverse consequence was that the war on terror led to the curtailment of many core liberties and freedoms in the leading Western democracies: whether or not it reached the intended destinations, democracy was being exported out of its home base.

Media Credibility

The credibility of the British and U.S. media suffered a steady erosion because of their coverage and analyses of the Iraq War. Sections of the media became cheerleaders for the humanitarian warriors. Tellingly, "of Rupert Murdoch's 174 newspapers worldwide, not one editorially opposed the war; and, once the invasion began, many of their commentaries became hysterically supportive."[59] In effect, patriotism supplanted journalism through such questionable techniques as "embedded" reporters. The U.S. and British security services repeatedly planted fabricated stories in the all-too-gullible mainstream media, which failed to carry out any sort of due diligence on government claims.[60] Media critics were held accountable for minor flaws and gaps in stories, but officials whose lies and incompetence caused immeasurable loss of life in an unnecessary war got medals of freedom.

The giants of American media collaborated with the Orwellian redefinition of common understandings of torture after 9/11. A group of journalism students at Harvard University analyzed the usage of key terms by the *Los Angeles Times*, the *New York Times*, *USA Today*, and the *Wall Street Journal*. In the seven decades before 2002, they routinely described waterboarding as torture (81 and 96 percent for the *New York Times* and *Los Angeles Times* respectively). After 2002, when the United States itself began to engage in the practice of waterboarding under official sanction and approval from the administration, the *LA Times, NY Times, Wall Street Journal,* and *USA Today* called it torture in only 4.8, 1.4, 1.6, and 0 percent of cases, respectively. The nationalist slip of the major U.S. newspapers showed in another way. When other countries engaged in waterboarding, the *LA Times* and *NY Times* called it torture in 86 and 91 percent of their articles, falling to 8 and 11 percent when the United States itself resorted to the practice.[61]

It is fair enough for journalists, analysts, and officials to insist on the strict body count rather than the best available scientific estimates of excess deaths, provided they are consistent in applying this stricture to all conflicts. What the rest of the world sees is that when the victims die from U.S. violence, the lowest confirmed toll is used. But for anti-Western regimes, the phrase "up to X thousand may have been killed" is substituted to plant the upper end of casualty estimates. Do we think they do not notice and care, or is it simply that we do not care about what they think? The distinguished Middle East journalist Rami Khouri, after pointing out that he learned his journalistic craft and values in the United States, writes after a month-long working visit there that "any impartial assessment of the professional conduct of most American media outlets in covering the Iran situation would find it deeply flawed and highly opinionated to the point where I would say that mainstream media coverage of Iran in the U.S. is professionally criminal."[62]

Soft Power Erosion

The growing loss of U.S. media credibility translates into a corresponding erosion of U.S. soft power. After 2003, there was a startlingly precipitous worldwide decline in U.S. global leadership.[63] Rarely has a U.S. administration faced such isolation and loss of public support among its closest allies from essentially pro-American publics as the Bush administration following the Iraq War. All cross-national opinion polls showed plummeting confidence in U.S. credibility and leadership. In an interview with an Australian newspaper, outgoing Deputy Secretary of State Richard Armitage noted poignantly that among his biggest regrets was that after 9/11, "instead of redoubling what is our traditional export of hope and optimism we exported our fear and anger. And presented a very intense and angry face to the world."[64] As Senator Byrd put it, "America's true power lies not in its will to intimidate, but in its ability to inspire."[65] As Joseph Nye observes, "Soft power depends upon credibility.... [It] may appear less risky than economic or military power, [but] it is often hard to use, easy to lose and costly to re-establish."[66] America's reputation for competence and support for human rights took a big hit.

U.S. credibility on human rights suffered a calamitous collapse with the publication of photographs from the Abu Ghraib prison, graphically depicting the extent to which the war had brutalized the U.S. military. The abuses were not isolated incidents but reflected a systemic malaise.[67] Thus Rob Corddry of the satirical *Daily Show* said, "Remember, it's not important that we did torture these people. What's important is that we are not the kind of people who would torture these people."[68]

Marine Major-General Michael Lehnert was the first commander of the task force that opened the U.S. detention camp in Guantánamo Bay at the U.S. naval base in Cuba in January 2002. The United States held 779 men at the detention facility altogether and 162 remained there as of the end of 2013, twelve years later. In a newspaper column after retirement, he wrote that the camp was opened because the United States was "legitimately angry and frightened" after the attacks of 9/11. Even in the early days, however, he became "convinced that many of the detainees should never have been sent in the first place. They had little intelligence value, and there was insufficient evidence linking them to war crimes." He added:

> In retrospect, the entire detention and interrogation strategy was wrong. We squandered the goodwill of the world after we were attacked by our actions in Guantánamo, both in terms of detention and torture. Our decision to keep Guantánamo open has helped our enemies because it validates every negative perception of the United States.[69]

CONCLUSION

The Iraq experience confirms that, as with terrorism, a war of aggression is an unacceptable tactic no matter how just the cause. The Bush administration pulled down the four pillars of post-1945 U.S. foreign policy: a commitment to international law; consensual decision-making; moderation; and the preservation of peace.[70] The ouster of Saddam Hussein flowed from strategic, not ethical, calculations. The United States is a great power, and a great power has strategic imperatives, not moral ones. Washington is motivated to act internationally not because it cares about foreign people, but because it cares about its own interests. The United States is consistent in its foreign policy, remarkably so — but strategically consistent, not morally so.[71]

"In theory, there is no difference between theory and practice. In practice, there is," observed Yogi Berra in his infinite wisdom. The optimistic assumptions behind Washington's Iraq folly can be summed up as: the people of Iraq will welcome and love the Americans as liberators with the ouster of Saddam Hussein; the United Nations will fall flat on its face and the countries of the world will flock to join the coalition as soon as the WMDs in Iraq are found and displayed; and Iraq will virtually rebuild itself with petrodollars. All proved to be wrong. As the *New York Times* commented, "What all our loss and pain and expense in the Iraqi invasion has actually proved is that the weapons inspection worked, that international sanctions — deeply, deeply messy as they turned out to be — worked, and that in the case of Saddam Hussein, the United Nations worked."[72]

NOTES

1. Barbara Tuchman, *The March of Folly: From Troy to Vietnam* (New York: Random House, 1984).

2. For my own collection of newspaper op-eds, see Ramesh Thakur, *War in Our Time: Reflections on Iraq, Terrorism and Weapons of Mass Destruction* (Tokyo: United Nations University Press, 2007).

3. Luke Harding, "Iraq Suffers Its Deadliest Year Since 2008," *The Guardian*, January 1, 2014.

4. Unnamed Bush administration official, quoted in Bob Herbert, "Bush's Blinkers," *New York Times*, October 22, 2004.

5. See Joseph Cirincione, Jessica T. Mathews, and George Perkovich, with Alexis Orton, *WMD in Iraq: Evidence and Implications* (New York: Carnegie Endowment for International Peace, January 2004).

6. Richard A. Clarke, *Against All Enemies: Inside America's War on Terror* (New York: Free Press, 2004), 231–32; Ron Suskind, *The Price of Loyalty: George W. Bush, the White House, and the Education of Paul O'Neill* (New York: Simon & Schuster, 2004), 72–75; and Bob Woodward, *Plan of Attack* (New York: Simon & Schuster, 2004), 9–23.

7. The speech can be found at: http://www.youtube.com/watch?v=TY2DKzastu 8&feature=youtu.be (accessed July 22, 2014).

8. Quoted in Tuchman, *March of Folly*, 7.

9. John Howard, "We Were Right to Invade Iraq," *Canberra Times*, April 9, 2013.

10. Ramesh Thakur, "US Test of UN Relevance," *Japan Times*, February 9, 2003.

11. Jonathan Owen, "Tony Blair and Iraq: The Damning Evidence," *Independent*, April 7, 2013.

12. "The Secret Downing Street Memo," *Sunday Times*, May 1, 2005.

13. Chaim Kaufmann, "Threat Inflation and the Failure of the Marketplace of Ideas: The Selling of the Iraq War," *International Security* 29, no. 1 (2004): 5–48.

14. Howard, "We Were Right to Invade Iraq."

15. Charles Dickens, *Bleak House* (London: Penguin Classics, 1996), 183.

16. "Iraq: 10 Years After Invasion," *Costs of War*, http://costsofwar.org/iraq-10-years-after-invasion (accessed July 23, 2014).

17. "The War in Iraq: 10 Years and Counting," *Iraq Body Count*, http://www.iraqbodycount.org/analysis/numbers/ten-years/ (accessed July 23, 2014).

18. Gilbert Burnham, Riyadh Lafta, Shannon Doocy, and Les Roberts, "Mortality After the 2003 Invasion of Iraq: A Cross-Sectional Cluster Sample Survey," *Lancet* 368, no. 9545 (2006): 1421–28.

19. Les Roberts, Riyadh Lafta, Richard Garfield, Jamal Khudhairi, and Gilbert Burnham, "Mortality Before and After the 2003 Invasion of Iraq: Cluster Sample Survey," *Lancet* 364, no. 9448 (2004): 1857–64. The team was from Johns Hopkins University's Bloomberg School of Public Health and was assisted by doctors from al-Mustansiriya University Medical School in Baghdad. Coalition governments disputed the findings but failed to provide their own estimates of civilian casualties whose accuracy could be assessed against those in the *Lancet* article. The methodology employed is called clustered sampling, which is the rule in public health studies of, for example, epidemics. The alternative technique, called passive-surveillance systems, relies on waiting for reports of deaths to come in, which tends to seriously undercount mortality, in epidemics as in violence. Experts consulted by the *Economist* — not one's average left-wing anti-war propaganda tract — confirmed that the study had been carried out to the standard professional level. See "Counting the Casualties," *Economist*, November 6, 2004.

20. Opinion Research Business, "More Than 1,000,000 Iraqis Murdered Since 2003 Invasion," press release, September 16, 2007, https://zcomm.org/znetarticle/more-than-1-000-000-iraqis-murdered-since-2003-invasion-by-orb/ (accessed August 4, 2014).

21. "Iraq Study Estimates War-Related Deaths at 461,000," BBC News, October 16, 2013, http://www.bbc.co.uk/news/world-middle-east-24547256 (accessed August 4, 2014). See also Michael Todd, "A Better Stab at Estimating How Many

Died in the Iraq War," *Pacific Standard*, October 15, 2013, http://www.psmag.com/politics/better-stab-estimating-many-died-iraq-war-68419/ (accessed August 10, 2014).

22. Alisa Roth and Hugh Eakin, "They Fled from Our War," *New York Review of Books*, May 13, 2010: 26; and Deborah Amos, *Eclipse of the Sunnis: Power, Exile, and Upheaval in the Middle East* (New York: Public Affairs, 2010).

23. William Dalrymple, "Iraq's Disappearing Christians Are Bush and Blair's Legacy," *Guardian*, November 12, 2010: and Robert Fisk, "Exodus: The Changing Map of the Middle East," *Independent*, October 26, 2010.

24. Joseph E. Stiglitz and Linda J. Bilmes, *The Three Trillion Dollar War: The True Cost of the Iraq Conflict* (New York: W.W. Norton & Company, 2008).

25. These statistics can be found on the Costs of War website: http://costsofwar.org/ (accessed August 10, 2014).

26. The text was published in full in 2005: "Rumsfeld's War-on-Terror Memo," *USA Today*, May 20, 2005.

27. Christopher Adams, "Bush Is al-Qaeda's 'Best Recruiting Sergeant', Declares Ambassador," *Financial Times*, September 21, 2004. The speech was described as a "gaffe," thereby proving the saying that a gaffe is the truth spoken by mistake.

28. Raymond Bonner, "New Attacks Expected to Hit Southeast Asia," *International Herald Tribune*, November 25, 2003.

29. Seumas Milne, "It Is an Insult to the Dead to Deny the Link with Iraq," *Guardian*, July 14, 2005; and Andrew Murray, "Cause and Consequence," *Guardian*, July 27, 2005.

30. Paul Kennedy, *The Rise and Fall of the Great Powers: Economic Change and Military Conflict from 1500 to 2000* (New York: Vintage, 1989).

31. The three points of view are articulated in separate chapters by Ruth Wedgwood (legal and legitimate), Charlotte Ku (illegal but legitimate), and David Krieger (illegal and illegitimate), in Ramesh Thakur and W.P.S. Sidhu, eds., *The Iraq Crisis and World Order: Structural, Institutional and Normative Challenges* (Tokyo: United Nations University Press, 2006).

32. "Wolfowitz Comments Revive Doubts Over Iraq's WMD," *USA Today*, May 30, 2003.

33. U.S. Department of Defense, "Deputy Secretary Wolfowitz Interview with Sam Tanenhaus, Vanity Fair," Session Two, May 10, 2003, http://www.defense.gov/transcripts/transcript.aspx?transcriptid=2594 (accessed January 7, 2014).

34. The report can be downloaded at: http://www.cia.gov/cia/reports/iraq_wmd_2004.

35. For his own version of the Iraq story, see Hans Blix, *Disarming Iraq* (New York: Pantheon, 2004).

36. Margaret Swieringa, "Howard Ignored Official Advice on Iraq's Weapons and Chose War," *Sydney Morning Herald*, April 12, 2003.

37. Gaby Hinsliff, "Blair Blow as Secret War Doubts Revealed," *Observer*, April 24, 2005; Michael White, "Opposition Goes on Iraq Offensive," *Guardian*, April 25,

2005; and John Ware, "MI6, Jack Straw, Defence Staff: Blair Ignored Them All," *Guardian*, March 26, 2005.

38. For a critique of how Washington has ridden roughshod over international law and the failure of the Blair government to exercise any restraining influence, see Philippe Sands, *Lawless World: America and the Making and Breaking of Global Rules* (London: Allen Lane, 2005).

39. "Iraq War 'Crime of Aggression,'" BBC News, March 24, 2005.

40. Robert C. Byrd, "The Truth Will Emerge," Senate floor remarks, May 21, 2003, http://www.thenation.com/article/truth-will-emerge (accessed August 10, 2014).

41. See Steven R. Ratner and Jason S. Abrams, *Accountability for Human Rights Atrocities in International Law: Beyond the Nuremberg Legacy* (Oxford: Clarendon, 1997); and Aryeh Neier, *War Crimes: Brutality, Genocide, Terror, and the Struggle for Justice* (New York: Times Books, 1998).

42. Danilo Zolo, *Victors' Justice: From Nuremberg to Baghdad*, translated by M.M. Weir (London: Verso, 2009). Originally published in Italian in 2006.

43. See Max du Plessis, "The African Union, the International Criminal Court and al-Bashir's visit to Kenya," *Institute for Security Studies*, September 28, 2010, http://www.issafrica.org/iss-today/the-african-union-the-international-crim inal-court-and-al-bashirs-visit-to-kenya (accessed August 10, 2014); and "The AU Seeks Clarity on Immunity of State Officials Under International Law," *Institute for Security Studies*, March 16, 2012, http://www.issafrica.org/iss-today/ the-au-seeks-clarity-on-immunity-of-state-officials-under-international-law (accessed August 10, 2014).

44. Helena Smith, "Greeks Accuse Blair of War Crimes in Iraq," *Guardian*, July 29, 2003.

45. Noelle Knox, "Rumsfeld Warns Belgium about War-Crimes Law," *USA Today*, June 13, 2003. U.S. officials ignored the directly equivalent practice of U.S. courts in subjecting foreign officials and officers to the jurisdiction of American courts. See Robert H. Bork, "Judicial Imperialism," *Wall Street Journal Europe*, June 18, 2003.

46. Desmond Tutu, "Why I Had No Choice but to Spurn Tony Blair," *Observer*, September 2, 2012.

47. Alexander Cockburn, "It Should Be Late, It Was Never Great," *Nation*, December 22, 2003.

48. See Ramesh Thakur, "Multilateral Diplomacy and the United Nations: Global Governance Venue or Actor?" in *The New Dynamics of Multilateralism: Diplomacy, International Organizations, and Global Governance*, eds. James P. Muldoon, JoAnn Fagot Aviel, Richard Reitano, and Earl Sullivan (Boulder, CO: Westview, 2011), 249–65.

49. See Ramesh Thakur, "United Nations," in *The Oxford Companion to American Politics*, vol. 2, ed. David Coates (New York: Oxford University Press, 2012), 388–96.

50. Salim Lone (the former director of communications for the U.N. mission in Iraq and among the injured in the August 19, 2003, bombing of the U.N. compound), who adds that "the U.N. effectively sanctioned the invasion after the fact with resolutions that accepted U.S. occupation goals in Iraq," in "One More Casualty of the War on Terrorism," *Washington Post*, August 29, 2004.

51. Robin Cook (who resigned as U.K. foreign minister over the war issue), "Bush Will Now Celebrate by Putting Falluja to the Torch," *Guardian*, November 5, 2004.

52. And not just the United States. In the United Kingdom, fifty-two distinguished former diplomats published an open letter to Prime Minister Tony Blair on April 27, 2004, urging a major rethink of policy toward the Middle East; in the United States, fifty-three former American diplomats did the same on May 4, 2004; and in Australia, a group of forty-three former service chiefs and ambassadors published an open letter on August 8, 2004, critical of the government's deceptions in the lead-up to the war. All were without precedent in their respective countries.

53. Susan Page, "USA TODAY Poll: Opposition to Syrian Airstrikes Surges," *USA Today*, September 9, 2013. See also Gabriel Debenedetti, "Americans Want Diplomacy on Syria, Are Unmoved by Obama Speech: Reuters/Ipsos Poll," Reuters, September 13, 2013.

54. Andrew Tilghman, "Troops Oppose Strikes on Syria by 3–1 Margin," *Military Times*, September 12, 2013.

55. Wilson Andrews, Aaron Blake, Darla Cameron, and Kennedy Elliott, "Where Congress Stands on Syria," *Washington Post*, September 11, 2013.

56. Quoted in Elizabeth Rigby, James Blitz, and Richard McGregor, "Cameron Lays Out Case for Syria Strike," *Financial Times*, August 30, 2013.

57. Quoted in Kiran Stacey, Elizabeth Rigby, and Jim Pickard, "Memory of Iraq Colours Commons Debate," *Financial Times*, August 30, 2013.

58. *Newsweek* (international edition), July 24, 2006: 5.

59. Alison Broinowski, *Howard's War* (Melbourne: Scribe Publications, 2003), 27.

60. See Nick Davies, *Flat Earth News: An Award-Winning Reporter Exposes Falsehood, Distortion and Propaganda in the Global Media* (London: Vintage Books, 2009).

61. Neal Desai, Andre Pineda, Majken Runquist, and Mark Fusunyan, *Torture at Times: Waterboarding in the Media*, Harvard student paper (Cambridge, MA: Joan Shorenstein Center on the Press, Politics and Public Policy, April 2010).

62. Rami G. Khouri, "The Pain of Following Iran in the U.S. Media," *Daily Star* (Beirut), April 6, 2013.

63. "Instead of isolating Saddam Hussein, we seem to have isolated ourselves. We proclaim a new doctrine of pre-emption, which is understood by few and feared by many": Robert C. Byrd, "The Arrogance of Power," Senate floor remarks, March 19, 2003, http://www.americanrhetoric.com/speeches/wariniraq/robertbyrdhiraq 31903.htm (accessed August 14, 2014).

64. Greg Sheridan, "Reflections of a Straight Shooter," *Australian*, January 20, 2005.

65. Byrd, "The Arrogance of Power."

66. Joseph S. Nye, "Hard, Soft, and Smart Power," *The Oxford Handbook of Modern Diplomacy*, eds. Andrew F. Cooper, Jorge Heine, and Ramesh Thakur (Oxford: Oxford University Press, 2013), 568.

67. See Seymour M. Hersh, *Chain of Command: The Road from 9/11 to Abu Ghraib* (New York: HarperCollins, 2004).

68. Quoted by Eric Alterman, "Hawks Eating Crow," *Nation*, June 7, 2004.

69. Michael Lehnert, "Here's Why It's Long Past Time That We Close Guantánamo," *Detroit Free Press*, December 12, 2013.

70. Robert W. Tucker and David C. Hendrickson, "Iraq and US Legitimacy," *Foreign Affairs* 83, no. 6 (2004): 18–32.

71. See George Monbiot, "The Moral Myth," *Guardian*, November 25, 2003.

72. "Bulletin: No W.M.D. Found," editorial, *New York Times*, January 13, 2005.

5

THE IRAQ INVASION AND U.S.-U.N. RELATIONS

Roger Coate

MISSION NOT ACCOMPLISHED: TEN YEARS LATER

When President George W. Bush gave his "mission accomplished speech" from the flight deck of the USS *Abraham Lincoln* on May 1, 2003, the only "mission" that had been accomplished was regime change. No weapons of mass destruction (WMDs) had been discovered and destroyed, no terrorists had been found and eliminated, no democratic government had been established, and there was and would be no foreseeable peace or end to the killing and violence in Iraq. Three years later to the month would be the bloodiest month of the war until that date, with 1,400 people killed in targeted killings, following April, when over 1,100 had been killed. Ten years later and today, there are numerous terrorist groups, including al-Qaeda, operating within the country. There are no meaningful stores of WMDs, but then, there were none at the time of the invasion. The intelligence was fabricated and made to fit the policy.

The costs of the Iraq War have been exceedingly high. In terms of loss of human life, the Iraq Body Count estimates that 184,000 deaths from violence had occurred as of the end of 2013. But this figure seems vastly understated. A scientific study by a joint American-Iraqi team from the Johns Hopkins School of Public Health and Iraqi medical doctors estimated that well over 650,000 "excess deaths" had occurred in the first three years

(2003–06) alone.[1] Millions of others have been displaced either internally or externally as refugees from their homes. The financial costs of the war are even more difficult to assess, but it is safe to say that the war has cost the United States well over US$1 trillion. Incalculable costs have incurred in terms of Iraqi national and regional destabilization and spreading terrorism throughout the region. The Shiite majority government verges on authoritarianism, not pluralist, open democratic governance. It is closer to and more co-operative with America's main adversary in the Middle East, Iran, than with the United States. In brief, the Iraq invasion turned out to be a nightmare, not the envisioned neo-conservative dream.

Iraq has been the second longest war in American history, with the related war in Afghanistan being the longest. In this context, the Iraqi invasion of March 2003 and subsequent military action there, such as the so-called "surge," impacted substantially on the Afghan conflict. The invasion represented "taking the eye off the ball" in Afghanistan, and diverted focus and resources from the war on terrorism. At one point in 2004–05, troop levels in Afghanistan fell to fewer than ten thousand, while 130,000 troops were amassed in Iraq. At the height of the Iraqi surge, there were 160,000 troops in Iraq but only twenty-six thousand in Afghanistan. The Taliban and al-Qaeda made a resurgence, and the United States and NATO forces were hopelessly still bogged down in Afghanistan three years after the withdrawal from Iraq.

The main focus of this chapter is on several additional "costs" of the war. Specifically, the Iraqi incursion and occupation have impacted on three critical aspects of contemporary international politics: the rule of law governing intra- and inter-state behaviour; U.S.-U.N. relations; and the United Nations as an instrument for promoting and maintaining international peace and security and dealing with breaches of it.

IMPACT ON THE RULE OF LAW NORM

The U.S.-led invasion and subsequent occupation challenged and served to undermine three important aspects of the respect for international norms related to the rule of law. The first and perhaps most profound is the norm of the illegality of waging aggressive war, as embodied in the U.N. Charter and other legal instruments. The second is the promotion and respect of fundamental international human rights. And the third is the evolving principle of the "responsibility to protect."

The Illegality of Waging Aggressive War

Both former U.N. secretary-general Kofi Annan and former chief weapons inspector Hans Blix have been forceful in their assessments of the aggression against Iraq and have argued that the invasion was a violation of the U.N. Charter and a tremendously costly mistake.[2] The cost being referred to here was not merely in monetary terms. It was the cost to one of the most fundamental principles of contemporary international law and relations — the illegality of waging aggressive war as an instrument of foreign policy. This norm was over a century in the making and is associated with the set of norms, including individual and collective self-defence, regarding a general prohibition on the use of force as a tool of foreign policy and the conditions under which states legally can resort to war.

These norms were given explicit legal substance in the Charter of the United Nations. By signing and ratifying the U.N. Charter and joining the world body, member states commit themselves to "settle their international disputes by peaceful means" and refrain in their international relations from the threat or use of force against the territorial integrity or political independence of any state, or in any manner inconsistent with the purposes of the United Nations (Articles 2.3 and 2.4). These norms were built on for more than a century of international conferences and customary and treaty law that increasingly narrowed the legality of the use of force except for self-defence — including the Hague conferences; the collective security provisions of the League of Nations Covenant, which did not outlaw war but acknowledged the need for mechanisms to prevent and deal with it; and the U.S.-French instigated Kellogg-Briand Pact of 1928, which condemned recourse to war as an instrument of policy. The U.N. Charter outlawed war except in narrowly defined instances of individual and collective self-defence or when authorized under the collective security provisions of the Charter.

In the U.S. National Security Strategy of September 2002, the Bush administration argued that states "need not suffer an attack before they can lawfully take action to defend themselves against forces that present an imminent danger."[3] The National Security Strategy went on to argue that the United States had a right to act "pre-emptively" in dealing with suspected cases of possible acquisition of weapons of mass destruction by terrorists, even in the absence of imminent threat or clear proof.[4] In delineating the new doctrine of acting preventively against terrorists and perceived rogue states that harbour them, and then invading Iraq, the Bush administration placed the United States in direct opposition to both the intent and the letter of the U.N. Charter and the international legal principles that underlie it — which occupy the domestic legal status of "supreme law of the land" under Article 6 of the U.S. Constitution.

Waging unprovoked aggressive war is illegal, short and simple. At the close of the Second World War, the victorious allies established the Nuremberg war crimes tribunal and the International Military Tribunal for the Far East (Tokyo Tribunal) in order to bring justice in regard to war crimes, crimes against humanity (genocide), and crimes against the peace (waging aggressive war). In the Geneva Conventions and other legal instruments over the years, these concepts have to a greater or lesser extent taken concrete form, especially in regard to war crimes and genocide. The concept of crimes against the peace has remained much more woolly and has proven difficult to codify. Nonetheless, the provisions of the U.N. Charter provide a general basis for the principle of non-aggression and non-use of force in foreign policy. The invasion of Iraq stood in clear violation of this principle.

It is not by chance that the Bush administration chose the language of "pre-emption." The legal principle of launching a pre-emptive attack in self-defence had been evolving since the mid-nineteenth century. It had first been enunciated in 1842 by U.S. secretary of state Daniel Webster in the *Caroline* case with England. As articulated by Webster and generally accepted, pre-emptive attack is justified only in a case where "the necessity of that self-defense is instant, overwhelming, and leaving no choice of means and no moment for deliberation."[5] The doctrine being enunciated by the Bush administration had none of these features. It was a prescription in support of U.S. unilateral aggression as a preventive measure in support of fending off a possible future threat to U.S. national security — illegal aggressive war, pure and simple.

In terms of impact on this essential element of the rule of international law, it is important to note that the Bush doctrine has not been repeated in other venues. However, given its position as the most important "structural" leader in the world, how the United States behaves matters a great deal. As Gregory Raymond and Charles Kegley have argued:

> How the United States acts is an enormous influence on the behavior of others. When the reigning hegemon promotes a new code of conduct, it alters the normative frame of reference for virtually everyone else.... As Stanley Hoffmann ... has put it, rules *of* behavior become rules *for* behavior.[6]

In this context, the debate over the evolving norm of the responsibility to protect (R2P) has come to occupy centre stage. The 2005 World Summit helped to provide at least a little meat on the R2P skeleton. But as we have seen recently in the case of Syria, responding to cases of gross failures of R2P is neither straightforward nor automatic.

International Human Rights

Another crucial impact of the Iraq War was on the international human rights regime. The words *GTMO* (pronounced *gitmo*; the detention centre at the United States Naval Station Guantánamo Bay, Cuba), *Abu Ghraib*, *rendition*, and *black sites* conjure up images of torture and detainee abuse. Using the formulation "unlawful enemy combatants," the Bush administration long stood by the claim that the legal provisions of the Geneva Conventions did not pertain to those non-uniformed troops captured in military actions. As the world stood by and watched, the United States openly flaunted its violations of international human rights law in regard to those captured in wartime in Afghanistan and Iraq. It is not important to repeat that history here, but it is important to note that under the U.S. watch in Iraq, egregious violations of human rights, including torture and prisoner abuse, were not only tolerated but apparently covered up.

In February 2006, the former human rights chief for the U.N. Assistance Mission for Iraq (UNAMI) John Pace charged that the U.S. military in Iraq had been violating the Geneva Conventions in regard to prisoner

internment. Referring to the practice of massive round-ups and internment of individuals, Pace estimated that 80 to 90 percent of the detainees
were innocent but still being interned without recourse to the legal protection of the Geneva Conventions.[7] The following year, in October 2007, as
the United States had intensified its air strikes in Iraq, the UNAMI Human
Rights Report charged that U.S. air strikes within densely populated areas
killing innocent civilians were illegal under international humanitarian
law. As more evidence of human rights violations and torture surfaced
in the Iraq War Logs released by Julian Assange of WikiLeaks, the U.N.
Special Rapporteur on torture, Manfred Nowak, called on President Barack
Obama to order a full investigation of U.S. troops' involvement in torture
and other human rights abuses.[8] The picture got even bleaker in December
2013, when the European Court of Human Rights issued a unanimous
decision that a German citizen of Lebanese origin had been sodomized,
shackled, and beaten by U.S. Central Intelligence Agency (CIA) agents. The
court found that the victim had been subjected to forced disappearance,
unlawful detention, extraordinary rendition outside any judicial process,
and inhuman and degrading treatment.[9]

Perhaps the most serious impact of these blatant violations of international human rights law has been on the moral authority of the United
States. This was occurring at the same time that the U.S. government was
refusing to become party to the International Criminal Court and shunning
the newly created U.N. Human Rights Council. In the latter case, paradox-
ically a main argument in opposition was that states that were gross violators of human rights were being elected as members of the council. At the
same time, the United States was condoning and even participating in such
gross violations of international human rights laws.

Finally in regard to human rights is the issue of the U.S. failure in
its responsibility to protect citizens and international personnel in Iraq.
Shortly after 9/11, the International Commission on Intervention and State
Sovereignty issued its report, *The Responsibility to Protect*.[10] In the aftermath of Rwanda, East Timor, and Kosovo, the concept rapidly picked up
international normative steam. Washington's humanitarian justification for
waging illegal war, in the context of the evolving R2P norm, stands in sharp
contrast to its failure to do just that as an occupying military authority.
As was implicit in the death toll discussed above, the United States as the

occupying force that had dismantled the Iraqi military, police force, and justice system failed in its responsibility to protect. Sadly, along with the tremendous loss of Iraqi civilian lives, in August 2003 this failure resulted in bombings at the Jordanian embassy and U.N. headquarters in Baghdad, killing and injuring many dozens of civilians, including Sergio Vieira de Mello, the U.N. high commissioner for human rights.

IMPACT ON U.S.-U.N. RELATIONS

At the time, the 2002–03 crisis over Iraq appeared to represent a defining moment in U.S.-U.N. relations, as the United States marginalized the United Nations and the international legal norms on which it is based and launched an aggressive attack on Iraq. But even in doing so, the Bush administration attempted to wrestle some legitimacy for its aggression from the world body. The administration argued that since Iraq was in material breach of several previous Security Council resolutions, the United States and its "coalition of the willing" had the implicit authority to go to war. Throughout the pre-war period, the U.N. Security Council served as the international forum of choice for debates over what to do with the situation in Iraq. As military success became obvious it was never really questioned, and the Bush administration came to realize that building permanent peace and stability in Iraq was not possible without the assistance of the United Nations.[11]

Almost simultaneously with the U.S. declaration of the end to its formal war campaign, the U.N. Security Council voted on May 22 to lift economic sanctions against Iraq, to cede wide-ranging authority to the United States and United Kingdom over governing Iraq, and to authorize a new role for the United Nations in rebuilding the war-ravaged nation. The official U.S.-led invasion might have been over, but violence and insecurity prevailed. As mentioned above, on August 19, 2003, in a major failure of U.S. forces to provide security in the area, the U.N. special envoy in Iraq, Sergio Vieira de Mello, and eighteen other U.N. staff members were killed in the bombing of the U.N. headquarters in Baghdad.

On October 16, 2003, the members of the Security Council unanimously adopted Resolution 1511, expanding the U.N. role in the transition to self-governance process in Iraq and authorizing a U.S.-led multilateral force:

... to take all necessary measures to contribute to the maintenance of security and stability in Iraq, including for the purpose of ensuring necessary conditions for the implementation of the timetable and program as well as to contribute to the security of the United Nations Assistance Mission for Iraq, the Governing Council of Iraq and other institutions of the Iraqi interim administration, and key humanitarian and economic infrastructure.

Furthermore, the resolution underscored the temporary nature of the U.S.-occupation's Coalition Provisional Authority and invited the Iraqi Governing Council to provide the Security Council with a timetable for drafting a new constitution for Iraq and for the holding of democratic elections. The resolution represented a compromise between the United States and its coalition allies, who wanted an internationally approved mandate for a U.S.-led multilateral force, and France, Germany, and Russia, who wanted a larger role for the United Nations and a clear timetable for transition of governance to self-rule.

But the real carnage in Iraq was just getting started, and would plague efforts by the United Nations as well as occupying forces to rebuild what the U.S.-led invasion had destroyed. Post-conflict peace-building required a secure environment to prosper, but security was elusive. As mentioned above, the U.S. attempt to deal with the situation drained the military effort in Afghanistan, causing disaster for both undertakings.

The United States is indeed an exceptional political power in the world. However, the American neo-conservatives' arrogance about the United States's exceptional role in shaping the world in its own image through the use of preponderant military power, and their abuse of the United Nations, not only severely hampered U.S.-U.N. relations, but also the attainment of vital American national security interests such as regional stabilization and the containment of terrorism. Richard Perle has perhaps stated this position most clearly in regard to Iraq:

Saddam Hussein's reign of terror is about to end. He will go quickly, but not alone: in a parting irony, he will take the U.N. down with him. Well, not the whole U.N. The "good works" part will survive, the low-risk peacekeeping bureaucracies will remain, the chatterbox on the Hudson will continue to bleat. What will die is the fantasy of the U.N. as the foundation of a new world order. As we sift the debris, it will be important to preserve, the better to understand, the intellectual wreckage of the liberal conceit of safety through international law administered by international institutions.[12]

Unilateralism was the flavour of the day and dominated the U.S. approach to dealing with major international security issues throughout the Bush administration. The United States withdrew from the 1972 U.S.-Russian Treaty on the Limitation of Anti-Ballistic Missile Systems and moved forward on the development of a missile defence system. It renounced the Comprehensive Nuclear-Test-Ban Treaty and rejected the Kyoto Protocol on the environment. As mentioned above, it refused to become party to the International Criminal Court. It declined to move forward on a biological weapons treaty and denied the applicability of the Geneva Conventions in regard to the post-9/11 prisoners held in custody at Guantánamo Bay, Cuba.

U.N.-U.S. relations were further strained by President Bush's congressional-recess appointment of John R. Bolton as U.S. permanent representative to the United Nations in mid-2005. Bolton reinforced the image of the United States as arrogantly unilateralist with his performance at the 2005 World Summit, where he set about, among other things, to strip every mention of Millennium Development Goals from the draft outcome document. Although Bolton was forced to leave the position after it expired in 2007, the new U.S. permanent representative, Zalmay Khalilzad, continued the same general policy lines but in a much less bullying manner.

As Thomas Weiss, Presidential Professor at the Graduate Center, University of New York, and one of the leading experts on humanitarian intervention, asked in a special essay on U.S.-U.N. relations in 2006, "Where does that leave U.S.-U.N. relations, especially as regards the politics of high security and the use of force, the main reason the world organization was founded?"[13] Weiss suggests there are two "world organizations": the United Nations (global in membership) and the United States (global in reach). Each needs the other in order to act effectively in peace-enforcement decisions.

A major problem is that neither of these two world organizations has the capacity to act as a cohesive and coherent unitary actor. Much of U.S. policy toward and action in the United Nations is conditioned and constrained by domestic political forces. So while the president can, for example, bring the United States into a consensus with other members of the Security Council in terms of a new peacekeeping initiative requiring substantial resource commitments, the actual implementation may well be contingent on Congressional authorization and appropriation of funding. The decades-long major budget arrears of the United States to both the regular and peacekeeping budgets were indicative of Congress's tendency to attempt to micromanage and manipulate the world body. Congressional concern over U.N. reform seems way out of proportion to the role that the United Nations plays in U.S. foreign policy. But on the other hand, it indicates that the world body is indeed of importance — albeit in a negative way from the perspectives of some members of Congress.

The election of Barack Obama as president of the United States brought with it much hope for positive change in U.S.-U.N. relations. This hope was reflected barely two months into his first term when he was awarded the Nobel Peace Prize "for his extraordinary efforts to strengthen international diplomacy and co-operation between peoples." He, of course, had not had an opportunity to do anything to deserve the award, yet tremendous hope existed that the United States would now reassume its leadership role in multilateral affairs.

It has sought to re-engage with the U.N. on many levels and ... has been a strong and measured voice on the council. On issues like Libya and Sudan, the Obama team has laid great stress on UNSC [U.N. Security Council] approval for any outside intervention. At the same time, however, the Obama administration seems to be under no illusion as to what the U.N. can accomplish, hence its approach has been pragmatic and inconsistent. It has not hesitated to resort to controversial unilateralism, as in drone attacks in Pakistan and Yemen, where it believes its security interests are threatened. The Obama administration has not joined the ICC ..., taken a hands-off approach to Sudan, boycotted a meeting on racism in solidarity with Israel, and failed to follow up on the Goldstone report out of the U.N. Human Rights Council which criticized Israeli and Palestinian actions in Gaza.[14]

The Obama administration moved for significant multilateral action in the case of Syrian use of chemical weapons, but when consensus in the Security Council proved impossible, it rattled its sabre and made loud noises about unilateral action as the world's moral leader. To many, this brought back grim reminders of the Bush administration and Iraq. The United States is a "hyperpower,"[15] and when the other world organization cannot act, it reserves the right to police the world as it sees fit.

In conclusion, U.S.-U.N. relations have been rocky for years. U.S. politicians, interest groups, and policy-makers have used and abused the United Nations as a pawn in domestic intra-governmental political struggles and the elusive search for a coherent foreign policy. U.S. exceptionalism and unilateralism have served to undermine the authority of the United Nations as well as of the United States itself, resulting in largely ineffectual global governance mechanisms and processes in many important areas, including peace and security.

IMPACT ON THE UNITED NATIONS

Ian Johnstone, dean and professor of international law at the Fletcher School, Tufts University, and former U.N. official, has argued that "Iraq was a bridge too far. The result is a seriously damaged U.S.-U.N. relationship, but one which may yet recover because the broader normative and institutional framework remains intact."[16] In arguing this, Johnstone is on the money when he suggests that the reason is because U.S. interests are the same as those of the United Nations and are embedded in it.

The post–Second World War world order, including the U.N. system, is indeed a product of American values, visions, and structural capabilities. Concentrating on the United Nations' peace and security mission, it is important to distinguish between the United Nations that most of the members of the international community and world society want, and the United Nations that actually exists. Most member states desire an organization that can act effectively for the good of all, using enforcement powers when needed, but only when absolutely needed, to protect from incursions by others on territorial sovereignty, and/or assist as requested with domestic disturbances or interference in domestic affairs.

President Franklin D. Roosevelt envisioned a rather different organization, as he made clear in mid-1944: "We are not thinking of a superstate with its own police forces and other paraphernalia of coercive power."[17] In Roosevelt's vision, the world would be policed by the major powers — the "Four Policemen," acting through the new institution when and as needed and deemed appropriate.[18] A year earlier, he had reflected this way:

> [I]t is my thought that time is essential in disseminating the ideals of peace among the very diverse nationalities and national egos of a vast number of separate peoples who, for one reason or another over a thousand years, have divided themselves into a hundred different forms of hate.... Therefore, I have been visualizing a superimposed — or if you like it, a superassumed — obligation by Russia, China, Britain and ourselves that we will act as sheriffs for the maintenance of order during the transition period.[19]

At the creation of the United Nations, both the Soviet Union and the United States demanded the right to veto unwanted actions. Thus the organization they were responsible for designing had the requisite attributes and rules. There was no utopian vision of one for all and all for one. The world body was based on and designed with war-time pragmatism, tempered by American-style liberalism. The Security Council was to be the body of last resort unless there was great power consensus for collective action.

Such consensus, of course, proved impossible during the Cold War, as the two ideologically opposed sides moved to divide the world into hostile camps. After the Cold War passed and the United States emerged as the hyperpower in a unipolar world, the world had changed so dramatically from that of the 1940s that the United Nations and its security machinery became largely anachronistic. Seventy years later the world's "power" distribution had been transformed in such a diverse way that, hyperpower or not, the United States found that it could not unilaterally act as the world's sole policeman. Moreover, the other member states of the United Nations were not about to permit it to act that way, should it try. Well, it tried in Iraq, and failed miserably.

As Thomas Weiss has argued, "Critics of Hegemony ... argue that enforcement decisions should be based on U.N. authority instead of U.S. capacity. But the two are inseparable."[20] The Iraq War has highlighted the need to bolster the United Nations' credibility and make its structures more representative of the international community. Yet it is clear that Security Council reform, including the expansion of membership — both permanent and non-permanent — to reflect more closely the geopolitical realities of the contemporary world, still would not resolve the issues surrounding the relationship between the United States and the United Nations. Expansion of the veto system would only complicate the need for consensus. Besides, it is politically improbable-to-impossible, given the requirements for Charter revision.

The real problem is based more on capacity issues. The world body simply is not, and intentionally was not, equipped with the capacity for undertaking any but small-scale security operations. In this unipolar world of the early twenty-first century, only the other world organization — the United States — is so equipped on a global basis. Moreover, it is not clear that many member states of the United Nations wish to endow the world body with such capacity, given the nature of the global power distribution and the current and ongoing state of play of world politics.

As Hans Blix has argued, it is fortunate that the U.N. Security Council did not "green light a war that was justified by false evidence."[21] The United Nations stepped up to the plate to bail the United States out of one of the largest messes of recent times. As reflected in the beginning, the only main goal achieved by the war was an unstated one: regime change. Yet that change bore very little resemblance to any meaningful attempt at promoting values. As Ramesh Thakur has poignantly queried:

> What answer to those who claim that aggression abroad was matched by repression at home, with serious cutbacks to many liberties that U.S. citizens, residents and visitors alike had come to take for granted for decades? The role of business cronies in shaping public policy had corrosive impact on public faith in government … this too failed to inspire Iraqi confidence in U.S.-style democracy.[22]

In all of this mess, the United States has severely squandered its soft-power capabilities. It has turned much of the Arab-speaking world against it. It has made the road to democracy in the Arab Spring much more rocky.

Thakur has further argued:

The U.S. has been deeply divided from world opinion, with a startling precipitous worldwide decline in U.S. global leadership. U.S.
soft power has been eroded. The problem of U.S. credibility with the
Islamic world is still more acute. Muslims are embittered, sullen and
resentful of a perceived assault on Islam.... U.S. credibility suffered
a calamitous collapse with the publication of abuse photographs
from the Abu Ghraib prison, graphically depicting the extent to
which war had brutalized the U.S. military. The abuses were not
isolated incidents, but reflected a systemic malaise. Washington is
yet to regain the moral high ground lost with the pornography of
torture.[23]

CONCLUSION

The debate over the U.S.-led war on Iraq in the United Nations brought the
world organization to centre stage as it had seldom been before. Contrary to
myopic American perceptions, it may well be that the United Nations' legitimacy has been strengthened and not weakened by the Bush administration's
flagrant and arrogant refusal to work co-operatively through the multilateral
institution. As Ramesh Thakur astutely observed, "The more the Americans
protested about U.N. irrelevance, the more the rest stubbornly dug in their
heels to demonstrate its increasing relevance."[24] Seen from the perspectives
of most member states, the real challenge posed is to the legitimacy of the
United States as world leader, not to that of the United Nations.

But has there been any real organizational learning in the United States
as a result of the Iraq debacle? Why has there been so much silence and
lack of reflection in America? The great hope placed on President Obama
during and immediately after his election has dwindled. Contrary to
beliefs put forth during his political inception, he has in turn embraced
targeted killings by drones as a normal course of events, even when these
actions violate the territorial sovereignty of crucial allies. He has condoned
the targeted killings of American citizens in clear violation of the U.S.

Constitution. Even though in this way Barack Obama bears resemblance to George W. Bush in his disregard for the rule of law, the American public remains quiet. Former vice-president Dick Cheney continues his litany of deception in justification of the war. Surprisingly or not, many Americans continue to believe him.

A 2012 scientific survey of American public opinion conducted by YouGov in conjunction with Dartmouth College, for example, found that over 57 percent of Americans either believed that Iraq had weapons of mass destruction when the United States invaded in 2003 or said they did not know. Over 82 percent of the Republicans polled held such beliefs, with 62.9 percent responding that they believed Iraq had WMDs and another 19.6 percent saying they did not know.[25] This was more than a year after the Bush administration's key source for its WMD claims — a disgruntled Iraqi defector who wanted to see Saddam Hussein deposed — publicly admitted he had lied, and long after it was clear that no appreciable WMDs had been found.

So, where does this leave us? The world is in need of an effective partnership among the two world organizations. Yet such a partnership requires mutual trust and respect, as well as a commitment that is dependable and binding. Unfortunately, none of these conditions seem to prevail in the current world political climate in regard to feelings and perceptions about the United States. A significant part of the Muslim world has been estranged by U.S. words and deeds. Much of what the United States promotes and focuses on in the Security Council and other U.N. bodies deals with affairs in Islamic-culture countries. And in reality, carnage continues in Iraq. Afghanistan spirals out of control. U.S. relations with Pakistan are strained. Similarly, an intransigent Israel continues to be elevated as a preferred regional partner, at the expense of its historical rivals.

The U.S. stance on Palestinian membership in the United Nations and other international organizations has further alienated the Muslim world. It was the United States and Britain that forced through quick membership for Israel in 1949. However, sixty years later the United States stands as the major obstruction to Palestine's admission to the world body. And when Palestine was admitted to UNESCO (United Nations Educational, Scientific and Cultural Organization) as a member in 2011, the United States immediately ceased funding for the agency — as John

Oliver on the *Daily Show* put it, cutting off its own nose to spite its face in terms of important U.S. national interests as well as further alienating Islamic-culture countries and making it easier for radical Islamic groups to recruit anti-American terrorists.

The two world organizations need each other. Yet U.S. hegemony, underpinned by its current foundations in unilateralism and exceptionalism, continues to strain U.S.-U.N. relations. At the same time, the United Nations is mired in an organizational structure and institutional norms that are nearly three-quarters of a century old. Discussions of reforming the Security Council to produce a more effective global entity continue to occur, but with inconclusive results. On the American side, there is not even serious talk about reforming the way or the norms with which the United States relates to the United Nations and the rest of the world. But on a positive note, the global political climate is rapidly being transformed. In this context, by midcentury there may well be only one world organization. The odds are, if either of the current two world organizations is to persist, it may well be the United Nations, assuming its reform is possible.

NOTES

1. *Iraq Body Count*, www.iraqbodycount.org (accessed January 7, 2014); and Gilbert Burnham, Shannon Doocy, Elizabeth Dzeng, Riyadh Lafta, and Les Roberts, *The Human Cost of the War in Iraq: A Mortality Study, 2002–2006* (Baltimore, MD: Center for International Studies, MIT, 2006).

2. Hans Blix, "Iraq War Was a Terrible Mistake and Violation of U.N. Charter," CNN, March 15, 2013; and "Iraq War Was Illegal and Breached the U.N. Charter, Says Annan," *Guardian*, September 15, 2004.

3. U.S. Department of Defense, *The National Security Strategy of the United States of America* (Washington: Government of the United States, September 17, 2002), 15, http://www.state.gov/documents/organization/63562.pdf (accessed August 10, 2014).

4. Ibid.

5. Daniel Webster to Lord Ashburton, August 6, 1842, in *A Digest of International Law*, vol. 2 , ed. John Bassett Moore (Washington: Government Printing Office, 1906), 412.

6. Gregory Raymond and Charles Kegley, Jr., "International Norms and Military Preemption: Implications for Global Governance" (paper prepared for delivery at the International Symposium on International Norms for the

21st Century, Aix-en-Provence, September 11–14, 2003), 15; and Stanley Hoffmann, "International Law and the Control of Force," in *The Relevance of International Law*, ed. Karl W. Deutsch and Stanley Hoffmann (Garden City, NY: Doubleday-Anchor, 1971), 34–66.

7. "Exclusive: Former U.N. Human Rights Chief in Iraq Says U.S. Violating Geneva Conventions, Jailing Innocent Detainees," *Democracy Now*, February 28, 2006, http://www.democracynow.org/2006/2/28/exclusive_former_un_human_ rights_chief (accessed August 14, 2014).

8. "Iraq War Logs: U.N. Calls on Obama to Investigate Human Rights Abuses," *Guardian*, October 23, 2010.

9. "CIA 'Tortured and Sodomized' Terror Suspect, Human Rights Court Rules," *Guardian*, December 13, 2013.

10. International Commission on Intervention and State Sovereignty (ICISS), *The Responsibility to Protect* (Ottawa: International Development Research Centre, 2001).

11. See, for example, Shashi Tharoor, "Why America Still Needs the United Nations," *Foreign Affairs* 82, no. 5 (2003): 67–80.

12. Richard Perle, "Thank God for the Death of the U.N.," *Guardian*, March 21, 2003.

13. Thomas G. Weiss, "U.S.-U.N. Relations and the Use of Force After the World Summit," in *U.S.-U.N. Relations* (New York: National Committee on American Foreign Policy, August 2006), 19.

14. Thomas G. Weiss, David P. Forsythe, Roger A. Coate, and Kelly-Kate Pease, *The United Nations and Changing World Politics* (Boulder, CO: Westview Press, 2013), 140.

15. Tim Dunne, "Society and Hierarchy in International Relations," *International Relations* 17, no. 3 (2003): 303–20.

16. Ian Johnstone, "U.S.-U.N. Relations after Iraq: The End of the World (Order) As We Know It?" *European Journal of International Law* 15, no. 4 (2004): 814.

17. Cited in Townsend Hoopes and Douglas Brinkley, *FDR and the Creation of the U.N.* (New Haven, CT: Yale University Press, 1997), 128. On the same point, see Georg Schild, *Bretton Woods and Dumbarton Oaks: American Economic and Political Postwar Planning in the Summer of 1944* (New York: St. Martin's Press, 1995), 57.

18. Hoopes and Brinkley, *FDR and the U.N.*.

19. Franklin D. Roosevelt to George W. Norris, September 21, 1943, in *The Roosevelt Letters*, vol. 3, ed. Elliott Roosevelt (London: George G. Harrup & Co., 1952), 473–74.

20. Thomas G. Weiss, "R2P After 9/11 and the World Summit," *Wisconsin International Law Journal* 24, no. 3 (2006): 754.

21. Blix, "Iraq War Was a Terrible Mistake."

22. Ramesh Thakur, "Fast Forward to the Past? The Line in the Sand from Iraq to Iran" (working paper no. 7, Centre for International Governance Innovation, August 2006), 5.

23. Ramesh Thakur, "From Iraq to Iran" (occasional paper series [online], no. 4, Australian Centre for Peace and Conflict Studies), December 2006.

24. Ibid.; and Ramesh Thakur, "The United Nations: More Relevant Now Than Ever," *Japan Times*, March 23, 2003.

25. Benjamin Valentino, *Data Sets: Survey on Foreign Policy and American Overseas Commitments*, http://www.dartmouth.edu/~benv/data.htm and http://www.dartmouth.edu/~benv/files/poll%20responses%20by%20party%20ID.pdf (both accessed August 14, 2014).

6

THE U.S. ALLIANCE OF STRATEGIC COUSINS

John Blaxland

An orthodox interpretation of the origins of the war in Iraq emerged following the U.S.-led invasion in 2003. This view portrayed the event as a major folly, a fiasco, which could be attributed squarely to the American neo-conservatives led by President George W. Bush. This view seemed obvious and compelling. Indeed, the widespread view was that had Al Gore been elected as president in 2000, there would have been no invasion of Iraq.

Frank P. Harvey, in his book *Explaining the Iraq War: Counterfactual Theory, Logic and Evidence,* has challenged this view, demonstrating that all major decisions from 2002 to 2003 were endorsed by Al Gore, his team, and most other senior Democrats in power at the time. Harvey does not argue that Gore's behaviour would have been identical to Bush's. Instead he argues that the differences would have been largely inconsequential in competition with the pressures to make the same big decisions that produced the path-dependent outcome.[1] Harvey's observations point to the merits of reconsidering the orthodox views on Australians and Canadians and their approach to security issues concerning the United States. This is particularly the case over the decision of whether or not to go to war in Iraq. Indeed, the intervention of both Canada and Australia in Iraq in 2014, performing similar air and ground roles, reinforces the argument.

The contrasting responses in Canada and Australia to Bush's call for allies has been described by Brendon O'Connor and Canadian scholar Srdjan Vucetic as "another Mars-Venus divide," drawing on a metaphor used in Robert Kagan's famous essay in 2003,[2] which in turn had borrowed the metaphor from the international bestseller *Men Are from Mars, Women Are from Venus*.[3] According to this view, Australians are instinctively more hawkish than the peacekeeper Canadians. O'Connor and Vucetic argue that in both Canada and Australia, the Iraq decisions followed the dominant views within the ruling party.[4] This view is not in contention. But the electoral balance in both countries was not nearly as one-sided as this point would suggest, for in both countries a change of government took place a few years later that saw the ruling party soundly defeated and the political polarities inverted, with the Conservatives beating the Liberals in the Canadian federal elections in 2006 and the Australian Labor Party beating the Coalition in the 2007 federal elections.

O'Connor and Vucetic also claim that the decisions over the Iraq War in 2003 followed the dominant strategic culture among the elites. On this point, I would argue, they are on shaky ground. To be sure, there was vocal and widespread opposition to the war among the elites in both countries in 2003. But in Australia's case the elites had little, if any, influence on the decision. Moreover, few would argue that this influence tipped the scales in the subsequent Australian federal elections in 2003 or the ones in Canada in 2004. In both cases, the ruling parties retained office largely over domestic matters.

In response to the claims by O'Connor and Vucetic, Harvey's argument provides a useful launching point for an interesting counterfactual on what Canada might have chosen to do had Stephen Harper come into office as prime minister earlier — in time to make the fateful decision on going to war in Iraq. Given his enthusiastic backing of the return deployment to Afghanistan in 2005 and 2006, and his criticism of the Liberal government's decision on Iraq in 2003, it is not unreasonable to surmise that he would have committed Canada to a calibrated force contribution to the Iraq War, much as was the case for the Gulf War in 1991.

Indeed, Prime Minister Jean Chrétien himself appealed to Bush for a few more weeks to muster sufficient consensus for United Nations support. Had Bush been more patient, or Gore been in the chair instead, the outcome for Canada likely would have been quite different. What this counterfactual example illustrates is that the argument that Canada's position was largely preordained by its political predisposition is demonstrably contestable. Events leading up to the decision provide some significant pointers as well.

Despite coming from opposing poles of the political spectrum (if politics can be so reduced to just one dimension), the initial responses in Canada and Australia to the events on September 11, 2001, were remarkably similar in many ways. For Canada the events were geographically much closer, and Canada played a more direct and immediate role when aircraft were grounded at airports across North America. Also for Canada, the incentive of keeping an open border for its vital cross-border trade was the most obvious motivation. This incentive became obvious when U.S. border posts and airports were immediately blockaded in September 2001. In contrast, for Australia, its isolation, growing sense of regional hostility, and perceived need to work harder at preserving its alliance with the United States spurred co-operation. The fact that Australian prime minister John Howard was in Washington, D.C., on 9/11 made his decision that much more forceful and immediate.

The United States began to hunt down and defeat al-Qaeda operatives wherever they could be found. The American response presented the governments of Australia and Canada with a range of significant challenges as they sought to respond and adapt to the new geostrategic environment. But despite coming at the issue from different directions, as they had so many times in the past, Canada and Australia ended up responding to the 2001 invasion of Afghanistan in virtually the same way. Both deployed similar-sized task forces to Afghanistan late in 2001 and into 2002.

Australia and Canada both played important supportive roles alongside U.S. forces in the Arabian Sea with their navies, and in Afghanistan. Their contributions included elements of both Canadian and Australian special forces — a 150-man Australian SAS (Special Air Service) team and a forty-man Canadian JTF2 (Joint Task Force 2) team. Canada also deployed a light infantry battalion. These forces were involved in operations aimed to "smoke out" al-Qaeda operatives. The mission was Canada's largest ground offensive since the Korean War. The mission also pointed to the similar imperatives that had once again drawn Australians and Canadians to work with their major allies and alongside each other, yet with little forethought.[5]

From 2002 onward, however, Bush's assertive and unilateralist inclinations over Iraq clearly were poorly received in Ottawa, and Prime Minister Chrétien read the domestic political winds very well in objecting to Bush's overtures in the lead-up to the war. But had Al Gore been the U.S. president and felt compelled to launch a war against Iraq, as Harvey argues, Gore's manner likely would have been more consensual than that of Bush, and possibly could have persuaded Chrétien of the merits of at least a token contribution. Obviously, we will never know for sure, but the point is that the contrast over Iraq between Canada and Australia can easily be overstated, and that overstatement can be misleading for those seeking to compare and contrast these two remarkably similar New World, federal, constitutional-monarchical U.S. allies that are also part of the British Commonwealth.

RECONFIGURING NATIONAL SECURITY AND DEFENCE FOR THE "WAR ON TERROR"

For Australia, the effect of the events of 9/11 and the Bali bombing in October 2002, which killed nearly one hundred vacationing Australian citizens, led the government to prepare and issue *Defence Update 2003*. The paper, released by Defence Minister Robert Hill on February 26, 2003, argued that, while the threat of direct military attack on Australia remained small, "geography does not protect Australia from rogue states armed with weapons of mass destruction and ballistic missiles or from terrorism" — including al-Qaeda and its regional offshoots and affiliates.[6]

Australia's Department of Foreign Affairs and Trade also issued a white paper in 2003 entitled *Advancing the National Interest*. This focused largely on Australia's need to fight terrorism and global threats to its security, including weapons of mass destruction proliferation. The paper stressed the value of collaborating with the United Nations and other multilateral groupings to facilitate Australia's national security.[7]

The underlying assumption behind these white papers was a significant reassessment of the dynamics at work in the United States. By 2003, the United States had become, according to a senior Australian defence policy adviser, Brendan Sargeant, "a strategic reality as present and pervasive as geography" — and geography has been a factor that has always dominated strategic thinking in Australia and Canada to an equal extent.[8] Similar views were being expressed in Canadian defence circles as well. One officer opined that "in the global interconnected Western world, the house under threat is no longer geographic, but geopolitical — no longer physical, but perceptual and cultural."[9]

For Australia, this increase in strategic value also manifested itself in the nation's growing importance to U.S. strategic plans in the Asia-Pacific. Presciently, U.S. deputy secretary of defense Paul Wolfowitz indicated that in conjunction with Japan, Australia acted as the foundation of a U.S. strategic triangle in the Pacific that may result in a greater U.S. military presence in Australia, with increased military exercises and increased sharing of Australian naval and air facilities.[10]

In contrast to Australia, and despite the observations made above, Canada showed little enthusiasm for significantly reworking its defence policy or increasing defence spending in the light of new and greater demands on the use of its forces. For instance, in contrast to the periodic reviews conducted in Australia, Canada took until 2009 to publish a Defence white paper to replace the one released in 1994. Some Canadian Defence officials defended the lack of a more recent review, arguing that the issues addressed and conclusions reached in the 1994 white paper remained pertinent for the post-9/11 world. Indeed, the Canadian government conducted a security review (but not a defence review) after the events of September 11, 2001, which resulted in a "Smart Border" agreement with the United States to facilitate the trade flow between the two countries. For Canada, like Australia, multilateralism had always been viewed as an attractive means to achieve broad foreign policy objectives. Despite the search for distinctiveness, prior to and after the invasion of Iraq, Canada followed the U.S. lead pretty closely.

The Australian comparison aside, Canada's geography and circumstances pointed to ongoing security co-operation with the United States as a tremendous economic imperative. Canada's overwhelming trade ties with the United States meant that American priorities had a significant impact on the security and foreign policy priorities that Canada set for itself. As Canada's Department of Foreign Affairs and International Trade's policy statement, *A Dialogue on Foreign Policy*, indicated in January 2003, no international relationship "is more important than the one we share with the United States." Indeed, "we will continue to work with the U.S. and other allies to protect the values that we hold in common, such as freedom, tolerance and respect for cultural diversity."[11]

In the face of post-9/11 security dynamics, defence policy priorities changed and pressure grew for closer Canadian co-operation with the

United States. Canada and Australia both saw their security interests largely aligned with the United States, and interoperability featured prominently as an issue critical to enhanced collaboration. At the same time, both countries faced the need to reconcile popular opinion and idealism with the dynamics of *realpolitik.*

The events of September 11, 2001, suddenly made North American defence of vital importance to the United States. Fiery and controversial Canadian military historian Jack Granatstein observed, "There are iron laws we [Canadians] must accept: We are part of North America; our economic prosperity depends on the United States; and North America will be defended with or without our consent."[12] These apparently conflicting imperatives had a significant effect on Canada's defence and security policy formulation — both in encouraging conformity and co-operation and in driving a desire for Canadian distinctiveness and protection of sovereignty, however ill-defined that may have been.

Canada, like several of its European NATO partners, recognized that radical Islamic extremism did not necessarily force "the West" to prove itself unified and coherent, as Soviet Communism once did.

Canadians and Australians struggled with reconciling their liberal internationalist predispositions with the often harder-nosed American reckoning of power politics in international affairs. For Canada, comfortable in its secure and benign environment under the largely U.S.-provided security umbrella, the apparent absence of direct and imminent threats meant being able to pick and choose which international military missions it would support. Nonetheless, the "war on terror" appeared to make Canada more vulnerable, at least to economic disruption, as the airport and border closures attested. Concerned about its apparently more unpredictable and volatile region, the Australian government felt greater certainty in backing U.S.-led efforts to extend the war on terror to Iraq.

MILITARY CONTRIBUTIONS TO THE IRAQ WAR

Canada was willing to strengthen some of its military links with the United States but was not prepared to go as far as Australia in support of U.S. military actions in Iraq. In early 2003, two thousand Australian troops deployed as part of the so-called "coalition of the willing" to the Gulf region and subsequently participated in the U.S.-led war against Iraq. Lead elements of special forces deployed into Iraq two days before the opening salvo of the war to track key military targets and destroy them as well as capture the Al Asad Airbase west of Baghdad with the support of Australian F/A-18 aircraft.[13] The Australian task group included members of the SAS Regiment, a force protection team from 4th Battalion, Royal Australian Regiment (Commando), members of the Incident Response Regiment, Chinook helicopters, transport and surveillance aircraft, naval ships, and headquarters elements attached to the U.S. forces.

The Australians played a significant role in neutralizing the missile threat to Israel in the opening days of the war. In addition, the Australian F/A-18 aircraft performed similar roles as Canada's CF-18s performed in the Kosovo campaign in 1999 and the Gulf War in 1990–91.[14] The F/A-18s conducted strike missions and close air support with precision weapons and with no civilian casualties observed. This was the first time that Australian aircraft had dropped bombs in a war zone since the Vietnam War more than thirty years previously.[15] In the case of Canada, its aircraft had dropped a similar quantity of ordnance during the Kosovo campaign. Australia also maintained a force of several hundred troops in the region after the initial phase of the war in Iraq subsided in May. Sixty air traffic controllers deployed to Baghdad International Airport. In addition, sixteen defence specialists were committed in support of the efforts to locate and destroy weapons of mass destruction, and a seventy-five-person security detachment deployed to Baghdad to protect the Australian Representative Mission. A further three Australian Defence Force (ADF) representatives were committed to work with the Office of Reconstruction and Humanitarian Assistance. Additional commitments included two C-130 Hercules aircraft, two PC-3 Orion aircraft, and the frigate, HMAS *Sydney*, which remained on station in support of the operation.[16] Australian major-general Jim Molan, commenting on the inter-service teamwork displayed by the Australian forces in Iraq in 2003, observed that "it is our ability to 'do jointery', that makes us different from most of our neighbours and many other armies in the world."[17]

Putting aside for the moment the considerable controversy over the war in Iraq, it is conceivable that, in less contentious circumstances, Canada and Australia could have collaborated to form a combined joint task force, had the will and greater awareness of compatibilities been evident. After all, Canada also maintained ships in the Gulf and deployed a comparable number of staff officers to the same U.S. headquarters. Instead, and in contrast to Australia, Canada sought to avoid being part of what some described as the "coalition of the coerced" and therefore committed up to three thousand troops to relieve U.S. forces in Afghanistan instead.[18] By so doing, the Canadian government cunningly attempted to side-step the issue of direct military support for U.S. plans in Iraq. Some observers suggested that Canada's reluctance had more to do with concerns about being too closely positioned with the Anglophone countries, which a majority of Quebeckers (facing a provincial election that was held during the war) were eager to avoid.[19] Such arguments point to the enduring concern in Canada over national unity.

There were, however, strongly held views in contrast to this one. Canadian scholar Douglas Bland, for instance, declared, "We rejected the American position in favour of the Security Council position, which is in fact the Russian/French position, thus making Canada, in effect, a French poodle."[20] Another similarly panned Chrétien's decision, saying, "We made a fetish of the United Nations."[21] While O'Connor and Vucetic point to a dominant culture among the elites opposed to supporting U.S. action in Iraq, such views clearly were not universally held.

The contrasting positions between Australia's Howard and Canada's Chrétien reflect a frequent difference in political orientation between the federal governments of both nations, with Canada's Liberal (progressive) government at variance with Australia under the Liberal (conservative) government. But such positions reflect a certain hard-nosed, short term–focused "realism" and do not necessarily reflect fundamental or permanent differences in values and orientations that would prevent closer co-operation in future. Indeed, Australian public sentiment, as in Canada and the rest of "the West," including among many Americans, shared the concerns about "the perils of empire."

Hypothetically, the military contributions to Iraq in early 2003 could have followed a different course. For instance, if Australia and Canada had previously scheduled exercises between their two countries' forces for a combined joint task force, and if the Quebec provincial elections of April 2003 had preceded the start of the war in Iraq, conceivably Australia and

Canada could have operated alongside each other — as a team, even — bolstering their combined diplomatic leverage. After all, Canadian Forces remained in the Gulf region throughout the war in Iraq, despite the Canadian government's public opposition to the war. For the sake of its ties with the United States, the Canadian government arguably could have been convinced to side with the United States in this conflict. Had Canada done so, a combined Australian-Canadian force may have made a significant contribution and retained considerable influence. As it turned out, with only two thousand troops involved, Australia's contribution remained relatively minor, not unlike Canada's contribution to the International Security Assistance Force (ISAF) in Afghanistan.[22]

Indeed, there is irony in the contrast to the Middle East crisis in 1956 over control of the Suez Canal, when Australia sided with Britain and France against the U.S. position, with Canada acting as the American proxy. The irony points to a distinction that reflects a continuing difference in the foreign policy dynamics of Australia and Canada. For Canada, distinctiveness, or at least a different stance to that taken by the United States, sometimes trumps alliance co-operation.

In light of these pressures to align with the United States, Paul Martin outlined his view of Canada's future foreign and defence policy in May 2003, arguing that "the time for multilateral initiative has never been greater," and yet "fixing multilateralism is not just a matter of strengthening the U.N. It also means identifying — and using — new arrangements and rules outside of the U.N." Martin suggested that:

There is an obligation for us to play our part in full to ensure that the global order remains open, stable, and able to deal with challenges and crises…. Merely rebuilding Canada's armed forces on old models will not suffice. We need to undertake a joint, systematic defence and foreign policy review to ensure that our defence objectives and capabilities match our foreign policy goals…. We have our interests too. We have joined alliances to preserve and protect them. We have fought wars to defend them. And we have worked diplomatically for an international system that embodies and extends them. We are internationalist in outlook, humanitarian by disposition, pragmatic in implementation, and always mindful of the limits of acting alone.[23]

Reflecting similar concerns, Canadian historian Margaret MacMillan lamented what she considered the loss of a clear sense of Canada's mission in the world. She pointed to the preoccupation with Quebec's place in Canada, arguing that "a lot of our best minds were turned inwards." The superpower polarity of the Cold War reinforced the sense that there was not much Canadians could do about it. But with the Cold War over and separatist sentiment at low ebb, Canadians, MacMillan argues, "show signs of being ready to reengage with the world."[24] Martin's and MacMillan's comments hint at the prospects of closer collaboration between Canadians and their "cousins down under" — equidistant to the twenty-first-century emerging great powers and potential "hot spots" of Northeast Asia. (Few appreciate how much the Mercator projection of the world, with Germany at the centre of the map, distorts perspectives on geographic proximity and the significance of Asia and the Pacific to Canada.)

Such comments about Canada's readiness to move beyond its national introspection and re-engage in international defence and security affairs arguably augur well for the prospects of collaboration between the Australian and Canadian forces, as well as with those of the United States. Indeed, despite Canada's reluctance to join the U.S.-led coalition in Iraq in 2003, its interests remained intrinsically aligned with those of the United States and its key allies. In fact, the contrasting positions over the war in Iraq tended to obscure the fundamental but often unnoticed similarities in outlook shared by Canadians and Australians that have remained extant for over a century. These similarities are enduring and numerous, even taking into account the occasional differences of opinion. The similarities demonstrate that Australia and Canada have a stronger interest in looking more closely at each other than has been the case for many years.[25]

Still, Canada's unwillingness to join its traditional allies in Iraq early in 2003 left Canadian policy-makers with a significant challenge. One American commentator argued in mid-2003:

It's stunning how much goodwill there is towards Britain and Australia, but not necessarily for Canada and New Zealand. It goes deeper than just historical ties or the English language. It has more to do with the idea that certain countries have not become post-modern yet. They're still muscular, they still have values and see the world as still a dangerous and tragic place. We in America don't necessarily always care what the exact material contribution of those countries is. It's got more to do with a shared kindred spirit.[26]

Such remarks reflected a heightened emotional sensitivity at the time. These high-spirited views would fade over time, particularly in light of what Canada would do next.

In the meantime, that lack of demonstrated Canadian "kindred spirit" over the Iraq War in 2003 and the American reaction left Australian policy-makers wary, in the short term at least, of closer engagement with Canada. Anecdotal accounts indicate Americans shunned their Canadian military counterparts, at times turning their backs on them in silent protest where once there had been close collaboration. Prime Minister Chrétien and his successors, Paul Martin and Stephen Harper, understood clearly the ramifications of the decision not to participate in Iraq, and made a concerted effort to compensate. This was most tangibly demonstrated by their forward-leaning support for the United States through their military engagement in Afghanistan.

LESSONS LEARNED

For the ADF, the experience in Iraq reinvigorated concerns about the need to refine and enhance its war-fighting capabilities. The carefully calibrated and time-constrained contribution to the combat phase of operations also saw the Australians emerge virtually casualty-free. This was a time of significant reflection on "lessons learned" and implications for the future of the ADF from the experience. In 2003, the ADF published a position paper entitled *Future Warfighting Concept*, touted as a "stake in the ground" for ADF concept development. The concept, known as "Multidimensional Manoeuvre," incorporates three components that reflect a strong American influence — "the Seamless Force, effects-based operations, and network-centric warfare."[27] Like Canada, Australia faces significant pressures and incentives to enhance interoperability with its American counterparts, and this is reflected in such definitions. Yet, regardless of what changes may occur, the same kinds of requirements remain extant for

Australian and Canadian soldiers. The concept paper acknowledged that "only a disciplined armed force capable of warfighting has the necessary skills and equipment to contribute to the full range of possible operational contingencies and peacetime tasks."[28]

Reflecting the complexity referred to, the spectrum of agencies involved or associated with military operations had grown in response to the challenges presented. Capturing the essence of at least part of the span of complexity, a term emerged for operations that were "joint, inter-agency, multilateral," or "JIM." These were operations involving all three armed services (joint); international organizations, non-governmental organizations, and other government aid; security and intelligence agencies (inter-agency); and multiple nations (multilateral). The conflict and post-conflict challenges in Afghanistan and Iraq over more than a decade suggest that this likely will be a continuing trend. This inter-agency approach engendered a co-operative effort among defence, foreign affairs, and the respective government aid agencies as well as the forces from other nations. Canada's deployment to Afghanistan also represented Canada's most conspicuous contribution to the U.S. "war on terror." For Australia, this would also come to be the case following the draw-down of forces in Iraq in 2007. In addition, the Afghanistan commitment represented the Canadian government's main calling card when it came to rebuilding credibility with Washington after sitting out the invasion of Iraq.

Canada's defence budget increased from around C$11 billion in 2001–02 to about $21 billion by 2010–11. Australia's defence budget grew commensurately as well to more than AU$25 billion. Over the following decade, the Canadian Armed Forces and the ADF underwent major recapitalization programs. Billions of dollars were committed. These investments strengthened some key operational capabilities. As combat operations in Afghanistan for Canada and Australia concluded, they both stood as the twelfth and thirteenth largest military spenders in the world. In both cases, their defence spending remained below the ostensible target of 2 percent of GDP. Yet even with the cessation of combat operations in Afghanistan by both the Australian and Canadian forces, the war there remained their largest and most dangerous military effort.[29]

Approximately 41,000 Canadian Forces personnel served in Afghanistan between 2001 and 2013 in support of the U.S.-led and NATO-mandated mission with ISAF. Australia had deployed 26,500 personnel to Afghanistan during the same period. The price Canada paid for having to make up for not participating in Iraq arguably can be quantified in a number of ways. But in terms of casualties, Canada sustained, after the United States and the United Kingdom, the third largest number of fatalities in Afghanistan among the forty-eight ISAF countries — 158 killed and more than 1,800 wounded. This is nearly four times the number of Australians killed there.

Although Canada's combat mission ended in 2011, nearly one thousand trainers and support personnel remained into 2014 to train Afghan National Security Forces. For Australia, approximately four hundred personnel remained beyond 2013 to perform comparable tasks in 2014 as well. With over a decade on operations in Afghanistan to their name, the Canadians can be confident that the United States is no longer interested in shunning them.

LOOKING AHEAD

Robust multinational operations such as the Afghanistan mission can be complex, lengthy, dangerous, and costly. They also can involve a high degree of interoperability with allied forces, and often result in combat and casualties. Although the framework of future deployments remains unknown, Canada and Australia can be expected to continue to face a range of military challenges in an unpredictable and volatile international security environment. Engagement alongside U.S. armed forces is therefore considered highly likely by the forces of both countries not just in Afghanistan but elsewhere, particularly in the Indo-Pacific region.

Australia's experience in the Regional Assistance Mission Solomon Islands in 2003 and in East Timor in 2006 reflects the high operational tempo that has affected both countries' forces. In the Solomon Islands, 1,500 Australian navy, army, and air force personnel, alongside military personnel from Fiji, Tonga, New Zealand, and Papua New Guinea provided security for police assisting the local government to restore law and order.[30] The experience in the Solomon Islands, while not involving Canadian or U.S. forces, demonstrates the kind of international activism in which Canada has long participated, seeking to proactively restore stability beyond its own shores out of enlightened self-interest. Desmond

Morton was correct when he observed that investment in sealift and airlift, better communications, precision-guided munitions, and light but robust military vehicles were precisely what would be needed in the future.[31] Similarly, other Canadian defence policy papers emerged which noted that "amphibious or littoral warfare capability is vital for any nation that wishes to deploy self-supporting military forces on operations overseas."[32] This is exactly the direction that the ADF has taken in recent years.[33]

As with Australia, the United States is eager to engage Canada as a partner in the Indo-Pacific region. Beyond that, however, some thought is also being given to the potential for further direct Canadian engagement with Australia and other powers in the region. The Australian Strategic Policy Institute and the Canadian Centre for International Governance Innovation have jointly commissioned a study exploring avenues for further trans-Pacific collaboration between Canada and Australia, to bolster regional security and stability and foster economic openness and prosperity.[34] The report points to the utility of remaining engaged with the United States while also reaching out for greater and deeper engagement with other regional powers, notably including China, India, Japan, and South Korea, as well as the countries of the Association of Southeast Asian Nations. The report is aspirational but points to the enduring relevance and significance of Canada and Australia seeking to explore opportunities to collaborate with each other in fostering regional security and stability as well as economic openness and increased trade.

Both countries already operate intimately alongside the United States armed forces, with integrated senior officers working in the United States Pacific Command headquarters in Hawaii, for instance. They both also have very close trading and economic ties with the United States, which tend to reinforce the enormous cultural influence from Hollywood on both countries.

Australia and Canada indeed are similar countries with, at times, different policies. But the focus on the differing decisions over whether to join the United States in invading Iraq has tended to distort perceptions of just how similar these two countries' policies have tended to be. More than a decade of working alongside each other in Afghanistan has reinforced the truism that despite being on opposite sides of the Pacific, Canada and Australia remain, in effect, "strategic cousins," with much in common and much to share for their mutual benefit.

NOTES

1. Frank P. Harvey, *Explaining the Iraq War: Counterfactual Theory, Logic and Evidence* (Cambridge: Cambridge University Press, 2012), 20.

2. Robert Kagan, *Of Paradise and Power: America and Europe in the New World Order* (New York: Alfred A. Knopf, 2003).

3. John Gray, *Men Are from Mars, Women Are from Venus* (New York: HarperCollins, 1992).

4. Brendon O'Connor and Srdjan Vucetic, "Another Mars-Venus Divide? Why Australia Said 'Yes' and Canada Said 'Non' to Involvement in the 2003 Iraq War," *Australian Journal of International Affairs* 64, no. 5 (2010): 526–48.

5. The Australian campaign in Afghanistan is considered in John Blaxland, *The Australian Army from Whitlam to Howard* (Melbourne: Cambridge University Press, 2014).

6. Senator Robert Hill, *Australia's National Security: A Defence Update 2003*, http://aseanregionalforum.asean.org/files/library/ARF%20Defense%20White%20Papers/Australia-2003.pdf (accessed August 10, 2014).

7. See Department of Foreign Affairs and Trade, *Advancing the National Interest* (Canberra, ACT: Commonwealth of Australia, February 2003), www.geneva.mission.gov.au/files/gene/2003_whitepaper.pdf (accessed August 10, 2014).

8. Brendan Sargeant, in discussion with the author.

9. Major Jeff Tasseron, "Facts and Invariants: The Changing Context of Canadian Defence Policy," *Canadian Military Journal* (Summer 2003): 22.

10. Stratfor, "Australia's Growing Importance to U.S. Strategic Plans," www.stratfor.com (accessed June 4, 2003).

11. Department of Foreign Affairs and International Trade, *A Dialogue on Foreign Policy* (Ottawa: Government of Canada, 2003), 5–6.

12. J.L. Granatstein, "Why Go to War? Because We Have To," February 20, 2003, www.jewishtoronto.com/page.aspx?id=39323 (accessed December 17, 2013).

13. Associated Press, "Australia Put Troops into Iraq Before War," *Globe and Mail*, May 10, 2003.

14. The Canadian Forces flew more than 5,700 hours including some 2,700 combat air patrols and 56 bombing sorties in the Gulf War in 1991. In Kosovo in 1999, CF-18s flew 678 combat sorties (air-to-ground bombing and combat air patrol) for more than 2,500 flying hours. See Samuel J. Walker, "Interoperability at the Speed of Sound: Modernising the CF-18 Hornet," in *Over Here and Over There*, ed. David Haglund (Kingston, ON: Queen's Quarterly, 2001), 258, 267.

15. Australian FA-18s flew 350 combat sorties over Iraq and dropped 122 precision-guided weapons: "Hornets Come Home," Defence public relations media release, May 15, 2003 (released from mediacentre@defence.gov.au).

16. See "Operation Catalyst: Australia's Defence Contribution to Iraq's Rehabilitation,"

Defence public relations media release, April 30, 2003 (released from mediacentre@defence.gov.au); and Australian Minister for Defence Media Mail List, "Operation Catalyst Comes into Effect Tomorrow," July 15, 2003, 89/2003.

17. Major-General Jim Molan, "Op Falconer — War Against Iraq — Winning Concepts," *Army: The Soldiers' Newspaper*, April 24, 2003.

18. See Sarah Anderson, Phyllis Bennis, and John Cavanagh, *Coalition of the Willing or Coalition of the Coerced?* (Washington: Institute for Policy Studies, February 26, 2003).

19. See, for instance, William Thorsell, "Canada Can No Longer Ignore the World's Siren Call," *Globe and Mail*, April 7, 2003; and Kim Lunman, "Canadians 'Dead Split' on Supporting War, Poll Reports," *Globe and Mail*, April 7, 2003. Lunman reported that a survey conducted from April 1 to 3, 2003, by CTV/the *Globe and Mail* found that only 29 percent of those surveyed in Quebec expressed support for the U.S.-led war in Iraq, compared to 54 percent in the rest of Canada.

20. Douglas Bland, "Military Interoperability," in *The Canadian Forces and Interoperability*, ed. Ann L. Griffiths (Halifax, NS: Centre for Foreign Policy Studies, 2003), 61.

21. Andrew Cohen cited in John Geddes, "Smart Guy, Eh?" *Maclean's*, June 23, 2003.

22. See Jim Wallace, "Iraq Lesson Can Help Correct Defence Policy," *The Age*, April 20, 2003.

23. Honourable Paul Martin, "Transcript: Canada's Role in a Complex World" (speech to the Canadian Newspapers Association, April 30, 2003).

24. Margaret MacMillan cited in Geddes, "Smart Guy, Eh?," 24.

25. This is the argument made in John Blaxland, *Strategic Cousins: Australia and Canadian Expeditionary Forces and the British and American Empires* (Montreal: McGill-Queen's University Press, 2006).

26. Geoffrey Blainey, "After Iraq: The Road from Baghdad," *Policy Magazine*, September 9, 2003.

27. Department of Defence, *Future Warfighting Concept* (Canberra, ACT: Australian Government, 2003), 2–3, www.defence.gov.au/publications/fwc.pdf (accessed August 10, 2014).

28. Ibid., 14.

29. Martin Auger, "Canadian Military Operations Into the 21st Century" (Ottawa: Library of Parliament, 2011), www.parl.gc.ca/content/lop/researchpublications/cei-17-e.htm (accessed December 17, 2013).

30. See Blaxland, "Operations in Solomon Islands from 2000," chapter 5 in *The Australian Army from Whitlam to Howard*.

31. Desmond Morton, *Understanding Canadian Defence* (Toronto: Penguin Canada, 2003), 211.

32. Canadian Alliance, *The New North Strong and Free: Protecting Canadian Sovereignty and Contributing to Global Stability* (Ottawa: Defence Policy White Paper of the Official Opposition, House of Commons, Spring 2003), 34.

33. See John Blaxland, "Game-Changer in the Pacific: Surprising Options Open Up with the New Multi-Purpose Maritime Capability," *Security Challenge* 9, no.3 (2013): 31–41, www.securitychallenges.org.au/ArticlePDFs/SC9-3Blaxland.pdf (accessed December 17, 2013).

34. See "Canada Needs Long-Term Plan to Benefit from Australian Support in Indo-Pacific Engagement, Says New CIGI-ASPI Report," *Centre for International Governance Innovation*, www.cigionline.org/articles/2013/09/canada-needs-long-term-plan-benefit-australian-support-indo-pacific-engagement-says (accessed December 17, 2013).

7

AUSTRALIA'S INTERNATIONAL DEPLOYMENTS IN HISTORICAL PERSPECTIVE

William Maley

Australia has a long history of involvement in wars beyond its shores.[1] The Australian War Memorial in Canberra houses the medals of an Australian who served in the second Anglo-Afghan War of 1879–80, and there may well have been Australians serving abroad even before that. What underpins this commitment to expeditionary force is perhaps less clear. Australia is physically remote from many of the areas in which its troops have served, and in a number of cases one could argue that no serious Australian interests were engaged by the situation into which Australian forces were thrust. When one looks in detail, however, at some of the specific situations in which Australia has become involved, what led to the involvement becomes more obvious. Rarely is the story a straightforward one. Rather, what one witnesses is a mixture of commitments and expectations derived from past experience, together with calculations by political elites, which themselves reflect sensitivity to the expectations that the wider public has been perceived to hold. In this respect, Australia's involvement alongside the United States in the invasion of Iraq in 2003 was not a surprising development; indeed, it would have been more startling if the then Australian government, a Liberal Party-National coalition led by Prime Minister John Howard, had decided *not* to become involved.

Nonetheless, it is important also to recognize that the kinds of factors that have shaped Australia's expeditionary involvements have changed over time. In the nineteenth and early twentieth centuries, involvement in foreign wars had a great deal to do with a sense of shared identity with people of British ancestry in different parts of the world. In this sense, oddly enough, earlier Australian deployments were underpinned by a kind of cosmopolitanism. This sense of identity is no longer anywhere near as potent as once it was, although Australia's new prime minister, Tony Abbott, has on occasion sought to revive the idea of an "Anglosphere."[2] By the late twentieth and early twenty-first centuries, a different set of factors come into play, derived from a "realist" conviction that "great and powerful friends" are required to guarantee Australia's security in an uncertain world.

This chapter explores these shifts. It is divided into five sections. The first examines a number of major overseas deployments from the nineteenth century onward, exploring the reasons why they were undertaken. The second focuses specifically on Australian involvement in the Middle East, noting that this has been an area of surprisingly active engagement given its relative remoteness from Australia, and the presence in Australia's more immediate surroundings of a range of challenges which one might think would have absorbed much of its strategic attention. The third is concerned with the way in which Australia has conducted operations authorized by the United Nations Security Council, either as part of classical peacekeeping operations, or pursuant to binding decisions of the Security Council made under Chapter VII of the Charter of the United Nations. The fourth explores in some detail the ways in which Australia's alliance commitments to the United States in particular have shaped its disposition to become involved in foreign wars. This emerges as by far the dominant consideration leading to Australia's involvement in Iraq from 2003. The fifth section offers some brief conclusions.

AUSTRALIA AND FOREIGN WARS: SOME HISTORY

Australia was born into war. The Boer War was already underway when the Commonwealth of Australia came into existence on January 1, 1901, pursuant to the provisions of the Commonwealth of Australia Constitution Act 1900, passed by the Parliament at Westminster. Australians had already by this stage volunteered for service in South Africa, and during the course of the conflict, some sixteen thousand Australians served and 589 died. In terms of mortality, the costs to Australia of the Boer War exceeded both the Korean War (with 340 dead) and the Vietnam War (with 521 dead). However, the Australians who served in South Africa did so under British command, and this may be one reason why the commitment has been largely forgotten except among professional historians.[3] It was nonetheless important as a marker of expeditionary inclination. Those who served in South Africa were volunteers, and the tug of Empire clearly meant something to them — it would be difficult to argue that Australia had significant strategic interests at stake in the Boer War.

This was not the case, oddly enough, with the First World War. There, Australia had significant strategic interests at stake because of the proximity of the German colony of New Guinea. Securing New Guinea, indeed, was one of Australia's very first actions once the war broke out. It was not this engagement, however, but rather the April 1915 Gallipoli landings that came to be of canonical significance in shaping Australians' understanding of the conflict. While the Dardanelles campaign proved to be a failure and cost the young Winston Churchill his position as First Lord of the Admiralty in London, the landings themselves provided Australia with a series of inspirational tales that continue to this day to contribute to a sense of identity among new generations. Nonetheless, the main carnage that Australia experienced was not at Gallipoli but on the Western Front. A total of 61,513 Australians perished in the war, and virtually every Australian country town contains within it a war memorial inscribed with the names of locals who died in the conflict. Yet despite the scale of this sacrifice, when referenda proposing conscription were held in 1916 and 1917 by the government of Prime Minister William Morris Hughes, the public voted the proposals down.

During the Second World War, by contrast, the Australian Labor Party (ALP) of Prime Minister John Curtin (1941–45) introduced conscription with little controversy, for the very obvious reason that Australia itself came to be directly threatened by Japanese power following the bombing of Pearl Harbor. On February 19, 1942, 188 Japanese planes attacked the northern city of Darwin, dropping a greater tonnage of bombs than had been used in the Pearl Harbor attack. Some 243 people were killed, and this was simply the first of sixty-four air attacks on the city, as well as on targets in Western Australia and on the Queensland cities of Cairns and Townsville. Wartime censorship ensured that news of the raids did not spread too far, but it was indisputably the case that Australians felt far more directly threatened by the war in the Pacific than by any other event in Australia's history. It is notable, however, that Australia's entry into the war came not with the Pearl Harbor attack in December 1941, but with the German invasion of Poland in September 1939. Prime Minister Robert Menzies, broadcasting to the Australian people, stated that it was his "melancholy duty" to inform them officially that "in consequence of a persistence by Germany in her invasion of Poland, Great Britain has declared war upon her, and that, as a result, Australia is also at war."[4] This was an unusual form of words, but Hitler's Germany constituted a very unusual form of threat. Adolf Hitler, as French premier Paul Reynaud later put it to his Cabinet, was "Genghis Khan."[5] Public opinion in many of the dominions, skeptical of involvement in Europe at the time of the 1938 Czechoslovak crisis, had shifted seismically with the German occupation of Prague in March 1939, and Australia was no different.

Australia's other major overseas commitment in the three decades following the Second World War, in Vietnam, could hardly have been more different. Australian leaders at the time saw it as strategically vital to encourage the United States to remain engaged in Asia.[6] But whether Vietnam was the best venue for such engagement was another question: some very well-informed critics raised doubts well before the fall of South Vietnam in 1975.[7] The Vietnam War was deeply controversial within Australia, but conscription *was* employed and there was a palpable sense of shock in early 1966 when the first Australian conscript was killed in Vietnam. The effects of Vietnam on domestic politics were not felt immediately. Harold Holt, who had succeeded Sir Robert Menzies as prime minister following Menzies's retirement in early 1966, won a landslide victory in the election held at the end of that year, not least because the Labor Party was clearly divided on a range of issues. But as the situation in Vietnam deteriorated, especially following the Tet Offensive of 1968, the war became more and more of a burden for the Liberal-Country Party coalition. When the ALP was elected to office in December 1972, one of the first steps it took was to abolish conscription, and no serious political figure has suggested its revival since.

In this very brief catalogue, three kinds of reason for Australian deployments abroad loom prominently: emotional, strategic, and political. A number of commitments were most strongly underpinned by emotional factors relating to identity and values. These were almost certainly the most significant for those who volunteered to serve in South Africa and during the First World War. There is no doubt that by the late nineteenth century, a sense of Australian identity had begun to crystallize. In 1894, Ethel Turner (1870–1958) published a novel entitled *Seven Little Australians* that has remained in print ever since[8] and captures very clearly the sense of Antipodean distinctiveness that was waxing palpably. Yet at the same time, some Australians retained a strong sense of British identity as well, at a time when this seemed more like recognition of family membership than allegiance to a foreign power. This was, of course, much more noticeable among those of English or Scots descent than among the Irish-Catholic element of the Australian population, but was not a trivial factor. Thus, in the twentieth century, an Australian leader such as Menzies could simultaneously have a sense of Scots identity, British identity, and Australian identity, all of which were grounded in respect for shared institutions, their histories, and the values they embodied.

This did not imply or entail subservience to the priorities of any particular British government, for a sense of identity could easily be overwhelmed by compelling strategic logic. It was Menzies who, in a speech on April 26, 1939, observed that "what Great Britain calls the Far East is to us the Near North."[9] No matter how strong the ties of Empire, a threat in Australia's immediate strategic vicinity would command top priority in response. Curtin, Menzies's Labor successor, was equally seized by such strategic logic, and this produced a wartime turn to the United States as a key strategic partner that remains unreversed to this day.

But beyond both emotional ties and strategic logic could lie political calculations. Strategic challenges can demand action, but more often than not, there is a range of possible options available to political leaders to respond to such challenges. How exactly a leadership will choose to respond can depend on a wide number of factors, such as ideological affinity, prior relationships, and the complex arrays of interests that may contribute to constituting relationships with different actors in the world. In circumstances such as Australia faced in early 1942 when its territory came under direct attack, there may have been relatively few options available. It is hard to make the same claim about the situation that Australia faced in Asia in the early 1960s, even taking into account the instability of Indonesia at that particular time. More recently, the consolidation of multilateral institutions has provided a clear alternative to balance-of-power thinking and simple "realism" as a response to strategic threats. Yet as we shall see shortly, Australian politicians, to a significant degree, have remained locked in a mindset that prioritizes alliance with the seemingly strong over alternative ways of promoting world order. Australia's entanglement in the Bush administration's Iraq adventure in 2003 was a very plain manifestation of this mindset.

AUSTRALIA AND MIDDLE EAST CONFLICTS

Even with its long history of expeditionary involvement, one might well query why Australia would become involved in conflicts in the Middle East. The countries of the Middle East hardly constitute Australia's backyard. While with careful planning one can now fly out of Australia in the morning and arrive in London in the evening of the same day, a flight to the Middle East remains exhaustingly long. Until the 1970s, most Australians would have had to undertake a lengthy sea trip to reach that part of the world. Furthermore, there are good reasons for seeing the Asia-Pacific region as much more relevant to Australia's immediate strategic concerns than the Middle East. Yet despite this, for a very long period of time Australia *has* taken an interest in the Middle East, although for reasons that have varied over time as well. Australia's involvement in the Middle East during the First and Second World Wars was essentially a reflection of the global nature of those conflicts, with different theatres of operation materializing given the nature of the enemy. Thus, when the Ottoman Empire joined the Central Powers on October 30, 1914, the territories it controlled became potential sites of conflict. This explains Australia's involvement in the Gallipoli landings, discussed earlier in this chapter, as well as in Palestine, where the famous Australian Light Horse served.[10] Similarly, during the Second World War, Australian forces served actively in the North African campaign, with the so-called "Rats of Tobruk" earning special fame, and it was only with the outbreak of the war in the Pacific in December 1941 that Australian priorities sharply shifted, with the 6th and 7th Divisions being returned to Australia.[11]

It was a long while before Australian troops were again to be deployed belligerently in the Middle East, but this did not mean that Australia's interest in the region had waned. On the contrary, Australia contrived to play an active role during the 1956 Suez Crisis, which ironically marked the end of the United Kingdom as a global power and set the scene for its subsequent withdrawal from east of Suez in 1967. The Liberal-Country Party coalition government led by Prime Minister Robert Menzies strongly supported the position of the Eden government in the United Kingdom following Egyptian president Gamel Abdul Nasser's nationalization of the Suez Canal. Free movement of vessels through the canal was seen as essential for Australia's economic well-being, although it was not clear that nationalization per se would threaten free movement of vessels (and the subsequent closure of the Suez Canal between 1967 and 1975 did not have a markedly detrimental effect on Australia's economic interests). Australia, however, found itself nearly as isolated as the United Kingdom once London and Paris, conspiring with the Israelis, dispatched forces to the canal zone. This action, astoundingly, had not been cleared with the Eisenhower administration in the United States, which took a very dim view of such a use of force on the very eve of a scheduled U.S. presidential election. British prime minister Anthony Eden was shortly thereafter obliged to stand down, and the entire episode came to be seen as a debacle of historic proportions. It did little harm to the Menzies government; Dr. H.V. Evatt, who as Opposition leader had roundly criticized the government's position, led the ALP to a catastrophic defeat at the 1958 election, and in 1960 relinquished the leadership of the Labor Party. What the Suez Crisis did do was drive home to Australia that it was now the United States that unambiguously carried the greatest weight in the world, and this was to have significant ramifications for Australia's deployments in other areas of the world, such as Southeast Asia. But this understanding, over time, was also to influence Australian orientations in other respects, especially toward the Israeli-Palestinian conflict that flared dramatically in the aftermath of the 1967 Six Day War.

It is easily forgotten that it was not until the advent of the Nixon administration in Washington in January 1969 that the United States began to support Israel in an uncritical fashion. President Harry Truman in 1948, urged on by his aide Clark Clifford, had moved swiftly to accord recognition of the new state of Israel, and friendly relations were quickly consolidated through the exchange of envoys. However, no Israeli prime minister could afford at this time to take U.S. support for granted. This changed after the Six Day War, although for complex reasons. On the one hand, the surge in terrorist activities by Palestinian groups such as Fatah and the Popular Front for the Liberation of Palestine, as well as by eccentric fellow travellers such as the Japanese Red Army, created a very bad impression in Western countries. On the other, despite President Richard M. Nixon's anti-Semitism, lobbying activity by vocal supporters of Israel grew strongly in the United States. This was to continue in particular during the term of the Reagan administration (1981–89).[12] Australia ultimately followed the American lead. This was not purely out of solidarity with Washington; ALP prime minister Bob Hawke (1983–91) was a lifelong supporter of Israel, and Liberal prime minister John Howard (1996–2007) was equally supportive but a good deal less critical in his support than Hawke had been. Indeed, in 2004, the Howard government in the U.N. General Assembly voted with only the United States, Israel, and three Pacific micro-states to oppose a resolution endorsing the Advisory Opinion of the International Court of Justice on the legality of the barrier wall built by Israel on territory occupied following the 1967 war.[13]

It was also, however, the case that a very active pro-Israeli lobby had emerged in Australia. Australia's Jewish community contained a wide range of opinions, but for historical reasons contained a large number of Holocaust survivors for whom Israel functioned as a beacon in the wider world.[14] A number of networks and groups vociferously pressed Australian politicians to adopt pro-Israeli positions and to support U.S. actions directed against states in the Middle East that these networks and groups saw as threatening to Israel. Iraq was certainly one of them, which was not surprising given that Saddam Hussein had fired Scud missiles at Israel in 1991. Whether Saddam in 2003 had anything like that capacity was doubtful, but this did not stop known supporters of Israel from pressing for action against Saddam, backed by claims that such action would be legal.[15] When the Americans ran into difficulty in Iraq, some of these advocates sought to distance themselves from their earlier advocacy, arguing that it had always been Iran that troubled them the most. This was somewhat disingenuous, and perhaps unnecessary as well, given that Prime Minister Howard almost certainly would have supported Washington even without the backing of this lobby. Nonetheless, it did supply him with a certain amount of community support to which he could point when the wisdom of his decisions was being contested.

AUSTRALIA AND U.N.-AUTHORIZED OPERATIONS

The key reason why this support was important was that the legal justi-fication for Australian involvement in Iraq was extraordinarily feeble, as Charles Sampford documents in his chapter. The fatal gap was the lack of appropriate endorsement from the United Nations Security Council.

Australia, like many member states of the United Nations, has a long history of involvement in supporting operations authorized through U.N. channels. A foundation member of the organization, it was represented at the San Francisco conference in 1945 by the ALP minister for external affairs, Dr. H. V. Evatt, who went on to become president of the General Assembly in 1948. Ever since, Australia has been an obvious target for requests that it become involved in supporting U.N. objectives, whether in the form of enforcement action authorized by the Security Council or in the form of classical peacekeeping or other forms of complex peace operation of the kind that have proliferated in the post–Cold War period. As early as August 1947, Australia deployed four military observers as part of the United Nations Good Offices Commission in the Dutch East Indies, a mission that ran until January 1, 1949.[16] Since then, Australia has been a vigorous contributor to peace operations, and, for the most part, these deployments have proved to be uncontroversial domestically.[17] Australia has also been involved in non-U.N. peace operations, most nota-bly those conducted by the Multinational Force and Observers in Sinai.

In addition, Australia found itself involved in more robust action under U.N. auspices. The most striking example was the Korean War (1950–53).[18] The division of the Korean Peninsula as a result of the Second World War created an unstable situation in which a Communist regime in the north faced a pro-Western regime in the south. Two developments in 1949 — the successful Soviet nuclear test on August 29 and the Chinese Communist takeover in Peking shortly afterward — shifted the calculus of the North Korean leadership under Kim Il Sung.[19] On June 25, 1950, North Korea launched a sustained attack on the south. Two factors facilitated Australia's subsequent involvement in the conflict. One was that the U.N. Security Council on June 27, 1950, adopted Resolution 83, which recommended that member states "furnish such assistance to the Republic of Korea as may be necessary to repel the armed attack and to restore international peace and security in the area." (This, ironically, happened only because, at the time, the Soviet Union was boycotting Security Council meetings in protest at the failure to allow Chinese Communists to occupy China's council seat, and as a result, the USSR was unable to use its veto power to block the resolution. It did not make that mistake again.) Australia was thus in a position to depict its involvement in Korea quite rightly as action in defence of binding international legal obligations and world order more generally. But beyond this, the Korean War was framed in a Cold War context.[20] The deterioration in East-West relations that had been flagged by Winston Churchill in his famous Iron Curtain speech in 1946 had only persisted, and the Korean Peninsula seemed simply to be the newest venue for competition between the Soviet Union and the United States. Australia was, throughout the 1950s and 1960s, on the side of the United States in this struggle, so it would have been exceedingly odd if Australia had not contributed support to the United States and its allies in Korea.

Given the veto power of the Soviet Union, Korea was the last case during the Cold War when action to contain Soviet power was carried out with Security Council authorization. Efforts at containment thereafter were justified legally by reference to the inherent right of individual or collective self-defence set out in Article 51 of the U.N. Charter. But with the end of the Cold War following the advent of Mikhail Gorbachev to the Soviet leadership in March 1985, and the fall of the Berlin Wall in November 1989, new opportunities for collective action authorized by the Security Council began to take shape.

The most important of these by far followed Iraq's invasion of Kuwait in August 1990. When Saddam Hussein dispatched forces to occupy his small neighbour, he may well have expected the Soviet Union to provide him with protection in the Security Council of the kind he could easily have expected during the Cold War period. Rarely has a ruler miscalculated so gravely. The Soviet leadership, which had no prior knowledge of the intended invasion, took a very dim view of Saddam's adventurism, not least because the Soviet foreign minister had had the humiliation of learning of the invasion from the U.S. secretary of state, who was visiting the Soviet Union at the time. As a result, the Security Council immediately adopted a resolution condemning the invasion and, ultimately, in Resolution 678 provided authorization for member states to use all necessary means to bring about the removal of Iraqi forces from Kuwait. Australia was not at this time a member of the Security Council, but the ALP Hawke government, with full support from the Opposition, wasted no time in condemning the Iraqi invasion, supporting the position the Security Council had articulated, and committing Australia to the wider objective of the liberation of Kuwait. While Australia was not a significant contributor of ground troops for subsequent military operations, Australian naval assets were deployed to the Persian Gulf in order to enforce specific sanctions on which the Security Council had agreed before the outbreak of Operation Desert Storm.[21]

Nonetheless, the government was obliged to tread with some care, not because it faced any opposition of significance in Parliament, but rather because within the ALP there were significant strands of opinion that saw the U.S.-led operations Desert Shield and Desert Storm as products of an American interest in protecting the flow of oil for the American economy. This skepticism led to demands that sanctions against the Iraqi regime be given time to work.[22] The downside of this demand, of course, was that if sanctions were imposed for a lengthy period of time but failed to procure an Iraqi withdrawal, there might be very little left of Kuwait to save. Indeed, when exacting sanctions were subsequently imposed upon Iraq, they caused a great deal of misery for ordinary people, and were notably ineffective in bringing about the collapse of Saddam's regime.[23] These arguments from the left cut little ice with the wider community, not least because the Iraqi invasion of Kuwait was an absolutely egregious violation of the prohibition on the threat or use of force contained in the Charter of the United Nations. Nonetheless, they were a significant pointer to a strand of opinion within the Labor Party that was to re-emerge, albeit with much stronger justification, in 2003.

More importantly, however, Australia's engagement with the United Nations to a degree redefined expectations or beliefs about the circumstances in which the expeditionary use of force was appropriate. The 1945 Charter had famously reconfigured the relevant international law relating to the threat or use of force.[24] It provided a general, overarching prohibition, combined with exceptions in two circumstances: self-defence (as covered by Article 51 of the Charter); and enforcement action authorized by the Security Council (under Article 42 of the Charter). When U.S. president George H. W. Bush in 1990 and 1991 consciously sought the approval of the Security Council for action against Iraq, and subsequently spoke of the possibility of a "new world order" in which the Great Powers would act co-operatively to promote a peaceful world, he gave a salience to Security Council authoriz-ation which many self-styled "realists" might have been inclined to contest. A consequence was that subsequent unilateral U.S. action, unsupported by an appropriate Security Council resolution, was likely to prove more contro-versial among allies than otherwise might have been the case. This indeed proved to be the case with most of Washington's friends of long standing. Yet in 2003 Australia bucked the trend by associating itself enthusiastically, although not in a bipartisan fashion, with the actions proposed by President Bush. In order to understand why this was the case, it is necessary, as fore-shadowed earlier, to explore the fundamental importance of *alliance* in the international thinking of a certain type of Australian political leader.

AUSTRALIA AND ALLIANCE PARTNERSHIPS

Australia's longstanding relationship with the United Kingdom before the Second World War is perhaps better seen as a kind of familial tie rather than as an alliance in the strict sense of the term. Underpinned by a sense of shared values and institutions, it also had a distinct legal character, given that the Australian Constitution had been embodied in an Act of Parliament at Westminster. But even before the Second World War broke out, these specific ties had begun to erode. In the legal realm, the 1931 Statute of Westminster saw the British Parliament formally abandon the right to legislate for the dominions unless specifically requested to do so. Moreover, in the political realm, conflicts of interest were beginning to surface, most dramatically over the issue of wool sales in the 1930s.[25] Yet these developments paled in the face of the shock that Australia experienced with the fall of Singapore in early 1942. This above all else prompted a reorientation of Australian foreign and strategic policy away from the United Kingdom and toward a working relationship, and ultimately an alliance, with the United States.

Alliances go beyond mere association, friendship, or common organizational membership. Alliances are constituted through some recognizable process or set of steps; reflect some shared purpose; involve a joint commitment of resources, either immediate or prospective; and involve some degree of joint decision-making. Alliances can be grounded in shared interests, ideologies, or values, in particular a desire to balance against a threat.[26] Any alliance relationship is likely to have both symbolic and practical dimensions, but the character of the alliance will most likely vary according to which dimension is the dominant. In some alliances, it is symbols that matter the most; in others, symbols are augmented by a potentially vast array of operational connections that are meaningful and useful to one or both parties on a regular basis. Symbols tend to be grounded in historical experience, although expectations can be grounded in a mythological or sanitized history. (The conviction expressed by some right-wing American commentators in 2003 that France owed the United States support on Iraq because of America's support for France during the Second World War overlooked the neutrality of the United States when the Nazis marched down the Champs Elysées from the Arc de Triomphe in June 1940; the diplomatic recognition that the United States accorded to the Vichy regime of Marshal Phillipe Pétain; and the inconvenient fact that it was Germany that declared war on the United States in December 1941, rather than the other way around.[27])

Australia's alliance relationship with the United States was formalized in the 1951 ANZUS (Australia, New Zealand, United States) Treaty, which was formally invoked by Prime Minister Howard following the September 11, 2001, terrorist attacks on the United States. Ever since it was signed, this treaty has served as the bedrock of the relationship between the two countries, but like many asymmetric alliances, it has its limitations as far as Australia is concerned. Where one alliance partner is in a dominant position, irrespective of the specific bases of its power, the other partners may find that things do not evolve in quite the ways they might have expected. In such circumstances, an alliance may matter more for one partner than another, or may matter equally but for quite different reasons. Where this is the case, the dominant partner may be in a position to dictate the terms upon which it meets its apparent obligations to the other parties. This is something that figures commonly in the politics of the powers. In 1969, for example, U.S. president Richard Nixon enunciated what came to be known as the Nixon Doctrine, which positioned the United States as ultimate guarantor of the security of its partners, but placed primary and initial responsibility upon local shoulders when threats needed to be met. This model, which in one respect involved special positions for pro-Western "regional policemen," unravelled badly with the fall of South Vietnam in 1975 and the 1979 Iranian revolution, but it does provide an illustration of how great power can bring with it at the very least a temptation to attempt to rewrite the terms of a relationship.

A more immediate and interesting example of the perils of asymmetry came in September 1999 with the crisis in East Timor that followed the announcement of the results of the popular consultation on that territory's future held under U.N. auspices on August 30, 1999. This was a crisis of tremendous significance for Australia. Public opinion, never as sympathetic to Indonesia's position on East Timor as had been successive Australian governments, manifested a high level of rage at the attacks on East Timorese civilians by armed militias plainly connected to the Indonesian armed forces. The Howard government, having earlier trumpeted its role in procuring the consultation, suddenly found itself under intense pressure to act to protect the voters who had gone to the polls in good faith.[28] However, its freedom of unilateral action was severely limited. Its de jure recognition of Indonesia's incorporation of East Timor remained in place, so that any unilateral deployment of Australian troops to the territory would, from Australia's point of view, amount to the invasion of a neighbouring country. For this reason, strong U.S. backing to pressure Indonesia to agree to an international deployment was of vital importance. However, this was not what Australia initially encountered. As James Cotton has put it, "The Pentagon and the Defense Secretary adopted the view that the United States had too many other commitments, and National Security Adviser Sandy Berger was positively opposed to any commitment."[29] Berger even trivialized the situation by comparing it to his daughter's messy college apartment.[30]

From Australia's point of view, this was truly chilling. It was facing its greatest foreign policy challenge since the ANZUS Treaty was concluded, and its strongest ally was opting to maintain a degree of distance. As things turned out, luck was on Australia's side. The Asia-Pacific Economic Cooperation (APEC) heads of government were about to meet in Auckland, and the meeting had the effect of extracting President Bill Clinton from the immediate influence of his more isolationist advisers and exposing him to the alarm of Asian regional leaders, prompting the U.S. administration to increase its pressure on Jakarta. It may well be that the fright that the Australian government received at this time was one factor which prompted it to enter a tighter embrace with Washington from that point onward. The key point here is that in an asymmetric relationship, the stronger partner enjoys some latitude to pick and choose whether and how it will give effect to such obligations as it feels toward its partners.

Yet alliances are not like bank accounts that can be replenished with fresh deposits. The French scholar François Heisbourg warned in 2003 that the United States might increasingly judge alliance partners not on the strength of what they had done in the past, but rather on the strength of what they were prepared to do in the future: "The sheriff composes his posse and if you don't want to be part of the posse you will be punished."[31] The former British foreign secretary Lord Douglas Hurd made the same point even more starkly when he referred to the supporters of the United States in Iraq as a "coalition of the obedient."[32] The Australian government doubtless believed that with other supporters very thin on the ground, the presence of Australian troops in the Iraq theatre of operations from March 2003 mattered far more in a symbolic sense than for any practical benefit that the small Australian force actually delivered. But how widely it was noted was debatable: an article by R.W. Apple, Jr. in the *New York Times* revealingly observed that without the support of the British, "American troops would be fighting alone."[33] Furthermore, what appeals to one administration may not appeal to its successor. Before becoming U.S. president in 2009, Barack Obama had been a forthright critic of the Iraq intervention.[34]

With all that said, the domestic politics of the alliance played in the Howard government's favour in net terms, at least in the short run. Prime Minister Howard's reckless claim in the House of Representatives on February 4, 2003 — "The Australian government *knows* that Iraq still has chemical and biological weapons"[35] — exposed him to the charge of being a liar; a subsequent investigation by a parliamentary committee concluded that the relevant evidence was much more equivocal.[36] But it was Opposition leader Mark Latham who suffered the greater harm from his approach to the alliance. Sensing — probably rightly — that large numbers of Australians viewed President George W. Bush as indolent, goofy, and fundamentally stupid, he publicly described the U.S. president as "the most incompetent and dangerous president in living memory."[37] This, together with his use of crude and vulgar terms to characterize those who supported Bush's position, boomeranged badly, suggesting a fatal lack of the kind of gravitas that Australians hope to see in a prime minister. The Howard government was fortunate that the 2004 election was out of the way by the time the situation in Iraq deteriorated severely, and by the time the 2007 election came around, it was clear that Howard had outstayed his welcome. For only the second time in Australian history, a serving prime minister lost his own seat. This was not, however, a direct consequence of Iraq, but of a wide range of contributing factors.

CONCLUSION

In opposing the Howard government's decision to join the Bush administration in its attack on Iraq, the Australian Labor Party (or at least its parliamentary wing) was able to draw on solid strategic arguments, some of them shared by conservative commentators wary of the reckless use of American power.[38] Nonetheless, the ALP leaders of that time found themselves out of step with both Australian public opinion and the wider disposition of the ALP to mimic the coalition in supporting the United States in a relatively uncritical fashion. The poor performance of the ALP at the 2004 Australian election, which led directly to the demise of Mark Latham as party leader, contributed to the resumption of bipartisan support for Washington and its key endeavours.

From this historical analysis, therefore, it emerges that the alliance between Australia and the United States remains, and is likely to remain in the future, central to Australia's expeditionary undertakings. This is not to say that Australia will shrink from involvements in other kinds of international activity. Elected as a non-permanent member of the U.N. Security Council in late 2012, it found itself exposed (like any significant non-permanent member of the Council) to the expectation that it would be willing to contribute personnel for peacekeeping operations when the Council had determined that such operations were necessary.

Furthermore, from time to time as a major power in the Pacific and as a significant actor in the Asia-Pacific region more broadly, Australia is likely to face pressure to pull its weight through the supply of troops for a range of purposes stretching from disaster relief to internal policing and reform in troubled states. But all of that said, when it comes to major contributions to operations outside these immediate spheres of activity, it will be the relationship with Washington that centrally determines what Canberra chooses to do. For the most part, when the United States chooses to flex its muscles, Australia will opt to keep it company, and when the United States chooses to cut and run, so will Australia.

NOTES

1. See Stuart Ward, "Security: Defending Australia's Empire," in *Australia's Empire*, ed. Deryck M. Schreuder and Stuart Ward (Oxford: Oxford University Press, 2008), 232–58; and Jeffrey A. Grey, *A Military History of Australia* (Cambridge: Cambridge University Press, 2008).

2. See Tony Abbott, *Battlelines* (Melbourne: Melbourne University Press, 2009), 160.

3. See Laurie Field, *The Forgotten War: Australia and the Boer War* (Melbourne: Melbourne University Press, 1979).

4. A.W. Martin, *Robert Menzies: A Life, Volume I: 1894–1943* (Melbourne: Melbourne University Press, 1993), 284.

5. Quoted in Ian Ousby, *Occupation: The Ordeal of France 1940–1944* (New York: St. Martin's Press, 1997), 19.

6. See Garry Woodard, *Asian Alternatives: Australia's Vietnam Decision and Lessons on Going to War* (Melbourne: Melbourne University Press, 2004), 290–92.

7. See, for example, David Halberstam, *The Making of a Quagmire* (New York: Random House, 1965); Townsend Hoopes, *The Limits of Intervention* (New York: David Mackay, 1969); and Bernard Brodie, *War and Politics* (New York: Macmillan, 1973), 157–222.

8. Ethel Turner, *Seven Little Australians* (Melbourne: Penguin Books, 2010).

9. *Sydney Morning Herald*, April 27, 1939, 9.

10. Joan Beaumont, *Broken Nation: Australians in the Great War* (Sydney: Allen & Unwin, 2013), 161–63.

11. See Gerhard L. Weinberg, *A World at Arms: A Global History of World War II* (Cambridge: Cambridge University Press, 2005), 331.

12. For background, see Anatol Lieven, *America Right or Wrong: An Anatomy of American Nationalism* (New York: Oxford University Press, 2005), 173–216.

13. See William Maley, "Military Intervention in the Middle East," in *Australia and the Middle East: A Front-Line Relationship*, ed. Fethi Mansouri (London: I.B. Tauris, 2006), 149.

14. See Danny Ben-Moshe, "Pro-Israelism as a Factor in Jewish Political Attitudes and Behaviour," in *Jews and Australian Politics*, ed. Geoffrey Brahm Levey and Philip Mendes (Brighton: Sussex Academic Press, 2004), 127–42.

15. See, for example, Darin Bartram et al., "The Case for a Legal Attack," *Australian*, March 18, 2003, together with the response of Lawry Herron (former legal adviser of the Department of Foreign Affairs and Trade); "Dated Resolutions Make Flimsy War Cover," *Australian*, March 20, 2003.

16. For background to this operation, see Maureen Dee, "Australia and UN Peacekeeping: Steady and Unwavering Support," in *Australia and the United Nations*, ed. James Cotton and David Lee (Sydney: Longueville Books, 2012), 230.

17. For further detail see Peter Londey, *Other People's Wars: A History of Australian Peacekeeping* (Sydney: Allen & Unwin, 2004); and David Horner, Peter Londey, and Jean Bou, eds., *Australian Peacekeeping: Sixty Years in the Field* (Cambridge: Cambridge University Press, 2009).

18. Robert O'Neill, *Australia in the Korean War 1950–53, Vol. I: Strategy and Diplomacy* (Canberra, ACT: Australian War Memorial and Australian Government Publishing Service, 1981).

19. See William Stueck, *The Korean War: An International History* (Princeton, NJ: Princeton University Press, 1995).

20. See William Maley, "The Cold War," in *War Since 1900: History, Strategy, Weaponry*, ed. Jeremy Black (London: Thames & Hudson, 2010), 209–27.

21. David M. Horner, *The Gulf Commitment: The Australian Defence Force's First War* (Melbourne: Melbourne University Press, 1992).

22. See William Maley, "The Gulf and the Australian Peace Movement," *Quadrant* 35, no. 10 (1991): 41–44.

23. Joy Gordon, *Invisible War: The United States and the Iraq Sanctions* (Cambridge, MA: Harvard University Press, 2010).

24. See Ian Brownlie, *International Law and the Use of Force by States* (Oxford: Oxford University Press, 1963); Thomas M. Franck, *Recourse to Force: State Action Against Threats and Armed Attacks* (Cambridge: Cambridge University Press, 2002); and Christine D. Gray, *International Law and the Use of Force* (Oxford: Oxford University Press, 2008).

25. See Kosmas Tsokhas, *Money, Markets and Empire: The Political Economy of the Australian Wool Industry* (Melbourne: Melbourne University Press, 1990).

26. See Stephen M. Walt, *The Origins of Alliances* (Ithaca. NY: Cornell University Press, 1987), 21–28.

27. See Evan Mawdsley, *December 1941: Twelve Days That Began a World War* (New Haven, CT: Yale University Press, 2011), 247–53.

28. See William Maley, "Australia and the East Timor Crisis: Some Critical Comments," *Australian Journal of International Affairs* 54, no. 2 (2000): 151–61.

29. James Cotton, *East Timor, Australia and Regional Order: Intervention and Its Aftermath in Southeast Asia* (London: RoutledgeCurzon, 2004), 95.

30. See Joseph Nevins, *A Not-So-Distant Horror: Mass Violence in East Timor* (Ithaca, NY: Cornell University Press, 2005), 124.

31. Mark Forbes, "US Has Changed the World Order: Strategist," *The Age*, March 13, 2003.

32. "People and Politics," BBC World Service, January 1, 2005.

33. R.W. Apple, Jr., "Bush's War Message: Strong and Clear," *New York Times*, April 9, 2003.

34. Barack Obama, *The Audacity of Hope: Thoughts on Reclaiming the American Dream* (New York: Crown Publishers, 2006), 295.

35. Australia, Parliament, House of Representatives, *Hansard*, February 4, 2003, 10645. Emphasis added.

36. See Parliamentary Joint Committee on ASIO, ASIS, and DSD, *Intelligence on Iraq's Weapons of Mass Destruction* (Canberra, ACT: Commonwealth of Australia, December 2003), http://www.globalsecurity.org/intell/library/reports/2004/australia_iraq-wmd-intell_01mar04_fullreport.pdf (accessed August 5, 2014).

37. Australia, Parliament, House of Representatives, *Hansard*, February 5, 2003, 10926.

38. See, for example, Owen Harries, *Benign or Imperial? Reflections on American Hegemony* (Sydney: ABC Books, 2004).

8

WAR AND THE CANADIAN LIBERAL CONSCIENCE

John English

In his brilliant lectures on British liberals and war, Sir Michael Howard used the British liberal historian George Macaulay Trevelyan to illustrate how a "profoundly pacific and kindly man" could possess a "passionate interest in military affairs." For Trevelyan, war was "the very stuff of history and he found no difficulty in reconciling it with his liberalism." Although British liberalism became a "transatlantic persuasion" in the late nineteenth century, its passage to North America sometimes resulted in local deformations. Although leading American liberals — notably Franklin D. Roosevelt, Churchill's "former naval person" in their wartime correspondence, and John F. Kennedy — celebrated the martial virtues, and in the latter's case embodied them, the major Canadian Liberal leaders — Wilfrid Laurier, William Lyon Mackenzie King, Pierre Trudeau, and Jean Chrétien — neither served in the military nor showed much interest in military matters. The Liberal King, the longest-serving prime minister, whose tenure extended through the Second World War, scorned those who exalted military values. According to military historian C.P. Stacey, when touring France after the war, King refused to leave his car to step onto the "battlefields" where Canadians had recently fought and died. Nervous about his own failure to serve in the First World War, deeply suspicious that Canadian generals had conspired with Conservatives to displace him, and bored by the military chitchat in which Churchill and Roosevelt delighted, King was a most unlikely warlord.[1]

Jean Chrétien, Canada's prime minister and Liberal leader when the United States patched together a coalition to overthrow Saddam Hussein in 2003, reflected King's caution when the Americans asked for Canadian support for the imminent war. Rising in the House of Commons on March 17, 2003, Chrétien announced that Canada would "not participate" in the coalition, even though its closest allies heeded President George W. Bush's appeal. His words brought thunderous applause from the MPs surrounding him and bitter scorn from Leader of the Opposition Stephen Harper, who attacked Chrétien for deserting "Canada's friends." Other contributions to this book describe the immediate circumstances surrounding Chrétien's decision. This essay will argue that it was not an aberration, but a reflection of a Liberal Party tradition that emerged when Canada was part of the British Empire and endured when the United States became its principal ally.[2]

Although Canadians pride themselves as the North Americans who went to war when the first shots were fired in 1914 and 1939, Canadian history is marked more generally by a reluctance to take up arms. John A. Macdonald, Canada's founding prime minister and a Conservative, complained in 1885 when William Gladstone's Liberals attempted to get colonial support for their disastrous attempt to save Khartoum from the Mahdi. The Australians had agreed to a contribution, but an angry Macdonald complained to his representative in London:

We do not stand in the same position as the Australians. The Suez Canal is nothing, and we do not ask England to quarrel with France and Germany for our sake.… Why should we risk men and money in this wretched business? England is not at war but merely helping the Khedive to put down an insurrection.… Our men and money would therefore be sacrificed to get Gladstone and Co. out of a hole they had played themselves into by their own imbecility.[3]

It was, however, Macdonald's final campaign in 1891, during which he clung to the Union Jack and proclaimed his devotion to the imperial link — not his defiant stand against Gladstone — that became his legacy to his twentieth-century successors.

A shrewd politician, Macdonald had built a coalition of English-Canadian and French-Canadian conservatives to assure his party's pre-eminence in the first decades after Canada's Confederation in 1867. But the balance tilted against the French Canadians after 1885, when Macdonald allowed the hanging of Métis leader Louis Riel, and his franco-phone support began to erode quickly. With the continuing support of the French Catholic hierarchy, he retained a base. In 1891, Macdonald won the election, but for the first time lost Quebec. When he died shortly after the election, the Conservative Party in Quebec gradually retreated to its anglophone fastnesses as Wilfrid Laurier, the first French-Canadian major party leader, began to erect a Liberal fortress in francophone Quebec.[4] In 1896, Laurier became Canada's first French-Canadian prime minister.

For Canadian Liberals, whose strength throughout most of the twen-tieth century and perhaps again in the twenty-first century has depended upon French-Canadian voters, the issues of peace and war have been profoundly difficult. The future problem became apparent not long after Laurier briefly flirted with the idea of a united Empire in 1897 when the imperial spirit at Queen Victoria's Diamond Jubilee Celebrations carried him away. To his later regret, he enthusiastically declared that "if a day were ever to come when England was in danger, let the bugle sound...."[5] Two years later, the bugle sounded in London and echoed loudly in Ontario and British redoubts throughout Canada. But among French Canadians, the bugle was muffled. The Boer War confronted Laurier with the funda-mental tensions underlying Canadian political history. Laurier's first polit-ical instinct was to refuse the entreaties of British colonial secretary Joseph Chamberlain, who asked for colonials to fight for the rights of English set-tlers in South Africa, but the pressure from the English Canadian press became too great for Laurier to resist. He hesitated, stifled debate, then finally agreed to send one hundred Canadian volunteers to South Africa, where they became part of the British imperial forces.

By the time the war ended, more than seven thousand Canadians had served and 267 died.[6] The Boer War framed the Canadian response to peace and war in the first half of the twentieth century. The Conservative Party was quick to respond to the imperial bugler's sound, while the Liberal Party lowered the volume but never stifled the call to duty. For his part, Laurier, like most Canadians, including many French Canadians at the time, was an admirer of the British parliamentary system and even the British Empire, which he believed had brought enormous progress and prosperity not only to Britain but to the world. But the hubris of new imperialists like Chamberlain and the concern among Laurier's fellow French Canadians of entrapment in a British colonial war were growing fears. Laurier's efforts to find a compromise brought strong condemnation from Conservative imperialists but went too far for his most brilliant young MP, Henri Bourassa, who resigned over the issue. In the House of Commons on March 13, 1900, Bourassa argued that Laurier had betrayed the traditions of British Liberalism, those of Burke, Fox, Bright, Gladstone, and the other "Little Englanders" who disdained the imperialists' attempt to impose British rule upon distant colonial peoples. Laurier, he argued, had not summoned Parliament, had not consulted Canadians, and had quickly and wrongly sent Canadians to fight a British colonial war. Bourassa's resolution condemning Laurier's action and requiring that Parliament approve any future commitment to British wars failed, gaining only ten votes.[7] Nevertheless, the terms of the debate were set for the dangerous new century. In the 1900 election, Laurier, despite Canada's growing prosperity, the troops in South Africa, his repudiation of Bourassa, and his Diamond Jubilee flirtation with imperialism, won only thirty-four seats in Ontario while the Tories won forty-seven of their overall sixty-nine. In Quebec, despite Bourassa's resignation and clerical opposition, Laurier took fifty-seven seats and the Tories only eight.[8] On this Quebec foundation, he won a majority government and did so again in 1904 and 1906.

In the years before the First World War, the Conservative Party of Canada was Canada's imperial party, advocating strong support for British imperial interests and reflecting ever more its political base among Canada's British Protestant majority. Laurier had responded to Bourassa in 1899 by pointing out that the volunteers sent to South Africa were not there in response to a British command but because English Canadians believed Canada should contribute. If Britain wanted to call directly upon Canada to fight, Canada should be represented in the councils in London where war would be decided. It was a clever response but disingenuous. When Chamberlain and his successors called Laurier to London, he was reluctant, ambiguous, and dilatory because he knew war would tear his Canadian political coalition apart. But in 1911 he took a risk: the Americans offered a reciprocal trade agreement that appealed strongly to rural Canada, already a Liberal stronghold, but that offended Canadian imperialists already wary of Laurier's reluctance to give Britain money to build dreadnoughts to confront Germany. Bourassa, now the leader of a burgeoning nationalist movement in Quebec, was furious because Laurier, typically, had offered the imperialists a compromise: a Canadian navy available when the Empire was truly threatened. Bourassa made an agreement to work with the Conservatives to strike down their mutual enemy. Laurier denounced the Quebec nationalist-Canadian imperialist pact as an "unholy alliance," yet it struck down the powerful coalition he had created. But the *mariage de convenance* between Bourassa's nationalists and Prime Minister Robert Borden's Conservatives did not endure. When war broke out in August 1914, the nationalist voice in Borden's Cabinet was absent.

However, the defeat of 1911 had chastened Laurier. When war broke out, his political instincts and deeply held beliefs caused him to cast aside rhetorical restraint. Although eminent British Liberals, notably George Trevelyan and Gladstone biographer John Morley, resigned their parliamentary posts in opposition to the war, Laurier expressed no hesitations in his first statements: "I have often declared that if the Mother Country were ever in danger, or if danger ever threatened, Canada would render assistance to the fullest extent of her power."[9] Laurier knew that his arguments that there had not been an "emergency" in 1911 were shattered by the guns of August 1914, and he promised Borden a political truce. In turn, he and the Quebec bishops received a commitment that there would be no conscription in Canada. But the war was too long, the casualties too many, and the volunteers too few.

By 1917 the political truce had shattered. Borden approached Laurier to form a coalition government to impose conscription. Laurier refused, and Borden formed a coalition with English Canadian Liberals who supported compulsory service. His so-called Union government won the election in December 1917, but the bitterest election in Canadian history profoundly divided the country. The Unionists won 134 seats in which there was a "British" majority but only two in which the majority of voters were French-Canadian. Laurier won sixty-two of sixty-five Quebec seats. German Canadians, traditionally Conservative, shifted strongly to the Liberals until the British Empire died.[10] Borden won the election but his Conservative Party mortgaged its future.

From Laurier's experience with the Boer War and the First World War, his successor, Mackenzie King, drew a clear lesson. In 1921, when he took office, most Canadians were of British origin (55.4 percent of the total population) and would respond when Great Britain was truly threatened, but French Canadians (27.9 percent) and other ethnic groups (14.2 percent) did not share the emotional link that bound most English Canadians to their mother country. The conscription crisis of 1917 and the "clash," as contemporaries called the bitter quarrels about the commitment to war, caused Canadians to divide on what were then described as "racial" lines. J.W. Dafoe, the Liberal editor of the *Manitoba Free Press,* deserted Laurier and enthusiastically promoted the Union government in 1917 while excoriating the traitors in Quebec. Four years later, in a brief biography of Laurier, Dafoe wrote that "the spirit" behind the movement had "passed with the war." The Union government was British Canada's victory, but it proved to be pyrrhic. Dafoe returned to the Liberal fold and joined others to construct a Canadian "nationalism" that found its effective, if not eloquent, voice in Mackenzie King. But in francophone Quebec, bitter memories endured. After Laurier's death in 1919, the leading Conservative organizer in Quebec warned Borden's successor, Arthur Meighen, that "it must be understood that ... the Liberal Party is looked upon by its adherents as the Party of French Canadians — in other words as a National Party." Laurier's legacy was enduring.[11]

King followed Laurier's path, refusing consistently throughout the interwar years to give the British a blank cheque for their imperial forays. When called upon by British prime minister David Lloyd George to send troops to assist in pushing back Turkish attacks on British and French troops guarding the neutral zone around the Dardanelles in 1922, King denounced the action and said that he should have been consulted first. In the following year, he turned to Laurier's biographer, Queen's University professor O.D. Skelton, as his principal foreign affairs adviser. Skelton, Norman Hillmer writes, "shared [King's] fears and insecurities" about the British, but they had a fundamental difference. Whereas King was wary of imperial linkages but cherished the British base of Canada's international personality, Skelton favoured what he termed "ultimate independence." King was horrified when Skelton expressed his views to him in 1923, and Skelton wisely retreated and took refuge in complexity. He was rewarded with the post of undersecretary of state for external affairs in 1925. Together, King and Skelton shaped Liberal and Canadian international policy in the interwar years, much to the consternation of imperialists in Canada and London.[12]

When he returned to office in 1935, King frustrated the British when they called upon the dominions to make commitments to a joint effort to face common foes. But King angered Skelton, who had surprisingly survived as undersecretary during the Conservative government of 1930–35. As war clouds darkened in 1939, King determined that Canada must stand at "Britain's side" as the "Britain of the West." Skelton, however, looked southward and saw Canada's future on the North American continent. Canada, Skelton told his wife, was "the safest country in the world — as long as we mind our own business."[13] But for King and most Canadians, Britain's fate remained Canada's business. The two agreed, however, that Canada must never again endure the bitter "clash" of 1917, and that the Canadian decision for war must be made by Canada's Parliament. When King summoned Parliament after the British declaration of war on September 3, 1939, the pacifist leader of the Co-operative Commonwealth Federation, J. S. Woodsworth, dissented; some Quebec MPs grumbled; but King's Cabinet held together, and his Quebec lieutenant, Ernest Lapointe, remained loyal as Canada declared war one week after Britain. Despite his doubts, Skelton remained a good soldier. Until he died, in January 1941, he stayed by King's side while he sought to limit Canada's commitment to Europe and to strengthen Canada's ties with the United States.

Like Laurier before him, King in wartime kept his gaze upon the delicate balance of domestic politics and away from the war councils in London and the battlefields in Europe. When Premier Maurice Duplessis of Quebec called an election four weeks after the declaration on the grounds that King's declaration of war exceeded his government's authority, Lapointe and the other Quebec ministers warned that they would resign if Duplessis won. The Quebec Liberals won a decisive victory on October 26, 1937. Shortly afterward, Liberals and Conservatives in the Ontario Legislature combined to condemn King's lack of "vigorous" prosecution of the war. Denouncing the Ontario resolution as irresponsible and divisive, King called a general election. On May 26, 1940, the Liberals won the largest majority in Canadian history. These two elections loosened King's hands, but he continued to move cautiously.[14] His war management was marked by hesitation and ambiguity, famously captured in his statement "not necessarily conscription but conscription if necessary." King, unlike Borden, had access to rich data on Canadian public opinion, including polling. He knew that the majority of Canadians favoured conscription for overseas service after the fall of France, and especially after the Japanese attack on Pearl Harbor brought the United States into war and conscription for Americans. King rejected the demands from English-Canadian leaders for a national government of leading Conservatives, Liberals, and independents or a referendum on conscription. Faced with pressure not only from the Conservative opposition and the English-Canadian press, he called a plebiscite, not on conscription but on whether voters would release the government "from any obligation arising out of any past commitments restricting the methods of raising men for military service." The conservative *Globe and Mail* railed against King's evasiveness and called upon him to make "the necessary decisions" rather than leave "the question to the people...." It concluded its ferocious attack in January 1942 with a prediction: "It can be said with certainty that this cowardly evasion of leadership will be recorded by posterity not as a pattern to imitate but as an example to deter." Not for the last time, the *Globe*'s editors erred.[15]

Although the plebiscite released King from his commitment of "no conscription" when approximately 63 percent of Canadians voted "yes," the overwhelming opposition of French Canadians and non-British groups in western Canada gave King grounds to delay a final decision on conscription.[16] When the casualties after D-Day created a political crisis in the fall of 1944, King finally assented to a policy that the majority of Canadians had strongly favoured for over two years. French-Canadian opposition was stronger than ever, but the creation of a third party, the Bloc populaire, by leading anti-conscriptionists including André Laurendeau and Pierre Trudeau, failed to bring down the King government. In the election of June 11, 1945, the Liberals more than 50 percent of the Quebec vote and fifty-four of its sixty-five seats, enough for another majority government. Cowardice to some, clever to others, King's obvious reluctance to become a "warlord" reflected the lessons he learned from Laurier and that he took from the Conservative Party's fate after 1917.[17]

These lessons influenced the postwar period as the British Empire faded and the new American empire rose. Their finest expression came in January 1947 when the University of Toronto, which was located at the heart of the city where imperial fires had burned most brightly and where support for conscription was strongest, invited Secretary of State for External Affairs

Louis St. Laurent to deliver the Duncan and John Gray Memorial Lecture. John Gray, a casualty of war, had learned French and been devoted to improving relations between English and French Canadians in his youth. St. Laurent, who emerged as the leading French Canadian in King's Cabinet, had supported conscription and would succeed King as prime minister in November 1948. St. Laurent began his lecture by paying tribute to Gray's generous appreciation of the role of French Canada in Canada's history. He then proceeded to set out the "foundations" of Canadian foreign policy. His first principle drew clearly upon his experience in wartime government and explicitly rejected the arguments that the *Globe and Mail* and eminent Torontonians had made during the conscription crisis. The first principle, St. Laurent declared, must be the preservation of national unity:

> The first general principle upon which I think we are agreed is that our external policies shall not destroy our unity. No policy can be regarded as wise which divides the people whose effort and resources must put it into effect. This consideration applies not only to the two main cultural groups in our country. It applies equally to sectionalism of any kind. We dare not fashion a policy which is based on the particular interests of any economic group, of any class or of any section in this country. We must be on guard especially against the claims of extravagant regionalism no matter where they have their origin. Our history has shown this to be a consideration in our external policy of which we, more even than others, must be perpetually conscious. The role of this country in world affairs will prosper only as we maintain this principle, for a disunited Canada will be a powerless one.[18]

"A disunited Canada will be a powerless one" was a principle that infused Liberal politics in future decades. The shock of the Cold War did unite Canadians in the 1940s and 1950s, and St. Laurent and Lester Pearson, his secretary of state for external affairs, faced very little dissent in their willingness to link Canada with both Britain and the United States to confront the Soviet Union. Still, national unity was carefully preserved by a new emphasis on multilateralism through the United Nations. Canada did fight in Korea, but St. Laurent emphasized that it was a United Nations commitment, and Canadian troops formed part of the British Commonwealth force. Again, careful balancing was the hallmark of Liberal policy. St. Laurent's test came when the British and French attacked Egypt in 1956 and calls came again from English Canada to stand behind Britain — or, at least, at its side. But St. Laurent lost his temper when the British deceived Canada about their intentions. His Liberal government refused to back the British-French invasion. In the House of Commons, Liberal MPs shouted down accusations of betrayal with chants of "ready aye ready" while St. Laurent rose to declare that the time was past when "the supermen of Europe could govern the whole world." It was true but was too direct and divisive. As the eminent historian Robert Bothwell notes, "He had waved a red flag at a political bull." The 1957 general election witnessed the last charge of British-Canadian patriotism, and it caused a Liberal defeat.[19]

Traditional British-Canadian Conservatives such as philosopher George Grant and historian Donald Creighton charged that the Canadian Liberals had "sold out" Canada to Washington, which had forced Britain and France to back down.[20] Their argument gained many adherents, but supporting evidence is weak. Indeed, Canada under Liberal governments proved to be a more reluctant participant in American wars in the second half of the twentieth century than in those fought by the British Empire-Commonwealth in the first half.

Canada, for example, refused to follow the bipartisan American policy of overthrowing Fidel Castro's Communist regime in Cuba in the 1960s. Although Lester Pearson came to power in 1963 in large part because of Conservative prime minister John Diefenbaker's quarrel with United States president John Kennedy over defence issues, Pearson made it clear to the United States that he would not participate in its imperial adventure in Vietnam. Canadian-American relations were soon in a shambles. Pearson, the only Canadian prime minister who served in a combat zone, not only refused to send troops to serve in Vietnam, but also criticized American war policy as early as April 1965. His speech at Temple University calling for a bombing halt created a lasting personal rift with Lyndon Johnson, which began with an encounter at Camp David, where Johnson literally shook up Pearson physically.

Critics on the left condemn Pearson for his leadership role in NATO, his hostility to Soviet Communism, and his acceptance of "quiet diplomacy" in dealings with the United States, while many on the right blame him for weakening the Canadian military and for the celebration of peacekeeping and "soft power." Like Laurier and King, Pearson was ultimately a prag-matist, and in the 1960s Canada's only Nobel Peace Prize–winner con-centrated on domestic policy, notably in responding to the challenge of Quebec nationalism and separatism. Like St. Laurent, Pearson knew that "a disunited Canada [would] be a powerless one." In normal times, Pearson would not have preferred Pierre Trudeau as his successor. Trudeau had resigned from the Privy Council because of his opposition to the Korean War; had condemned Pearson in 1963 as the "defrocked prince of peace" when the Liberal leader announced he would accept nuclear weapons for Canadian Forces; and had expressed hostility to Canada's alliances within Cabinet. But in 1968, times were very different, and Canada was in doubt.[21]

Pierre Trudeau's initial foreign policy initiatives profoundly irritated Pearson, but in the intellectual turmoil of the late 1960s they responded to the marked shift to the left in Quebec, where criticism of American foreign policy was pronounced, and to the stirrings of Canadian nationalism in English Canada. In a new time, Trudeau sought the middle. In a reflection of his own beliefs, Trudeau tried to persuade his Cabinet to withdraw Canada from NATO immediately after he took office in June 1968. When his effort failed as senior ministers threatened to resign over the issue, Trudeau dras-tically cut Canada's troop presence in Europe and called on the military to protect Canadian sovereignty.[22] Although Canada remained within NATO, Trudeau openly tried to find counterweights in recognition of China and the creation of a so-called contractual link with the European Common Market, or, less convincingly, in an embrace of a north-south dialogue and a global economic restructuring in which Canada would play a leading role. Those who had expected more of Trudeau were disappointed. Echoing earlier crit-ics of King, St. Laurent, and Pearson, Jack Granatstein, who then favoured NATO withdrawal, wrote in 1968, "The only charitable solution to unravel-ling the tangle of Trudeauvian statements on defence policy seemed to be that he was deliberately taking all sides of all questions, so that, when the review was completed, he could find support for its decisions somewhere in his past remarks."[23] Trudeau fit with surprising ease into the Liberal tradition.

In the 1970s, Trudeau took no notable foreign policy initiatives apart from an attempt to broaden Canada's relationship with Europe and the so-called Third World. Trudeau's relationship with Republican president Richard Nixon was brittle. When Trudeau learned that Nixon had called him an "asshole," he replied that "he had been called worse things by better people."[24] But Trudeau struck up a friendship with moderate Republican Gerald Ford, Nixon's successor, which was important in securing decisive American advocacy for Canadian membership in the G7. With the election of Ronald Reagan in 1980, Trudeau became a significant opposition voice within the G7 against the economic and defence policies of Prime Minister Margaret Thatcher and President Reagan.

Trudeau was not alone in criticizing Reagan's triumphant invasion of Grenada in 1983, but he was, in the words of American journalist Seymour Hersh, the "only" Western leader who spoke out against the American administration's quick assertion that the Soviet airmen who shot down the Korean Air Lines jetliner in September 1983 had known it was a civilian aircraft. Deeply concerned by a deteriorating international situation, Trudeau immediately launched a peace initiative that took him around the world in a fruitless pursuit of nuclear disarmament. The diaries of Canadian ambassador to the United States Allan Gotlieb report in considerable detail the growing hostility to Trudeau in Washington as the peace initiative unfolded. "Our prime minister," Gotlieb writes of the G7 meeting, "true to form, is playing the bad boy." Reagan wrote in his diary of the same meeting, "I thought at one point that Margaret was going to order Pierre to go stand in a corner." At Trudeau's final G7 summit in June 1984, Thatcher, the host, refused to let him speak. In Canada, however, Trudeau's assertive international policy in his final prime ministerial year brought him accolades from many Liberal loyalists and others who had criticized him for "going along" with the Americans too often in the past.[25]

With Progressive Conservative Brian Mulroney in power, Canada finally did join an American war — the first Iraq war — in 1991. Indeed, its contribution to Operation Desert Storm was larger than that of Australia, with significant air resources supplementing a naval commitment. The Canadian response was immediately and warmly welcomed by President George H.W. Bush, and he generously thanked Mulroney, a close friend, for the help. Faced with Mulroney's decision to go to war, the Canadian Liberal Party was deeply divided. In the House of Commons, the new Liberal leader, Jean Chrétien, was very ambiguous on the matter, in contrast to the offer of full support by Mulroney. Faced with a decision by the Conservatives that committed the government to accept a U.N. resolution that would permit war, Chrétien refused to give the government "a blank cheque." He told a Canadian Broadcasting Corporation interviewer that more time for economic sanctions was needed.[26] Former Liberal leader John Turner, who had been absent from the House since Chrétien's election as leader, suddenly appeared in Ottawa and, without mentioning Chrétien's stand, strongly backed Mulroney and called for Canada to join the United Nations effort in Iraq under American leadership.

In truth, the Liberal Party was divided in the summer of 1990. Its foreign policy critic, Lloyd Axworthy, was profoundly suspicious of American neo-conservatives and American military adventurism. Some other prominent members shared his strong views, and Chrétien himself regularly attacked Mulroney's too-close relationship with American presidents Reagan and Bush. In the end, Turner's opinion prevailed, but only after Chrétien's reluctant caucus bowed to media and other pressure.[27]

How, then, does the decision to say no to Iraq fit within a Canadian historical perspective? Obviously, a careful observer of Chrétien's words about Iraq in 1990 will see striking parallels with Chrétien's celebrated "no" in 2003. What is remarkable is that Canadian media regarded Chrétien's comments as astonishing and suggested that former leaders such as Lester Pearson would not have stepped away from Iraq in 2003. But there are clear patterns to the Canadian response to involvement in foreign wars.

1. Political alignments matter. In his refusal to send Canadians to Khartoum in 1884, Conservative Macdonald was clear that he did so in part because he disliked British prime minister Gladstone, the Liberal giant of the nineteenth century. Similarly, Conservative Brian Mulroney enthusiastically supported Republican George H.W. Bush's war on Iraq, although out of office Mulroney was a vocal opponent of Democrat Bill Clinton's decision to begin the Kosovo War. In the second Iraq War of 2003, Opposition leader Stephen Harper vehemently denounced Chrétien's "no." Moreover, he was ferocious in his defence of the Afghanistan commitment as long as Republican George W. Bush was president but cooled notably when Bush left office. Canada withdrew most of its forces by 2011.

2. The Canadian Liberals have demonstrated a historical nervousness about too close a relationship with the imperial centre, whether it be

London or Washington. Before the First World War, Laurier refused to give his support for any move to create imperial institutions. Mackenzie King continued such refusals in the interwar period. In the Second World War, despite major Canadian involvement, he refused to participate in Commonwealth gatherings in London — and unlike Australian prime minister Robert Menzies, avoided the political gatherings in London whenever he could. In the postwar period, Lester Pearson tried to constrain U.S. power within multilateral alliances, but when it failed, he spoke out. A speech on the expansion of the Korean War in 1951 ended his personal friendship with American secretary of state Dean Acheson; his speech on Vietnam in 1965 resulted in the worst encounter between a Canadian and American leader since Canadian Confederation in 1867. With Trudeau, relations were good with Democrat Jimmy Carter and even with Republican Gerald Ford, but poor with Republicans Richard Nixon and Ronald Reagan. On both sides, perceptions of the political views of the opposite leaders were a major factor as much as specific international policy differences.

3. For Liberals, domestic fears trump international demands. In his historic 1947 statement on Canadian foreign policy, Liberal Louis St. Laurent declared, "The first general principle upon which I think we are agreed is that our external policies shall not destroy our unity." That was precisely the principle on which Liberals and Conservatives had profoundly disagreed in the First and Second World Wars. The Conservative argument for conscription in 1917 and again in 1944 was that a minority should not block a policy that the majority of Canadians favoured and Canada's national interest compelled.

In the decision on Iraq in 2003, St. Laurent's basic principle continued to be observed. Chrétien's closest aide, Eddie Goldenberg, recounts receiving a phone call from the prime minister right after the announcement that Canada would not be taking part in military action. After Chrétien told him that Bush would be vindictive and that things might be rough, Goldenberg told the prime minister of a conversation he and I had recently had: "John [English] says the decision to stay out of the war has averted a potential major national unity crisis. English," he continued, "reminded me of how national unity is never far from the surface in Canada. Canadian participation in the war, he said, would have been extremely unpopular in Quebec," and could have affected the course of the heated provincial election campaign by allowing Bernard Landry of the Parti Québécois to claim it proved the existence of a profound gap between the values of Quebec and those of English Canada. According to Goldenberg, until I raised the subject, "there had never been any reference to Quebec in all the discussions on Iraq in Cabinet or in any of my own talks with the prime minister." None was needed. It was bred in their Liberal bones.[28]

NOTES

1. Although King has recently been described as a "warlord" in Tim Cook, *Warlords: Borden, Mackenzie King and Canada's World Wars* (Toronto: Allen Lane, 2012), the book discusses King's minimal interest in military affairs and makes clear that he was not at all a "warlord" in the traditional sense. See also Michael Howard, *War and the Liberal Conscience* (New York: Rutgers University Press, 1978), 10; and C.P. Stacey, *A Date with History: Memoirs of a Canadian Historian* (Ottawa: Deneau, 1982), 186–87.

2. Chrétien did emphasize that the failure of the United States and the United Kingdom to secure United Nations support was the principal reason for his stand: "If military action proceeds without a new resolution of the Security Council, Canada will not participate." Canada, Parliament, House of Commons, *Debates*, vol. 138, March 17, 2003, www.parl.gc.ca/HousePublications/Publication.aspx?Pub=Hansard&Mee=71&Language=e&Parl=37&Ses=2 (accessed August 5, 2014).

3. Quoted in Peter Pigott, *Canada in Sudan: War Without Borders* (Toronto: Dundurn, 2009), 74.

4. The finest study of this process remains H. Blair Neatby's *Laurier and a Liberal Quebec: A Study in Political Management* (Toronto: McClelland & Stewart, 1973).

5. Quoted in Réal Bélanger, "Sir Wilfrid Laurier," in the *Dictionary of Canadian Biography*, www.biographi.ca/en/bio/laurier_wilfrid_14E.html (accessed April 6, 2014).

6. The Canadian War Museum in its description of the war points out: "The Canadian government claimed at the time that this overseas expedition was not a precedent. History would prove otherwise." www.warmuseum.ca/cwm/exhibitions/boer/boerwarhistory_e.shtml (accessed April 6, 2014).

7. Bourassa's eloquent speech and Laurier's effective response is described and analyzed in Réal Bélanger, *Henri Bourassa: le fascinant destin d'un homme libre*

(1868–1914), (Quebec: PUL/ University of Toronto Press, 2013) 75–77.

8. It should be noted that the popular vote was not as decisive, with the Liberals getting 56.3 percent in Quebec and the Conservatives 46.7 percent. The margin in seats was caused by the concentration of Conservative votes in anglophone seats. See www.parl. gc.ca/About/Parliament/FederalRidingsHistory/hfer.asp?Language=E&Search=G (accessed April 15, 2014).

9. Quoted in J. Castell Hopkins, *Canada at War* (Toronto: Canadian Annual Review, 1919), 33.

10. The figures are taken from the *Canadian Parliamentary Guide* and the *Sixth Census of Canada* and are analyzed in John English, *The Decline of Politics: The Conservatives and the Party System 1901–1920* (Toronto: University of Toronto Press, 1977), 197–203.

11. J.W. Dafoe, *Laurier: A Study in Canadian Politics* (Toronto: Allen, 1922), 180. See also Ramsay Cook, "J.W. Dafoe at the Imperial Conference, 1923," *Canadian Historical Review* 41, no. 3 (1960): 19–40. Comment on the Liberals as a National Party is found in Sir William Price to Arthur Meighen, December 29, 1920, Meighen Papers, vol. 44, Library and Archives Canada.

12. Quoted with permission from Norman Hillmer, *O.D. Skelton: A Life in the Arena* (draft biography), 7.

13. O.D. Skelton to Isabel Skelton, September 16, 1938, quoted in ibid., 472.

14. Tim Cook has recently compared the different approaches of Borden and King in Cook, *Warlords.*

15. *Globe and Mail,* January 23, 1942.

16. Details of opposition are found in T.M. Prymak, *Maple Leaf and Trident: The Ukrainian Canadians During the Second World War* (Toronto: Multicultural History Society of Ontario, 1988), 163. The subject is also covered in greater detail in Ivana Caccia, *Managing the Canadian Mosaic in Wartime: Shaping Citizenship Policy 1939–1945* (Montreal and Kingston: McGill-Queen's University Press, 2010).

17. The election is discussed and results analyzed in Ray Argyle, chapter 9, in *Turning Points: The Campaigns That Changed Canada — 2011 and Before* (Kingston, ON: Waterside, 2011). The Liberal total in Quebec includes independent Liberals who supported the party but opposed its conscription policy.

18. Louis St. Laurent, "The Foundations of Canadian Foreign Policy" (Duncan and John Gray Memorial Lecture, University of Toronto, January 13, 1947), www.russilwvong.com/future/stlaurent.html (accessed April 20, 2014).

19. Robert Bothwell, "Louis St. Laurent," in *Dictionary of Canadian Biography*, www. biographi.ca/en/bio/st_laurent_louis_stephen_20E.html (accessed May 5, 2014). The 1957 election was analyzed in John Meisel, *The Canadian General Election of 1957* (Toronto: University of Toronto Press, 1962). Meisel supports the view that Suez hurt the Liberals because of the belief that the Liberals had "knifed" Britain

(56–59, and 254–55).

20. The two most famous expressions of this view are George Grant, *Lament for a Nation: The Defeat of Canadian Nationalism* (Toronto: McClelland & Stewart, 1965), and Donald Creighton, *The Forked Road: Canada 1939–1957* (Toronto: McClelland & Stewart, 1976).

21. On Pearson and Trudeau, see John English, *The Worldly Years: The Life of Lester Pearson 1949–1972* (Toronto: Knopf Canada, 1992), 383ff.

22. See John English, *Just Watch Me: The Life of Pierre Elliott Trudeau 1968–2000* (Toronto: Knopf Canada, 2009), 64–68. Pearson's irritation was expressed in his marginal comments on Trudeau's major foreign statement, *Foreign Policy for Canadians*. The copy was shown to me by his son, Geoffrey Pearson.

23. Granatstein as quoted in John Saywell, ed., *Canadian Annual Review for 1968* (Toronto: University of Toronto Press, 1969), 249.

24. A full account can be found in the *Toronto Star*, December 8, 2008.

25. Allan Gotlieb, *The Washington Diaries, 1981–1989* (Toronto: McClelland & Stewart, 2006), 160–62; Seymour Hersh, *"The Target Is Destroyed": What Really Happened to Flight 007 and What America Knew About It* (New York: Random House, 1986), 245; and English, chapter 7 in *Just Watch Me*.

26. The interview is held in the archives of the Canadian Broadcasting Corporation at: www.cbc.ca/archives/categories/war-conflict/1991-gulf-war/the-1991-gulf-war/canadian-opposition-to-the-war.html (accessed August 5, 2014).

27. Personal conversations in 1990 with Lloyd Axworthy and Liberal Party foreign policy adviser Michael Pearson.

28. Eddie Goldenberg, *The Way It Works: Inside Ottawa* (Toronto: McClelland & Stewart, 2007), 296–97.

9

WHY AUSTRALIA INVADED IRAQ:
A STUDY IN ALLIANCE MANAGEMENT

Hugh White

The two or three years that followed 9/11 were a strange time. Today, only a decade later, the decisions made back then already seem remote and hard to explain. Like the momentous decisions of distant eras, Australia's choice to join America and Britain in the invasion of Iraq already appears both inevitable and inexplicable. We wonder how we could possibly have supported such folly. But equally we wonder, how could we possibly have done anything else? In fact, there are good and interesting answers to both these questions, but little interest in exploring them. The furious debate about Australia's commitment to Iraq stopped once the fighting actually began in March 2003, and no one has been much interested since in looking back with the benefit of experience to see who was right, who was wrong, and what can be learned.

In this chapter I try to explain Australia's decision to join the invasion, and to evaluate that decision as a piece of strategic policy. I am interested primarily in why the decision was made and what the practical consequences of the decision have been, rather than the wider legal and moral questions that it raised. The legal and moral questions are important, of course, but they have already been widely discussed while the more pragmatic questions have been largely ignored. Moreover, we cannot reach firm conclusions about the moral and legal questions until we have a clearer idea about what actually happened and why, and what the consequences have been. If, like the pioneer political scientist Max Weber, you think judgments about public policy should reflect the ethic of consequences, and in most cases I do, then we generally need to understand the practical results of our actions before we can judge their moral merit. I think this is such a case.

Some of what follows, especially about the actions and motives of key figures like John Howard, is necessarily somewhat speculative. Until official papers are released, we have little to go on except statements made at the time and subsequent memoirs by those involved. Howard and others have given accounts of their decisions about Iraq, but they must naturally be treated with a little caution, and no investigative writing of the kind produced in the United States by Bob Woodward and others offers less partisan accounts. Nonetheless, by drawing on what we can know, and looking carefully at what was actually done and said, some reasonable conclusions can be drawn.

STARTING IN WASHINGTON

We need to start in Washington. As we will see, the relationship between Washington's decision to invade Iraq and Canberra's decision to take part is both complex and critical, but we need to get a few things straight about Washington's motives before we can understand Canberra's. And Washington's purposes remain rather perplexing, because during the year before the invasion the Bush administration explained them in terms which made little real sense at the time, and much less sense once Baghdad had fallen. The role of Iraq's weapons of mass destruction (WMDs) in America's decision to invade remains a key source of confusion. The popular view is that the Bush administration simply lied when they said that Iraq had WMDs, in order to justify the invasion. This is almost certainly wrong. The evidence clearly suggests that the administration really believed that Iraq did have active WMD programs and capabilities. would hardly have set itself up for the humiliation that followed the invasion had it known in advance that no weapons were going to be found.

But it is equally clear that WMDs were not the reason the United States decided to invade Iraq. Iraqi WMDs, had there been any, would certainly have been a problem, but not a serious enough threat to warrant the costs and risks of invasion. Even on Washington's rosy pre-invasion estimates of those costs and risks, the threat posed by the kind of WMD programs it believed Iraq to have would not credibly explain the strategic investment the Bush administration decided to make. So the WMDs were much more likely to have been a pretext rather than a reason to invade Iraq. They offered a legal, strategic, and political justification for the invasion, but its real purposes must be sought elsewhere. There are several possibilities. Some believe the invasion was primarily intended to secure Iraq's oil, others that George W. Bush was driven mainly by a desire to punish Saddam Hussein for trying to assassinate his father. Still others have argued that the main aim was to intimidate Iran. Perhaps each of these carried some weight in some decision-makers' minds, but none seems to offer a compelling explanation for such a momentous decision.

Only two reasons seem sufficient for that. The first was the need to do *something*. Bush's declaration of a "war on terror" had created a political imperative, and perhaps for the decision-makers themselves a psychological imperative, for large-scale military action. Nothing less seemed an adequate response to the attacks of September 11. For Americans, these imperatives had not been satisfied by the invasion of Afghanistan in late 2001. That was a clear tactical success, but it was strategically inconclusive, especially after it left Osama bin Laden uncaptured. The Bush circle felt a deep need to do something more — and something big — in response to 9/11, and Iraq fit the bill.

The other credible U.S. motive was more strategic. It sprang from neo-conservative ideas developed in the 1990s, when the end of the Cold War seemed to leave America with unchallengeable global power. The neo-conservatives believed that America could consolidate and perpetuate its triumph by turning the unipolar moment into a unipolar era. To do this, U.S. power should be used to transform those countries and regions that did not yet acknowledge U.S. primacy and accept the U.S.-led global order. Quite a few American policy-makers and analysts thought this way in the 1990s, but only the neo-conservatives contemplated the large-scale use of U.S. armed forces to drive the transformation. Many of them, however, ended up in powerful jobs in the Bush administration. After 9/11 they saw an opportunity. The imperative for some kind of large-scale military response to the terrorist attacks made ideas which had seemed far-fetched suddenly seem quite reasonable. The invasion of Iraq was just the first step toward the transformation of the Middle East into a region where peace and democracy would flourish under U.S. leadership. This was the purpose for which Iraq's WMDs provided the pretext.

OTHER PEOPLE'S WARS

Australia's decision to join the invasion of Iraq fits a pattern that stretches back to Federation, and we need to understand that pattern and what has driven it if we are to understand Canberra's actions in 2003. Since the Boer War, Australia has always been quick to send forces to support our major allies in distant conflicts. To some, this is a regrettable sign of Australia's continued dependence on "great and powerful friends" and a willingness to sacrifice our blood, treasure, and interests in "other peoples' wars." To others, it seems both strategically prudent and morally commendable to send forces to fight alongside our allies in defence of our values wherever they are threatened, because a threat to our values anywhere is a threat to us here. This has been described approvingly as "the Australian way of war," and such ideas were deployed to support Australia's involvement in the invasion of Iraq. The strategic-policy analyst might take a more detached view than either of these, simply noting that Australia has been so strikingly keen to take part in other people's wars for reasons which can be traced directly to fundamental aspects of our geostrategic situation.

Australia's strategic geography is characterized by distinctive problems of space and distance. Our continental-scale territory means that we have a huge space to defend, especially relative to the economic and demographic resources available to defend it. This has always led us to believe that we cannot defend the country without help from others. Issues of space mean we have always believed we must rely on the direct military support of allies for our security. Australia's location means we are a long way from Britain and America, to which we have successively looked for this support, and close to the large and potentially powerful countries of Asia, which, for most of our history and to some extent still today, are so easily seen as alien and threatening. Proximity to Asia has, for the past century, made us anxious about our security, and distance from our allies has made us uncertain of their support. The greater the distance, the more likely it has seemed to Australians that when we needed our allies' help they would be too preoccupied with problems closer to home to come to our aid.

Space and distance have, therefore, made Australia an anxious and eager alliance partner, always having been keen to do whatever we could to ensure that our distant allies had both the inclination and the capacity to provide the help we needed when we needed it. Australia has thus always feared abandonment much more than entrapment, and been willing to be entrapped in its allies' wars as the best way to reduce the risk of abandonment in its own.

All this makes Australia very different from Canada, of course. Canada shares with Australia the factor of space, but the factor of distance works for Canada very differently. Once its relations with the United States were settled in the early nineteenth century, Canada faced no local threats. At the same time, Washington increasingly took responsibility for the security of the whole western hemisphere from non-local threats, and took on the role of an ally for Canada. Canadians thus had no fear of abandonment, and have traditionally been much more wary than Australians about entrapment as a result.

SINCE 1972

Australia's eagerness to fight in other people's wars has persisted until today, but since 1972 it has taken a rather distinctive form. Between 1949 and 1972, when the Cold War raged in Asia, Australia found itself fighting other people's wars in our own region, which we did consistently under the policy of Forward Defence, under which Australian forces throughout this era were stationed in Southeast Asia, and committed to a series of conflicts in Korea, Malaya, and Vietnam, in support of Western allies. But President Richard M. Nixon's visit to China brought the Cold War in Asia virtually to an end, and American primacy in Asia became effectively uncontested. Australia found itself feeling more secure than at any time since the late nineteenth century, as Asia itself became more peaceful and settled, and our ally's position there became virtually unchallengeable. The alliance with America had until then had a distinctively regional focus, but after 1972 America faced no challenges in Asia that required our support. Not surprisingly, Australia reacted by widening its focus and offering America support farther afield where it did face strategic challenges. The most obvious way to do this would have been to join the U.S.-led collective effort to contain the Soviet Union, but, strangely enough, this never happened. Though Australian governments continued to identify themselves as strongly aligned with the West, Australian forces were never designed for operations against the Soviet Union, and there was no planning, commitment, or expectation that they would be sent if war broke out.

So, Australia sat out the Cold War after 1972. We did, however, find an easier, cheaper way to maintain and even enhance our credentials as a U.S. ally. America faced a new strategic challenge in the Gulf after the fall of the Shah in 1979. Under the resulting Carter Doctrine, the Gulf became the place where the United States was most likely to use armed force, albeit on a much more modest scale than would be required against the Soviets. This new commitment lacked the diplomatic and political clarity provided by the North Atlantic Treaty Organization, and America found itself eager to enlist allies in fulfilling the Carter Doctrine, not for the forces they could send, but for the diplomatic and political value of their flags.

Australia took this opportunity, and established a pattern in which we routinely — almost automatically — provided small, essentially token, force contributions to U.S.-led operations in the Gulf. After 1980, while Asia was at peace and we sat out the Cold War, this was how Australia maintained and even enhanced its alliance credentials in Washington. It was an extremely cost-effective model of alliance management, because the forces we sent were very small, the operations quick and cheap, and there were no casualties. In return, Australia's standing actually went up in U.S. eyes, putting us on par with Britain as America's favourite ally. Not surprisingly, this pattern of policy enjoyed strong bipartisan support. Under all these circumstances, it would have been surprising if any Australian prime minister had not been quick to say yes when George W. Bush asked for support in another foray into the Gulf.

AFTER 9/11

John Howard was the key figure in Australia's decisions on Iraq, and this account will focus on him because he was the only significant decision-maker. Much is often made of the fact that he was in Washington,

D.C., on September 11, 2001, celebrating the fiftieth anniversary of the signing of the ANZUS Treaty. It has been argued that this gave Howard an especially strong emotional stake in supporting the U.S. response to the attacks, and made him more willing to agree to join the invasion of Iraq. I am skeptical about this. Howard is a phlegmatic person and a cautious and canny calculator of political and policy costs and benefits in any situation. I see no evidence that his judgments and decisions in the years that followed were influenced by his experience in Washington on the day of the attacks. He readily agreed to support the initial U.S. response to the attacks by sending forces to join Operation Enduring Freedom in Afghanistan, but in doing so he showed no more enthusiasm than the leaders of many other countries. At this early stage, support for America's responses to 9/11 was more or less universal: even *Le Monde* had declared on September 12 that "we are all Americans now." Against this background, and in view of the well-established pattern of Australian support for U.S. operations in the region, it is clear that Howard would have sent forces to Afghanistan whether he had been in Washington that morning or not.

Even at this early stage, however, Howard showed some of his characteristic caution. He made it clear from the start that Australian forces would only stay in Afghanistan until al-Qaeda and the Taliban regime had been removed. He explicitly rejected the idea that the Australian Defence Force (ADF) would remain for protracted nation-building operations. Howard was determined that this commitment would conform to the long-established pattern by remaining — like all the previous ones — small, quick, cheap, and successful. By early 2002, it seemed likely that it would be. Australian forces started to withdraw soon after the fall of Kabul, and by the end of November 2002, the Australian contingent had been withdrawn entirely.

Like many others around the world, Howard was perhaps a little dazzled by the ease and speed of America's first apparent success in Afghanistan. It seemed to confirm that American military power was effortlessly omnipotent. The architect of the invasion, Defense Secretary Donald Rumsfeld, was widely hailed as a strategic genius. This no doubt affected Howard's reaction when the idea of invading Iraq was first raised with him by the Americans, which probably happened in February 2002. Howard made a quick trip to the United States at that time, arriving just a few days after

Bush's State of the Union address (January 29, 2002), in which he identified Iraq as a member of the axis of evil, and foreshadowed action against it.

Howard has always insisted that he gave no formal undertakings to join the invasion until the very eve of the operation itself, and there is no reason to doubt this. But it seems likely that in early 2002 he gave Bush a clear private undertaking of support for military action against Iraq, and soon after began to foreshadow Australian participation publicly and to argue in favour of the Bush administration's proposals. This meant that from an early stage Howard became locked into supporting an operation that he did not at that time fully understand. At this early stage, Howard probably assumed, as so many others did, that invading Iraq would not be very different from invading Afghanistan — and again, like so many others, he gave little if any thought to what would happen after the invasion. He had faith that America, and the U.S. military in particular, could make this work, and he saw no reason not to take part.

HOWARD'S REASONS

That way of putting it — "saw no reason not to" — is probably an accurate description of Howard's decision-making process at this point. Australia's long history of support for the United States in the Middle East meant that saying yes to such a request was the natural thing to do, and he assumed that this commitment would be as small, quick, cheap, and successful as all the others had been. The still-fresh memory of the searing trauma of 9/11 and of the intoxicating if incomplete and inconclusive tactical success in Afghanistan only strengthened the presumption to say yes. So, perhaps, did domestic political calculations. Howard had just won an election in which national security issues and his own image as a strong national security leader had played the central part. He probably calculated that more high-profile military operations would be good for him politically.

This account of Howard's reasons for agreeing to join the invasion imply, of course, that for him, just as much as for Bush, Iraq's WMDs provided a pretext rather than a reason. There is no reason to doubt that Howard genuinely believed Iraq had WMDs, but there is no reason to think that this was why he agreed to take part in Operation Iraqi Freedom. But his real reasons were different from Bush's. In Washington, Iraq's WMDs provided cover for the crusade to transform the Middle East, which even after 9/11 the administration was reluctant to reveal too plainly. Howard never signed up for the neo-conservative agenda, and was anyway instinctively unsympathetic to anything so grandiosely ambitious. He may not even have been clearly aware of it. It is quite possible Howard believed that America really was motivated by Iraqi WMDs. In a very real sense, however, America's purposes didn't really matter to Howard. His purpose in supporting the invasion was always going to be different from America's in mounting it. His aim was to bolster the alliance by supporting America in whatever it was doing, regardless of America's reasons for doing it.

Of course Howard could not say this — or at least he could not say it in quite such blunt terms. Like his predecessors, he did acknowledge support for the United States as a secondary reason to send forces to the Gulf, but he could not acknowledge this as the primary purpose. The nature of Australia's Middle East–centred alliance management strategy imposed a need to dissimulate about our real reasons for joining successive U.S. military deployments there. Australia's primary aim was always to burnish its alliance credentials by giving America something it valued. That was not the forces Australia actually sent — they were never operationally significant to the overall outcome. America sought the political and diplomatic value in both domestic U.S. and international debates of having Australia as a coalition partner, adding Australia's voice to America's in explaining why military action was justified. But Canberra could not provide this value if we admitted that we were only going along because America wanted us to. Australia has always had to claim that our purposes were the same as America's, otherwise our arguments would not help to support America's. To achieve our objectives in the Middle East, we have always had to misrepresent them.

Hence Howard had to claim that he, too, was motivated by the threat of Iraq's WMDs, and he, too, believed that this threat was serious enough to justify the invasion. As I have said, there is no reason to think Howard did not really believe Iraq had WMDs. Whether he believed that they were dangerous enough to warrant invasion and regime change is much harder to say. Quite possibly he never really thought about it, because it was not relevant to the real grounds on which he made his decision.

ASSUMPTIONS, SECOND THOUGHTS, AND GROWING CAUTION

It seems likely that when Howard made his personal and political commitment to support Bush in Iraq early in 2002 he had no clear understanding of what he was signing up for. He did not see that the undertaking that Bush was contemplating would be by far America's largest and most demanding military commitment since Vietnam, and the largest and most demanding by any power since the Soviets invaded Afghanistan in 1979. He believed that this would be just another short, cheap, and successful operation in which Australia would be called upon to do no more than contribute a token contingent to an effortless American triumph. He assumed that removing Saddam Hussein and liberating Iraq would not be much harder than the liberation of Kuwait following Saddam's invasion in 1990 had been. He probably also assumed that whatever America planned to do would eventually attract widespread international support and would not be opposed by the Labor Opposition in Australia.

If he had been right, his decision would now be generally regarded as wise and justified, a perfectly natural and appropriate example of Australia's approach to alliance management. But, of course, he was wrong, and these errors remain the most critical and, in a sense, the most mystifying element in the whole process that led Australia into Iraq.

The assumption that invading Iraq and creating a new, pro-U.S. political order there would be easy was a cardinal strategic error for which there is no real explanation — or excuse. Any staff college could explain the scale of the task and the mismatch between the resources required and those available. Indeed it had already been done. Back in 1990, it had been clearly recognized that invading Iraq, taking control of the country, and managing a radical and unprecedented political transformation was an immense task for which America was quite unprepared. That was why everyone agreed at the time that Operation Desert Storm should stop at the Iraqi border and not go on to Baghdad.

Even today, it remains a mystery how American policy-makers and the American policy process got this wrong when they looked at the question a second time in 2002. Howard himself had little strategic insight to draw on and his experience of easy tactical successes in East Timor and Afghanistan perhaps made him overconfident, but there can be little doubt that Howard was at first happy to assume that the Americans knew what they were doing. There is, moreover, no evidence that he sought or received any advice from Australian military or civilian officials on the wisdom of invading Iraq. Most likely Howard had already committed himself to support Bush before there was any chance to seek or receive such advice, and once the commitment was made, any advice that contradicted Howard's initial assumptions would have been distinctly unwelcome.

In fairness to Howard, it must be said that his assumptions about the feasibility of Bush's strategic plans were shared, not just by supporters of the invasion around the world, but also by many of its opponents. Criticism of Bush's plans over the coming months focused overwhelmingly on diplomatic, legal, and ethical questions, rather than on practical operational issues. Almost everyone assumed that America could do what Bush planned, and the debate centred on whether he should or not — and especially on whether he should invade Iraq without approval from the United Nations. This debate quickly flared both in Australia and overseas. Howard may well have assumed that his early expressions of support for action against Iraq would soon be followed by others. Australia had often in the past — such as in 1990 — been among the first to sign up for U.S. military initiatives, well before others who later overcame their initial doubts to become strong supporters. But by the middle of 2002, it perhaps started to dawn on Howard that the opposition to Bush over Iraq was not going to wither away as the idea gained momentum. From then it became increasingly clear that very few countries would join this "coalition of the willing," and that may have helped push Howard toward greater caution about the nature and scale of his commitment to Iraq.

The fact that Australia was one of only two countries to provide substantial support for Bush's invasion is very striking, but almost equally striking is the very modest and cautious nature of that contribution. Howard may have stuck steadfastly to his early decision to support Bush, but he also stuck equally steadfastly to his decision to limit Australia's contribution and hence its liabilities to the absolute minimum, and in this he was strikingly successful. The contrast with the other member of the coalition of the willing is stark. U.K. prime minister Tony Blair committed the largest forces Britain could possibly send to Operation Iraqi Freedom. Britain deployed a larger proportion of its regular forces to the Gulf than America did, and ten times the proportion that Australia sent. Howard resisted pressure from Washington and London to commit more troops, and he worked hard to minimize the risks of casualties. In this he was remarkably successful. The fact that Australia suffered no battle casualties in Iraq in 2003 was not just a tribute to luck and military skill, but to Howard's determination to keep the overall risks to Australian forces as low as possible.

Howard was also determined that Australia would not become entrapped in protracted post-invasion peacekeeping and stabilization operations. From mid-2002 he began to insist — as he had in Afghanistan — that Australian forces would be withdrawn soon after any invasion took place, and would not take part in subsequent nation-building. It may be that Howard insisted on this so forcefully precisely because he saw more clearly than Bush or Blair how long and painful the post-invasion entanglements might be. Overall, it seems at least possible that as the march to war stepped up during 2002, Howard became less and less certain of the wisdom of the invasion. He was not prepared to face the political costs of backing down from his early commitment to take part, especially because Labor's opposition to the invasion would make a U-turn by him look like a win for them. But he was determined to insulate Australia and himself as much as possible from the consequences of failure in Iraq. And when we compare his fate to Bush's and Blair's, we can only acknowledge that he succeeded.

SUCCESS AND FAILURE

A decade after U.S. forces entered Baghdad, it is clear that America's invasion of Iraq failed completely to achieve its primary aim of strengthening U.S. power in the Middle East, and it proved a political disaster for Bush himself. Iraq also played the biggest part in discrediting Tony Blair's prime ministership. And yet Howard's reputation survived the debacle, and Howard himself cheerfully defends his decision to this day. The contrast between Iraq's consequences for Howard and Blair is especially striking. It reflects deep differences in their approach to the issue. Blair, it seems, came much closer to supporting the Bush administration's underlying neo-conservative objectives in Iraq than Howard ever did, but Blair's primary objective was, like Howard's, to consolidate his country's relationship with the United States.

However, while Howard approached the operation with prudent caution, which grew as the problems and risks became more apparent, Blair became ever more recklessly enthusiastic as the invasion approached.

That is partly explained by big differences in temperament between the two men, but it also reflects deeper differences between Britain and Australia. Although both countries went to Iraq mainly to strengthen their alliances with America, they saw their alliances differently and were trying to use Iraq to achieve different things in relation to them. Blair, perhaps even more than his predecessors, hoped that Britain's alliance with America would help to preserve or even expand the vestiges of British global power. The idea was that as a close ally, Britain would influence America, and America would shape the world, just as in the Second World War Harold Macmillan had spoken of Britain playing Greece to America's Rome. But Blair's ambition to shape American policy required a much more active, costly, and risky contribution than Howard's more modest goal of simply supporting it. That drew Blair into making a proportionally much bigger military and political commitment to the invasion of Iraq, while ultimately failing to win for Britain much influence over U.S. policy, or bolstering its standing as a global power.

Compared to Bush and Blair, therefore, it might seem that Howard's decision on Iraq has been vindicated. His modest aim was to be seen as a good ally, and to judge from Washington's warm praise, he succeeded in doing this, even if the operation itself was a failure. It certainly worked for Howard himself politically. He won praise for his strong leadership and escaped blame for the mess because, at least superficially, it cost Australia very little. History might not be so generous, however. When we look closer, there is good reason to think that Australia's policy on Iraq was bad for our ally and bad for the alliance, and that there were other things Howard could have done when he was approached by Washington in 2002 that would have served Australia's interests much better.

Iraq was bad for the alliance because, to many people in Washington beyond the White House, the small size and cautious nature of Australia's military contribution was seen for what it was — tokenism, with a dash of cynicism. Australia's pattern of small, quick, cheap, and essentially symbolic deployments to U.S.-led coalitions in the Gulf worked fine as long as the operation itself was quick, cheap, and successful. But as it became clear that Iraq was turning out to be none of those things, the mismatch between

Howard's bold talk and timid actions became painfully clear. When Iraq's civil war spun out of control, Howard faced pressure to reverse his rapid withdrawals and send Australian forces back to Iraq and Afghanistan, which he did, but in both cases ensuring that the units deployed were restricted to relatively safe duties in relatively safe places. No Australians were killed in action in Iraq and very few in Afghanistan while Howard was prime minister. Americans were not impressed. It is too early to say what effect this will have on future alliance dealings with Washington, but it is a fair bet that the next time America asks for Australian support it will not be so easily satisfied by tokens.

The bigger point for historians, however, is likely to be not whether Howard's actions in Iraq were good or bad for the alliance in the longer term, but whether they were relevant to it at all. Support for U.S. operations in the Gulf became the benchmark for Australia's standing as an alliance partner only after 1972, when U.S.-China rapprochement ushered in an era of uncontested U.S. primacy in Asia. As China's power grows, it is increasingly distancing itself from the post-1972 understandings, and since 2008 it has begun more overtly to challenge U.S. primacy in Asia. America, in response, has pushed back with its "pivot" to Asia, aiming to resist China's challenge and reassert U.S. leadership. In doing this, it looks to Australia for support, and over the last few years America has begun once again to judge Australia's alliance credentials primarily on the basis of the support we provide to them in Asia, and especially in their steadily intensifying strategic and political contest with China. This raises immense diplomatic questions for Canberra, as it tries to meet U.S. expectations without alienating Australia's most important trading partner. Australia's contributions in Iraq — and Afghanistan — are increasingly irrelevant to these questions. No one in Washington in the future will care much about what we did in Iraq. Their focus will be on how we are supporting them against China.

This brings us to the most imponderable but perhaps most important of the longer-term consequences of Howard's decision to support the invasion of Iraq. The invasion has turned out to be bad not just for the Middle East but for America as well. Bush's gambit in Iraq was a test of the idea of American post–Cold War hyperpower, and the test failed. The idea was always flawed, of course. No matter what had happened in Iraq, America's role around the world faces a fundamental challenge from rising regional powers, especially China. How America responds to that challenge — with bellicose defiance, sulky withdrawal, or prudent adaptation — will be one of the biggest factors shaping the strategic affairs in many parts of the world in the coming decades. But it is quite possible that America's entanglement in Iraq and its failure there will prove a big factor in shaping its response to this very real challenge to its role in the world. America faces the challenge from China in worse shape — materially, financially, and psychologically — because it invaded Iraq. That could have huge consequences for the way America responds to China's challenge, and that, in turn, has huge consequences for Australia's future. Our security and prosperity depend on a stable order in Asia, and that depends on America continuing to play a strong role there while avoiding escalating rivalry with China. Iraq may have made that harder.

Does Australia, and John Howard specifically, carry any responsibility for all this? That depends on whether you think there was any chance that a different response from Howard might have dissuaded Bush from the invasion. Most people would dismiss that possibility, because in 2002 the idea of invading Iraq acquired such swift momentum in Washington that nothing could have stopped it. But that overlooks the fact that many key figures in Washington, including Colin Powell and many senior military figures, were very skeptical until close to the end. Contestability collapsed in Washington in 2002, but reviving it might not have required much effort. And perhaps — only perhaps — that could have been done if loyal allies like Australia and the United Kingdom had asked some searching questions before agreeing to sign up for the invasion. The questions they could have asked are clear not only in hindsight — they were being asked by many people at the time. Questions like, "What happens after we get to Baghdad?" and "How many troops would it take to pacify Iraq once Saddam has gone?" In the early months of 2002, no Australian prime minister would have given George W. Bush a flat no. But a wiser prime minister would have realized that "yes" was not the only alternative to no. He could have started asking such questions instead. Not doing so was, in Talleyrand's words, "worse than a crime: it was a blunder."

10

CHEERLEADERS OF FOLLY: AUSTRALIA'S MISGUIDED ATTEMPT TO BE A GOOD ALLY

Charles Sampford

Australians and Canadians share a great deal. In particular, they share two desires for the future: they no longer want to be British and they do not want to become American. The biggest difference is that Australians are more concerned about demonstrating the former, and Canadians the latter. There are many reasons for this inclination on the part of Canadians, including the two occasions when the United States sought in vain to incorporate some, or all, of Canada by the use of force, and the occasional suggestions that it might do so later.[1] This not only made Canada feel more vulnerable to the United States, but also more dependent on Britain. By contrast, the first American boots on Australian ground arrived by invitation — to repel a potential invader — rather than as an invader in 1812.

In the first half of the twentieth century, Australia and Canada were empire loyalists who joined most of the wars fought by the United Kingdom — though they were more likely to operate in wars and theatres close to their territory.[2] Over the last sixty-five years, they have joined several actions led by the United States (Korea, the first Gulf War, and Afghanistan). But there were a number of exceptions. During the Cold War, Canada, as one of three members of the International Control Commission meant to supervise the implementation of the 1954 Geneva Agreements, did not contribute troops to Vietnam as Australia did. However, as a member of the North Atlantic

Treaty Organization, Canada at the time maintained a mechanized brigade and twelve squadrons in Europe, prepared for a much bigger war in Europe. More recently and notably, Australia opted out of the Kosovo War in 1999[3] and Canada opted out of the Iraq War in 2003 — wars which were, if the vast majority of international lawyers are correct, the first and only illegal wars in which either country engaged.[4]

How should we account for this last difference? In both 1999 and 2003, Canada was led by Liberal prime minister Jean Chrétien, and Australia by Liberal prime minister John Howard.[5] In both cases, the United Kingdom was led by Tony Blair, a Labour prime minister. There were differences in American leadership. In 1999, the United States was led by a Democrat, and in 2003 by a Republican. One might conjecture that Howard was less inclined than Chrétien to go along with Democrat Clinton, and Chrétien less likely to join a Republican like Bush.[6] However, it should be noted that Australia and Canada joined in the 1991 Iraq War when the British were led by the Conservatives, the Canadians were led by the Progressive Conservatives, and the Australians were led by the Australian Labor Party. But the key difference between Canadian and Australian choices over going to war has virtually nothing to do with partisan politics; rather, the main influence on their final decision was the importance of the relative roles of the United States and the United Kingdom in the two middle powers' history, consciousness, and military politics.

Australia and Canada believed their forces had been squandered in the First World War by British generals, with the early years of the Second World War a repetition of the experience (most notably the 1942 disasters in Dieppe and Singapore). The stories during the rest of the Second World War were much happier. Canadians provided an army on the left flank in Normandy and the push into Germany. Australia was the first to stem and then reverse the Japanese tide on land.[7] Since the Second World War, both countries have enjoyed the mixed blessing of a great and powerful friend (and the United States is all three of those things — great, powerful, and, for the most part, a friend). The blessing is mixed because there is generally limited material benefit to the United States from allied participation, so there is little American gratitude if the United States is successful and even less if it is not. Canada has long been a loyal member of NATO, and Australia of the ANZUS security alliance and SEATO (South East Asia Treaty Organization), while the latter lasted.

If the United States is planning to go to war, that is a reason for both Australia and Canada to consider whether to go to war. Their alliances do not mean they are expected to join the United States in all cases, and they do not. While NATO is an integrated organization and ANZUS a loose alliance (one of whose three legs fell off in the nuclear-ship dispute between the United States and New Zealand in the 1980s), NATO obligations are greater than those of ANZUS but do not legally require the use of armed force.[8] However, preparedness to engage in some conflicts is clearly expected and is naturally relevant to any reciprocal aid if one of the security "consumers" is threatened.

A decision by America to go to war is a highly relevant consideration for Australia. While there is no legal obligation for the United States to come to the defence of Australia, it does not mean that it would not do so, or that Australian conduct is not highly relevant. So, which wars should Australia be prepared to join and what are the issues that should be considered? I will look at five such issues, the Australian debate, and what the government said about them.

1. Facts: The factual claims about Iraqi weapons of mass destruction (WMDs) — whether and to what extent Iraq had continued to retain and develop WMDs in breach of its obligations. These facts were largely a matter for intelligence and the reports of the weapons inspectors.
2. Options: If Iraq had WMDs, what responses might be made and what were the risks and benefits of those options?
3. Law: Which of the considered options were lawful under international law?[9]
4. Alliances: Were there obligations or expectations arising from Australia's alliances and other treaties that needed to be considered in choosing from options?
5. Commitment: If Australia did decide to take part, what forces should be deployed?[10]

I will argue that little effort was made to determine the facts or to consider options other than war or the risks, benefits, or legality of the option chosen. Alliance and friendship with the United States was the dominant issue. Australia entered the Iraq War on the assumption that helping the United States was in its interests and that it would be in America's interests to receive that help. Australia was wrong on both counts.

However, ignoring factual and legal arguments that an ally wishes to pretend away does not constitute the actions of a good ally. Australia tried to be a good ally and turned out to be a very bad one. The first three issues are, or should be, concerns for Australia and the United States alike. As an ally, Australia should seek to ensure, as far as possible, that the United States reaches sensible conclusions on those issues. It is in Australia's national interest to ensure, as much as possible, that it does — even to the point of forcefully arguing the contrary case. Cheerleaders of an ally's folly may be appreciated at the time but earn no credit in the long term. If the United States is weakened by the folly — as seems to be the consensus on the draining impact of the Iraq War on U.S. treasure and resolve — cheerleader allies are doubly compromised.

I will conclude by raising and partly addressing two questions: Could Australia have made a difference? What has Australia done to reduce the risk of similar mistakes in future?

Canadians may feel a sense of superiority in not entering the Iraq War. But with the Kosovo War in 1999, Canada engaged in a war many thought illegal. Until then, Australia had never engaged in an illegal war and had led the Cambodian and East Timorese missions appropriately and with an extraordinary degree of success.[11] The Australian attorney general strongly supported international law, emphasizing its importance in his opening address at the International Institute for Public Ethics biennial conference in Brisbane in October 2002. Within three months, Australia had taken part in a war whose legality had even less foundation and far less positive outcomes than the one in Kosovo. But herein lies another difference — whereas Canada sought to reflect on the 1999 war and established the International Commission on Intervention and State Sovereignty to consider the circumstances under which intervention might be justified,[12] Australia, on the other hand, has done nothing to learn from the mistakes made in the 2003 Iraq invasion, either by striking a national inquiry or taking the lead in international discussions of how it can do so collectively.

DIFFERENT REGIONS AND ALLIANCES

Canada's membership in NATO gave it a reason to be involved in Kosovo[13] but not Iraq. For Australia, by contrast, "fighting the wars of our great and powerful friend" is absolutely predominant and the region(s) shifts with the U.S. perception (often induced by Australia) of where Australia can be useful. Its engagement with the United States has seen two major phases — starting with noble causes and ending with major strategic blunders, with the nobility of the cause reducing and the scale of the blunder increasing.

The period 1942–72 started with joint involvement in the noble cause of resisting aggression by major powers in one of the most justifiable wars in history. The war had, of course, started with Japanese aggression in Manchuria, about which the major powers did nothing. Only the United Kingdom and France responded to German aggression against Poland. The United States entered the war when Pacific territories and the East Asian colony (the Philippines) were attacked. That war ended in a great victory for the Allies.[14] This period ended when the United States suffered a strategic defeat in the error-ridden Vietnam War — a war that Australia had encouraged in the hope of U.S. engagement providing protection to Australia. Instead, it ended with the Guam Doctrine,[15] which told Australia that it had to take the primary responsibility for its own defence.

The more recent Middle Eastern period started with a legal, legitimate, and largely justified war in response to clearly illegal aggression by Iraq against Kuwait in 1990. It ended seventeen years later with the greatest U.S. strategic blunder since the War of 1812 and its greatest strategic defeat ever.

The third period has fortunately not started with a war against China but with collaboration to bolster the U.S. strategic position in the region vis-à-vis China. It is not entirely clear how this collaboration will benefit Australia or the region. However, one thing is very clear: we cannot afford it to end in a strategic debacle like the first two periods of our collaboration. It is unlikely to start with success, and the danger of a truly disastrous end are clearly evident.

Of course, Southeast Asia is of particular importance to Australia, and it has been particularly keen for the United States to be involved there. General Douglas MacArthur made it quite clear to the Australian government that Australia's sovereignty and independence was not an interest of the United States.[16] He was interested in restoring U.S. prestige and reconquering the Philippines. Ever since 1942, Australia has wanted the United States to be engaged in the region so that any future threat to Australia will involve a challenge to the United States by going through territory or compromising interests the United States will fight to defend. However, Australia now has to be careful that U.S.

involvement in the region does not provoke a conflict that it may lose — a reversal of the usual rationale that U.S. involvement in the region will prevent conflict because any potential enemy is bound to lose. Such a loss is now a real possibility, not just as the relative strengths of China and the United States vary, but as the United States comes to realize that it is not rational for it to demand military hegemony on the doorstep of a power approaching its own size. If the United States comes to this rational conclusion after a conflict emerges, it could be disastrous for Australia. But even if it comes to this conclusion before a conflict emerges, Australia may still be left high and dry.

AUSTRALIA, NEW ZEALAND, UNITED STATES SECURITY TREATY

Like many Australians, I support an alliance with the United States and can trace family links to its genesis. My father was a senior intelligence analyst in the Combined Operations Intelligence Centre (COIC) at MacArthur's headquarters (work for which the United States decorated him — a rare honour for an Australian). He introduced me to his colleagues and junior officers on both sides of the Pacific, including then secretary for health, education, and welfare (and later defense secretary) Caspar Weinberger. As we entered the West Wing at the height of the 1972 Christmas bombing, my father anticipated John Cleese in *Fawlty Towers* by nearly three years in urging me not to mention the war — by which he meant the current war that was straining the Australian-American relationship, rather than the one that had forged it. As we flew home across the snow-covered landscape of the Midwest, my father turned to me and, in reference to the Vietnam War, said, "We have made a huge mistake, and it is time to recognize it." He hoped that our intelligence services recognized it too. This story illustrates three aspects of the U.S.-Australian relationship, namely shared values, the importance of good intelligence, and an expectation of mutual military support.

Shared Values

The alliance is supported by most Australians, based on the shared values on which it was forged and for which Australians and Americans fought. Among the shared values was concern for the international rule of law. This was recognized by both countries as co-signatories of the 1928 Kellogg-Briand Pact, which was enshrined in Article 2 of the U.N. Charter, the Nuremberg trials, and Article 1 of the ANZUS Treaty. President Dwight Eisenhower eloquently restated this core value:

> The time has come for mankind to make the rule of law in international affairs as normal as it is now in domestic affairs.... Plainly one foundation stone of this structure is the International Court of Justice. It is heartening to note that a strong movement is afoot in many parts of the world to increase acceptance of the obligatory jurisdiction of that Court.... One final thought on rule of law between nations: we will all have to remind ourselves that under this system of law one will sometimes lose as well as win. But ... if an international controversy leads to armed conflict, everyone loses.[17]

The rule of law means that the law applies to us as well as others. As the American prosecutor at Nuremberg aptly put it, "Let me make clear that while this law is first applied against German aggressors, the law includes, and if it is to serve a useful purpose it must condemn aggression by any other nations, including those which sit here now in judgment."[18]

Intelligence

Intelligence co-operation between the two countries commenced in 1942 with code-breaking activity and the formation of COIC. The analysis provided did not always accord with the expectations or views of high-ranking officers. But my father and his colleagues recognized both the temptation and the folly of telling their superiors what they wanted to hear rather than what they needed to hear. Doing the latter was neither disloyalty nor insubordination but their professional duty and the best service they could render to allies and friends.[19] To do otherwise risked lives, battles, and, in 1942, when the balance of forces was more even, the war itself. Subsequent history has shown the importance of this kind of professionalism in intelligence, and the dangers of intelligence officers telling superiors what they want to hear.

Intelligence co-operation has remained a significant part of Australian (and Canadian) alliances with the United States — through the location of facilities and the sharing of intelligence in the "Five Eyes"[20] and other arrangements. Geographic locations have been useful in different ways. Canada's propinquity allowed early warning and integrated defence during the Cold War, and Australia's remoteness provided a valuable location for global signals intelligence (SIGINT) and satellite monitoring.

Mutual Support

While the United States and Australia are not committed to joining in each other's wars, even in self-defence, there is a general expectation of mutual support in peace and war. The ANZUS provisions for consultation are not intended to be idle, and the joint exercises are not just for appearance. They give Australia a degree of comfort that U.S. assistance is likely if it is threatened, and this itself is likely to deter threats. The use of Australian bases in intelligence-gathering is assumed to continue even if Australia is not involved in a given war — and provides a further reason for the United States to defend it. More generally, it is assumed that the interests of each are the interests of the other — though neither will be expected to put the other's interests above its own.

HOWARD'S VIEW OF FACTS, OPTIONS AND LEGALITY

In a speech to the Lowy Institute on the tenth anniversary of the attack on Iraq, John Howard sought to justify the decision to go to war despite "mistakes" about Iraq's alleged WMDs, the lack of postwar planning, and other postwar mistakes.

1. Facts: Howard's government believed at the time that Iraq had WMDs, claiming that "the belief that Saddam had WMDs was near universal," citing a Rudd speech in late 2002[21] "that it was 'an empirical fact' that the Iraqis possessed WMDs," and quoting the Report of the Inquiry into Australian Intelligence Agencies that "prior to 19 March 2003, the only government in the world that claimed that Iraq was not working on, and did not have, biological and chemical weapons or prohibited missile systems was the Government of Saddam Hussein."[22]

2. Law: The Howard government "never saw the obtaining of a fresh Security Council resolution as a necessary legal prerequisite to action the removal of Saddam."
3. Options: Howard mentioned two options — war, and containment through sanctions.
4. The alliance: Howard saw it as even more important than usual because of a shared sense of threat from terrorists in New York and Bali and a recognition that leaving Saddam in power would come with the real risk that he would "provide WMDs to a terrorist group."

Howard rightly points out that the major party–political division was over the second point. That division mirrored debate among experts, in the media, and in public opinion.[23] This emphasis is partly because it is easier to debate issues of legality than intelligence. Intelligence and its sources are not public and are not subject to public evaluation and determination. On the other hand, legal sources are not only publicly available, but authoritatively ranked, and disputes can be resolved by open, transparent, and independent determination.

Of course, the two are not unrelated. The lawfulness of actions will often depend on facts and evidence — especially where the action taken is in response to an alleged breach by another. It is also relevant in considering options, in particular the seeking of further information. Before examining the legal arguments, therefore, let us assess the state of intelligence at the time.

INTELLIGENCE

Howard, and former foreign secretary Philip Flood before him, put great store by the fact that the only government that claimed Iraq neither had nor was working on WMDs was the government of Iraq itself. However, this does not mean that as of March 19, 2003, those countries believed Iraq had WMDs. Silence does not mean assent in logic — and even less so in diplomacy.

Diplomats are careful not to give any unnecessary offence by challenging the strongly expressed views of others, especially when the others are much more powerful than they are and no vital interest is served by speaking up. In any case, as Howard rightly says, there is rarely proof beyond reasonable doubt in intelligence estimates. So, it is doubly unsurprising that other countries would have avoided unequivocal statements. Silence could have, and as we later discovered, did cover a range of views about the extent and usefulness of Iraqi WMDs. Saddam Hussein had virtually no credibility. Despite the fact that he was the only one who knew for certain, his record of deceit was such that his support for a proposition generated further doubt as to its veracity. However, this did not mean that all claims by the United Kingdom and United States were accepted at face value — a likelihood reduced by each overstatement. In between, there were a range of scenarios to which various countries could have assigned a range of varying probabilities. Included among them was the possibility that Saddam had retained some largely useless material and weaponry that posed little threat and could be disposed of relatively easily.

Rather than trying to parse silence, it is more useful to consider what other nations did say. The U.N. Security Council unanimously passed Resolution 1441 (November 8, 2002) to give Iraq a final opportunity to comply with its disarmament obligations, empower weapons inspectors to go anywhere to find WMDs and ensure their destruction, and provide full Iraqi assistance to the weapons inspectors. This action established a process likely to render debates over Iraqi WMDs moot. Indeed, there was an almost perfect opportunity to combine intelligence with on-the-ground inspectors. The U.S. intelligence could guide the inspectors to the WMDs the United States confidently asserted were there. Under these circumstances, it would seem foolish to go out on a limb and make public statements that might be proven wrong either way.[24]

During this process, doubts about Iraqi WMDs started to emerge:

1. While countries were reticent to speak out, a range of Australians did, including Andrew Wilkie,[25] Rod Barton,[26] Paul Barratt,[27] Alison Broinowski,[28] and Ramesh Thakur (who sets out some of the other voices at the time).[29]

2. Claims were being invalidated, including the claim that Iraq's WMDs could be deployed at forty-five minutes' notice[30] and the claim made in Bush's State of the Union address (January 28, 2003) that "the British government has learned that Saddam Hussein recently sought significant quantities of uranium from Africa" (discredited on March

7, 2003, by the International Atomic Energy Agency, which revealed that the documents produced by the United States to substantiate the president's claim were patent and incompetent forgeries).[31] When a politician makes a statement based on intelligence sources, it is appreciated that this cannot be publicly verified, putting a premium on trust — trust that was rapidly evaporating.

3. Most important, the perfect opportunity to find WMDs was not producing any evidence. Instead, it was providing a test of the reliability of U.S. and U.K. claims — a test that they were failing. That failure increased the desire by the majority of states and their public for these inspections to run their course. Instead, the American insistence on war meant that the Hans Blix mission was cut short.

Blix started with a view that Iraq had WMDs. However, he knew that it was his job to gather evidence. The intelligence agencies that had concluded that Iraq had WMDs had a perfect opportunity to feed him information he could confirm on the ground. It is not entirely clear the extent to which they provided evidence that was not borne out, or the extent to which they did not provide evidence. Blix's criticisms of intelligence agencies was not that they were wrong or were necessarily lying. It is that they failed to exercise critical thinking, to challenge their sources, the evidence, and their conclusions.[32] Such procedures are part of the core of professional intelligence. Because one can be wrong, one should test one's theories and be open to being wrong.

Howard takes great offence at the suggestion that there was a lack of professionalism in various intelligence services.[33] But most blame politicians and their spin doctors. Even Howard acknowledges that some members of the Bush government had no basis for making the absurd claims about links between Saddam and al-Qaeda (lamely defending Bush personally because he himself did not make such claims). However, according to the standards of the amateurs who worked in COIC, the professionalism of some intelligence agencies leaves a lot to be desired. The famous "slam dunk" claim[34] by George Tenet has no place in a profession that Howard himself does not admit can provide proof beyond reasonable doubt. There is a temptation for politicians to seek, and a temptation for agencies to give, the facts they want to hear. Politicians of integrity do not give in to the former temptation. Intelligence professionals do not give in to the latter. Those who gave in to the latter temptation may have done so under pressure from politicians who had already given in to the former temptation. Any such failures should be subject to the most rigorous, independent, and external scrutiny. It would seem that the Office of National Assessments (ONA)[35] was not particularly critical but that the main problems occurred in and between U.S. and U.K. politicians. The concern is the extent to which Australian politicians sought to cite the less equivocal statements by U.S. and U.K. politicians and intelligence agencies rather than to press them for the kind of critical thinking required.

INTERNATIONAL LAW — LAWYERS AND OFFICIALS

Howard correctly stated that the main issue between the parties was whether U.N. approval would be needed for the war — as it was among lawyers, in the media, and in public opinion. While he makes much of the belief of other governments about WMDs, inferred from what they did not say, he fails to mention the views of other governments on this issue. Nor does he reflect on the massive weight of legal opinion and the public opinion polls (let alone protest demonstrations of record size). He says, "It was always our view that Resolution 678, dating back to 1990, provided sufficient legal grounds for the action ultimately taken. That was reflected in the formal legal advice tendered to the Government, and subsequently tabled in Parliament."[36]

Anne-Marie Slaughter[37] said that 80 percent of international lawyers concluded that the invasion of Iraq was unlawful.[38] The figure among Australian international lawyers would seem to be higher, starting with the forty-three who signed a letter to the *Sydney Morning Herald* to that effect and the three Australian signatories (Professors James Crawford, Christine Chinkin, and Deborah Cass) to a letter sent to the *Guardian* signed by sixteen international lawyers.[39] The number of international lawyers who expressed contrary views was extremely limited — of whom Professors Don Greig and Ivan Shearer are the only significant ones, and the latter's view could be taken either way.[40] The lack of support from lawyers who had taught, researched, or practised in international law was not remedied by a small group of volunteers without that expertise whose arguments were as likely to be as unpersuasive to a court of competent jurisdiction as they were to their peers.

What was even more remarkable was (U.K. attorney general) Lord Goldsmith's statement in his advice dated March 7, 2003 (not published until two years later), which indicated that this view was supported by few academics and only one state, the United States.[41] This disclosure not only implied that the British lawyers disagreed but that the Australians lawyers did as well — raising questions about whether a different view had been expressed by Australian government lawyers from that which was later published.[42]

Goldsmith subsequently issued a one-page statement that the war was legal after Admiral Michael Boyce, Britain's chief of defence staff, demanded such an opinion before he would order troops to invade Iraq.[43] It did nothing to sway international professional opinion and dealt with few of the issues ably and professionally canvassed in the first opinion from Lord Goldsmith.

Given this weight of opinion, it is not clear on what basis Howard could confidently assert in Parliament on March 6, 2003, that there was "ample legal authority" to go to war.[44] He would presumably have had a draft of the March 12 memorandum he tabled on March 18.[45] But why was this advice so clearly contrary to the bulk of international legal opinion (including the opinion of those more senior to the memorandum authors)?[46] On Slaughter's statistics, there was a one in twenty-five chance of getting two international lawyers to say going to war was legal. Based on Goldsmith's March 7 view, there was no chance unless they were American.

How are we to explain this statistical improbability?

1. Was it pure coincidence?
2. Had the government asked others and chosen to ignore their opinions?
3. Had other, more senior lawyers been deliberately bypassed?
   - The attorney general at the time believed that his heavy administrative load meant that he could not devote time to providing advice (something he would otherwise be eminently qualified to do as a former leading silk).[47] He considered that, in the Australian system of government, such advice should be provided by the solicitor general.
   - However, on Iraq, the solicitor general was not approached to give advice.

- Neither was there any sign of an approach to the next most senior lawyer — Henry Burmeister AO, QC, the general counsel to the attorney general's department.

4. Did it have something to do with unpublished instructions that the memorandum's legal drafters were given? It is interesting that Howard refers to the government view on legality being "reflected" in the legal advice. Unlike Goldsmith's first advice (and normal professional advice), it did not canvass alternative views, their relative strengths, or whether the advice would receive judicial support. Was this omission requested, hinted at, or made to please or avoid causing an upset? Were they aware that the governor general had asked the attorney general's legal advice on the issues and that their advice would be placed before him? [48]

Howard tried to bolster his case by referring to two earlier occasions when the United States and United Kingdom had engaged in limited bombing citing Security Council Resolution 678. However, this unilateral interpretation caused great disquiet and was one of the reasons that the Security Council was very cautious about giving any new authorization to use force in Kosovo[49] and, later, Iraq. It did not sway the majority who said the war was illegal, and was not used by the minority who thought it was.

The other disturbing possibility is that the Australian government did not much bother about the accuracy of the advice tendered to the governor general and Parliament. Did it give in to the temptation to seek, and the lawyers to give, the advice it wanted to hear? This temptation is generally severely constrained by the embarrassing prospect of a judge pointing out its flaws. But Australia had just altered its acceptance of the compulsory jurisdiction of the International Court of Justice (ICJ) in a way that would make it impossible for Iraq to sue Australia as Serbia had sought to sue NATO countries in 1999 (a suit that reached the court within ten days of the start of hostilities).[50] Australia's alteration to *Declarations: Recognizing the Jurisdiction of the Court as Compulsory* was lodged with the ICJ on March 22, 2002, just two weeks after the British Cabinet received unequivocal advice that the planned war would be illegal without a new Security Council resolution.[51]

This change by the Australian government is most unfortunate. The legality of an action is not determined by the legal counsel employed by the initiator of the action. It is determined by a court of competent jurisdiction. The inability of such a court to hear the case does not make the action legal — although it may create temptations for politicians to seek and for some lawyers to give, advice that is wrong, misleading, or otherwise inadequate. In international law, the opposite is the case. The long-standing limitations of international tribunals has been one of the factors that gives greater weight to academic opinion — raising it to a source of law. Where the vast majority of international law professors (and an even larger majority of the senior ones) endorse a legal proposition and are not contradicted by a superior source of law, it can be taken as an accurate statement of law. It can be displaced by the minority who differ if it is endorsed by a relevant treaty, a Security Council resolution or an international court of competent jurisdiction. Law develops when the majority view is challenged — but only when it *is* challenged and challenged *successfully*. Until then, the view of the vast majority of international lawyers stands. Howard's stated view to Parliament is right that Australia should never go to war contrary to international law. If he believed this to be so, he should have been prepared to defend it in court rather than blocking that path.

INTERNATIONAL LAW — MEDIA AND PUBLIC OPINION

Going to war without U.N. approval was highly unpopular. The demonstrations against the war were unprecedented, exceeding even the largest moratoriums against the Vietnam War. The BBC estimated 150,000 demonstrators in Melbourne[52] and several authorities cite figures of 250,000 in Sydney. (Apart from those in Montreal, Canadian demonstrations were much smaller — though the differences between February weather in our two countries might be relevant.)[53] While it is always possible for politicians to downplay such numbers by referring to the majority who did not come, opinion polls showed that in the lead-up to the war the "silent majority" of 68 to 76 percent of Australians and 65 to 67 percent of Canadians opposed war without U.N. approval, but 56 to 61 percent of Australians polled supported involvement if approved by the United Nations and 60 percent of Canadians supported a U.N.-sanctioned attack.[54]

Brendon O'Connor and Srdjan Vucetic argue that the reason this tactic was ineffective was a difference in opinion between Canadian and Australian "strategic elites."[55] Or was the real difference that Australia's newspapers were controlled by an American citizen totally committed to Bush and the Iraq War? According to Alastair Campbell's diaries, on March 11, Rupert Murdoch promised that all his newspapers would get behind the war if Prime Minister Blair was prepared to "come in" (i.e., to join the war).[56] The Murdoch papers hold around 70 percent of the capital-city daily circulation in Australia, which has a gravitational effect on the stories carried by other media. Their coverage was blatantly pro-war. Anyone reading the opinion pages of the *Australian* would have had the impression that the balance of opinion between international lawyers was the opposite of what it really was. The letter from forty-three international lawyers was first sent to the *Australian*, which held it for a week before its writers went to another paper (similarly, the *Times* of London refused to publish the letter by sixteen international lawyers). Tom Switzer, the editor of the *Australian*'s opinion page, claimed to provide balance with two op-ed pieces on the day the war began. On one side, there was an op-ed piece from an international lawyer giving the standard reasons why the war was illegal.[57] On the other side was a piece in favour of the war by what were described as "22 international lawyers," including seventeen Australians, of whom only three (all associate professors) had any background in teaching public international law and one in international economic law. The other thirteen do not appear to have ever taught, researched, or practised in any area of international law.

THE COMMITMENT WE MADE

Hugh White is correct that Australia paid a very small premium in terms of blood and treasure and that the limited commitment was not unnoticed.[58] However, it is not clear that this was fully intentional. It was reported that Howard had wanted to contribute an armoured division but had to back down because Australia did not have one and could not hope to create one in time. It is, however, very interesting that the mission to which Australia contributed was one that, if there had been any missile-mounted WMDs, would have been a very dangerous (and critically important) one. Preventing launches of WMD-armed Scud missiles onto Israeli territory would have been justifiable if there had been WMDs and Scuds in the western desert of Iraq. As there were no such WMDs and virtually no serviceable Scuds, it was one of the safest missions. Howard's actual beliefs about WMDs are, accordingly, crucial to understanding whether he was brilliantly, deviously, and effectively keeping the premium low while making it look large, or whether he was trying to commit Australia to a very risky contribution.

Whether Australian troops entered Iraq before the expiration of the Bush ultimatum to Saddam Hussein, demanding that he leave the country, is not central despite the strong words traditionally used for those who start wars without declaring them (most notably Franklin Delano Roosevelt's reference to December 7, 1941, as a "day of infamy").[59] Acts of aggression are contrary to international law, whether or not they follow the expiration of an ultimatum. The U.N. Charter prohibits both the threat and use of force other than in self-defence or with Security Council authorization. When war was still a legal option (a "continuation of politics by other means"), warnings, ultimatums, and declarations were part of the way that the right to make war was meant to be exercised. When war is not a legal option, threatening to invade in advance does not make it legal. Issuing of the ultimatum without legal justification (as argued by most international lawyers) is itself an illegal threat to use force.

On the other hand, if the war is legal (for example, in defending victims of aggression) it is legal as soon as the conditions for legality are met. Reasonableness, proportionality, and likely civilian casualties will often make an ultimatum necessary, but could also point in the other direction.

A useful analogy is that of terrorist hostage-takers. If they threaten to kill hostages if their demands are not met within an hour, the elapse of an hour does not mean that killing the first hostage is any less a murder — or that killing a hostage before the hour is up is any less legal. On the other hand, taking a head shot at the leader when the opportunity presents itself is legal whether or not the security forces purport to be negotiating with the terrorists.

ALLIANCE

Australia went to war to prove itself a good ally to the United States in an alliance that has wide public support. Australia entered the war on the basis that helping the United States was in its own interests and that it would be in the interests of the United States to receive that help.

Australia was wrong on both counts. The Iraq War did the United States enormous damage. It cost trillions; weakened the United States relative to potential rivals, increasing the possibility and rapidity with which it could lose its position as the number-one military and economic power; cost several thousand lives and significant multiples of that in Iraqi lives; significantly damaged U.S. soft power; reduced the likelihood of the United States sending forces abroad (including for the defence of Australia) in the future; did potential damage to the values both countries share; and provided a bad example for rising powers as to how to handle disputes with other nations.[60]

Those who care about the United States should care about this. Those who think that a strong United States is important to Australia should doubly care. Australia may have considered itself a loyal friend. But those who are cheerleaders for a friend's folly are not thanked when the folly is comprehended. A true friend warns against folly even at the risk of that friend's disapproval — as in Prime Minister Robert Menzies' warning that Australia would not fight over the Taiwan Strait.[61] This tactic requires courage — but no more courage than young intelligence officers sticking to their guns in front of high-ranking officers, and no more courage than a lawyer who advises a client that, while he has done his best to find a legal way for that client to do what he wishes, the action he contemplates is illegal. Indeed, intelligence and legal professionals consider such acts to be part of their professional duty. There is a temptation to seek and a temptation to give the intelligence and legal advice that the government wants to hear. But it is in the interests of both professionals and politicians to resist those temptations. Far too many gave way to those temptations in the United States, the United Kingdom — and, it would seem, Australia. In being an overly enthusiastic and uncritical supporter of that war, Australia rushed to endorse intelligence assessments and legal views despite their increasing untenableness. It did so in the mistaken belief that it was thereby being a good ally.

In so doing, Australia compromised values that were present at the birth of the alliance and which should have been at its heart ever since. And it compromised the professions that help to deliver those values. In doing so, it also engaged in a fundamental breach of the first article of the ANZUS Treaty, which obligates parties to settle all their international disputes by peaceful means in accordance with the U.N. Charter, and to refrain from the threat or use of force. It is very hard to argue that the alliance is a reason for doing something in fundamental breach of the first article of the treaty that formalizes it.

COULD AUSTRALIA (AND/OR CANADA) HAVE MADE A DIFFERENCE?

Some might respond that the United States was going to war regardless and there was nothing Australia (and/or Canada) could do to stop it. Nothing Australia did exacerbated the suffering of the Iraqi people, and its participation in the aftermath was limited and positive. This reflects the arguments of some ethical investors who believe that "engagement" is more effective than "disinvestment."[62]

In fact, it is very possible that Australia could have made a difference by pursuing some principled policies, for example:

1. If Australia had not altered its recognition of the ICJ, it could have sought high-level independent legal advice. On the basis of that advice, it could have privately told its American and British allies it had grave doubts about the legality of the war. If they were sure of their legal advice, Australia would take part, but only on the understanding that it would allow the claim of legality to be tested in the ICJ and would abide by the decision of the ICJ. Australia could have quoted Eisenhower and Article 1 of ANZUS in support of this position. This would have reinforced Blair's push for a new resolution authorizing the use of force (also based on legal advice) but would have made it impossible for him to back out of it. Australia's offer and the legal advice backing it would have either deterred or negated Goldsmith's inadequate and unprofessional, brief response. This would have led to the rejection of a war without U.N. backing by the House of Commons, and quite possibly Cabinet. And Boyce would not have marched. The United States might have gone ahead, but the pressure would have been intense and the possibility of "wiser heads" (there were some) might have prevailed. Blix may have been able to complete his task and discover in April what we now all know.

2. A simpler version might merely have been the seeking and publication of advice by the Australian government to justify why it was prepared

to go to war with a second Security Council resolution but could not do so otherwise.

Of course, friends are more persuasive when they join together. These tactics would have been much more effective if pursued jointly by Canada and Australia with the United Kingdom either leading or reluctantly following. If the United States ever again appears willing to pursue such folly, it is to be hoped that Australia will argue forcefully against it — in conjunction with other like-minded democracies concerned with promoting a rules-based international order, like India, Brazil, and South Africa. The United Kingdom might even take the lead — or, better still, the United States could do so, as in the 1940s.

LEARNING FROM OUR MISTAKES

Countries make mistakes. Howard has acknowledged that mistakes were made. We are accustomed to holding inquiries after disasters — natural, man-made, or mixed — to discover the causes, identify weaknesses in process, and recommend improvements. It should seem axiomatic that we would do so for the most critical decision we can make as a country — especially when it did not turn out all that well.[63] Indeed, Australia should take this farther and emulate Canada's international leadership in trying to deal with the issues generated by its participation in the Kosovo War.

The passage of time does not render the issues moot. Australia may be asked to engage in future conflicts in which the balance of forces are more even and the military and economic consequences more serious. It cannot rule out having to go to war again, or needing American military help. It must learn from the past to minimize the potential for mistakes in the future. Australia should inquire into its own approach to war to be a more effective friend and a country more secure and confident of its values. In future, the legal consequences could be more serious, too. From 2017, the International Criminal Court will have jurisdiction over the crime of aggression. If the majority of international lawyers are correct about Iraq, a repeat of that process could find key Australian decision-makers in the dock if they repeated their 2003 "mistakes."

NOTES

1. In 1775 and 1812, with concerns, which led to the British retaining a garrison and taking defensive measures, continuing until the 1860s. See Boyd L. Dastrup, *King of Battle* (Virginia: TRADOC Branch History Series, 1992).

2. In the Second World War, Canadians concentrated on convoy protection and the invasion of Europe. Australians concentrated on the Middle East and Oceania.

3. Any comparison of the 2003 decisions that ignores Canada's 1999 decision is fraught with risk. For example, Brendon O'Connor and Srdjan Vucetic's explanation that the reason Australia went to war and Canada did not was because of differences in "strategic culture" (in which Australia is from Mars and Canada is from Venus), has, if anything, less basis than the overgeneralized popular title from which it borrows. See O'Connor and Vucetic, "Another Mars-Venus Divide? Why Australia said 'Yes' and Canada said 'Non' to Involvement in the 2003 Iraq War," *Australian Journal of International Affairs* 64, no. 5 (2010): 526–48.

4. Vietnam was clearly a mistake in retrospect but not as clearly illegal. The war in Afghanistan would probably have been found to be legal if the matter had been brought before the International Court of Justice.

5. Confusingly, Canada's Liberal Party is centre-left while Australia's is centre-right (conservative).

6. O'Connor and Vucetic downplay the role of the relevant individuals by asking highly relevant (but not necessarily conclusive) counterfactuals of whether other leaders in those countries would have decided differently.

7. The point where it was turned was the most distant ripple of that tide: the Japanese were experienced and determined and the Australians were operating under terrible conditions and ignorant leadership. Roland Perry, *Pacific 360°: Australia's Battle for Survival in World War II* (Sydney: Hachette, 2012), 7.

8. See North Atlantic Treaty, April 4, 1949, Article 6.1.

9. For a discussion of the constitutional means for Australia to go to war, see Charles Sampford and Margaret Palmer, "The Constitutional Power to Make War – Domestic Legal Issues Raised by Australia's Action in Iraq," *Griffith Law Review* (2009): 350–84.

10. Australia made two controversial decisions: to employ minimal forces and, apparently, to enter Iraq before the expiry of the ultimatum.

11. Indeed, Australia had even managed to secure a high degree of success in Somalia. See Michael J. Kelly, *Restoring and Maintaining Order in Complex Peace Operations: The Search for a Legal Framework*, vol. 2, International Humanitarian Law Series (The Hague, Netherlands: Kluwer Law International, 1999).

12. In his Millenium Report to the U.N. General Assembly, Secretary-General Kofi Annan challenged the international communiy to address the real dilemma posed by intervention and sovereignty. The independent International Commission on

Intervention and State Sovereignty (ICISS) was established by the Canadian government in September 2000 to respond to the challenge.

13. Along with the more recent memory of Rwanda and Bosnia, where Canadian Forces were neutered witnesses to atrocities.

14. See Minutes of Prime Minister's War Conference, Melbourne, June 1, 1942, 2.

15. First publicly stated by President Richard Nixon in Guam on July 25, 1969.

16. Even here, General Douglas MacArthur made it clear that the United States was assisting Australia in defending itself only because it was in U.S. interests to do so.

17. Dwight D. Eisenhower, "Remarks Upon Receiving an Honorary Degree of Laws at Delhi Unversity" (speech, December 11, 1959), www.presidency.ucsb.edu/ws/?pid=11617 (accessed August 5, 2014).

18. Robert Jackson, Chief U.S. Prosecutor, "Opening Address at Nuremberg, The International Military Tribunal, " *Trial of the Major War Criminals before the International Military Tribunal (Blue Series): 14 November 1945 – 1 October 1946*, vol. 2 (Nuremberg: Hein, 1947; reprint, 1995), 154.

19. One of the examples published was by Zelman Cowen, one of my father's junior colleagues, in Sir Zelman Cowen, *A Public Life: The Memoirs of Sir Zelman Cowen* (Carlton: Melbourne University Press, 2006).

20. AUSCANNZUKUS (Australia, Canada, New Zealand, United Kingdom, United States).

21. Kevin Rudd, "Address to the State Zionist Council of Victoria" (speech, October 15, 2002).

22. Philip Flood, *Report of the Inquiry into Australian Intelligence Agencies* (Canberra: Australian Government, 2004), 177.

23. See the chapter by Ian McAllister in this volume on Australian public opinion on the Iraq War.

24. This does not deny that a small number of politicians were foolish in this sense.

25. Wilkie publicly resigned from the Office of National Assessment in 2003 and criticized the intelligence conclusions at the time. See Andrew Wilkie, *Axis of Deceit: The Extraordinary Story of an Australian Whistleblower* (Melbourne: Black Inc., 2004).

26. Former weapons inspector, special adviser to Hans Blix, and senior adviser of the Iraq Survey Group. See Rod Barton, *The Weapons Detective: The Inside Story of Australia's Top Weapons Inspector* (Melbourne: Black Inc., 2006).

27. Former secretary of the Department of Defence, Paul Barratt, "Address on Launching the Real Face of War" (video speech, March 6, 2003).

28. See Alison Broinowski, *Howard's War* (Melbourne: Scribe Publications, 2003).

29. Ramesh Thakur, "Gimmick Exacted a Great Cost from Iraq," *Canberra Times*, April 12, 2013.

30. *Iraq – Its Infrastructure of Concealment, Deception and Intimidation* (more commonly known as the Dodgy Dossier, the Iraq Dossier, or the February Dossier). Also see *Select Committee on Foreign Affairs Ninth Report*, www.parliament.uk.

31. Mohamed ElBaradei, "Statement to the United Nations Security Council. The Status of Nuclear Inspections in Iraq: An Update" (presentation to the United Nations, New York, March 7, 2003), http://edition.cnn.com/2003/US/03/07/sprj.irq.un.transcript.elbaradei/ (accessed August 10, 2014).

32. Bonnie Azab Powell, "U.N. Weapons Inspector Hans Blix Faults Bush Administration for Lack of 'Critical Thinking,' in Iraq," NewsCenter, March 18, 2004, http://berkeley.edu/news/media/releases/2004/03/18_blix.shtml (accessed August 10, 2014).

33. John Howard, *Iraq 2003: A Retrospective* (Sydney: Lowy Institute for International Policy, April 9, 2013), 9.

34. From a statement by George Tenet, then director of central intelligence for the CIA, that intelligence reports of WMDs in Iraq amounted to a "slam dunk" case, as first alleged in Bob Woodward, *Plan of Attack* (New York: Simon & Schuster, 2004).

35. The agency which concluded that Iraq "must have WMDs" as opposed to the Defence Intelligence Organization (DIO), which said it did not. ONA judgments were expressed with greater certainty and fewer qualifications than ones by DIO. Flood, *Report of the Inquiry into Australian Intelligence Agencies*, 176.

36. Howard, *Iraq 2003*.

37. Anne-Marie Slaughter is Professor Emerita of Politics and International Affairs at Princeton University. From 2009–2011, she served as Director of Policy Planning for the U.S. Department of State, the first woman to hold the position.

38. Presidential address to the annual meeting of the American Society of International Law, April 3, 2003.

39. "War Would be Illegal," *Guardian*, March 7, 2003.

40. Shearer's March 1 letter to the *Sydney Morning Herald* set out criteria for the legality of non-U.N.-sanctioned force validity, including proportionality, reasonableness, and transparent motives to advance the wider Charter objectives, "especially" human rights.

41. Lord Goldsmith, "Full Text: Iraq Legal Advice of March 7, 2003," *Guardian*, April 29, 2005.

42. While this might have implied that there had been no contact with Australian government lawyers, I am reliably but confidentially informed that there was "constant interaction" between government lawyers of all three countries.

43. The statement was issued on January 17, 2003, and can be viewed at https://web.archive.org/web/20080828073051/http://www.number-10.gov.uk/output/Page3287.asp (accessed August 10, 2014). Boyce said he had little confidence in the opinion but thought it might give him company in the dock if he were charged with war crimes; Antony Barnett and Martin Bright, "British Military Chief Reveals New Legal Fears Over Iraq War," *Observer*, May 1, 2005.

44. Australian Parliament, House of Representatives, *Hansard*, March 6, 2003, 1255.

45. Bill Campbell QC (first assistant secretary in attorney generals) and Chris Moraitis (a senior legal adviser in the Department of Foreign Affairs and Trade).

46. For example, Robin Cook, leader of the House of Commons and former foreign secretary, who resigned over the war.

47. This position needs some caveats — including his duty to provide certificates of legality for Executive Council decisions. This may have been the reason why Howard did not bring the decision to Federal Executive Council "for ratification" after the governor general asked the attorney general for his legal opinion on the proposed war. See Sampford and Palmer, "The Constitutional Power to Make War. "

48. Ibid.

49. This is discussed at length in Charles Sampford, "Sovereignty and Intervention," in *Human Rights in Theory and Practice*, ed. T. Campbell and B. M. Leiser (London: Ashgate, 2001).

50. Iraq was asking lawyers the day before the invasion if there was any country it could sue. Without the 2002 changes, it would probably have won before the British reached Basra.

51. The change involved restricting Australia's acceptance of the compulsory jurisdiction of the ICJ to those countries that had accepted the same jurisdiction for twelve months. "Australia Launches Anti-War Protests," BBC News, February 14, 2003.

52. "Australia Launches Anti-War Protests," BBC News, February 14, 2003.

53. O'Connor and Vucetic cite several sources for this figure in "Another Mars-Venus Divide?," 534.

54. O'Connor and Vucetic, "Another Mars-Venus Divide?"

55. Ibid.

56. See "The Alastair Campbell Diaries," extracted in the *Guardian*, June 16, 2012.

57. One of the forty-three signatories whom the *Australian* had ignored.

58. See his chapter in this volume

59. Franklin D. Roosevelt, "Day of Infamy" (speech, Washington, December 8, 1941), Records of the United States Senate, SEN 77A-H1(1941). Available at: www. archives.gov/historical-docs/ (accessed August 15, 2014).

60. For example, the dispute in the South China Sea is just the kind of matter that should go to the ICJ, but America's shunning of that court and the use of force means China is much less likely to do so.

61. Malcolm Fraser, "Politics, Independence and the National Interest: The Legacy of Power and How to Achieve a Peaceful Western Pacific," *Arena Journal* 39/40 (2012/2013): 49.

62. William Ransome and Charles Sampford, *Ethics and Socially Responsible Investment: A Philosophical Approach* (London: Ashgate, 2013).

63. See the Iraq Inquiry, www.iraqinquiry.org.uk (accessed August 15, 2014).

11

TAKING THE OFF-RAMP: CANADIAN DIPLOMACY, INTELLIGENCE, AND DECISION-MAKING BEFORE THE IRAQ WAR[1]

Timothy Andrews Sayle

In the lead-up to the Iraq War, and during the early months of the war itself, pundits heaped criticism on Prime Minister Jean Chrétien for not taking a clear position on whether Canada would join the invasion.[2] In retrospect, students of diplomacy and the history of international relations will surely find this criticism bizarre. Rare are the politicians and diplomat-ists who make rigid pronouncements amidst chaos, or stick to positions despite changing facts and analysis, or purposefully paint themselves into a corner. Chrétien's ambiguity over Canada's potential participation in the invasion was a conscious strategy for dealing with the uncertainty over the international community's support for the invasion of Iraq.

Chrétien recognized early that Canada needed an off-ramp in case the United States — so clearly determined on war with Iraq — failed to gain an international consensus for invasion. He began paving Canada's potential exit early and explicitly, telling both President George W. Bush and Prime Minister Tony Blair in 2002 that Canada would support military action against Iraq only if the international community was convinced invasion was necessary. By basing his test of support on overwhelming international approval — and not ruling out Canadian participation — Chrétien ensured that Canada remained a relevant player in pre-war international diplomacy, and left open the road for Canadian participation in an allied operation without United Nations sanction. Canada, after all, had participated in the 1999 bombing of Kosovo without a U.N. Security Council resolution approving the use of force. But when, in March 2003, international consensus on Iraq had not been achieved by the eve of war, the prime minister took the exit he had prepared over the previous six months and declared Canada would not participate.

The countdown to the invasion began in the dark days after September 11, 2001 (9/11). Shortly after the attacks, the Canadian ambassador to the United States, Michael Kergin, arrived in Ottawa to brief the government on the ramifications. He described the Manichaean worldview Washington had adopted in the wake of the attack, and warned that Canada must be prepared to deal with a United States whose international outlook was coloured only in black and white. The ambassador reported that Afghanistan would undoubtedly be the first target of the American response, but that American retaliation was not likely to be limited to one country.[3]

Soon after 9/11, Canadian officials noticed that American intelligence reports paid special attention to Iraq. The reports isolated Iraq from lists of other countries and noted Iraq's failure to express sympathy for the Americans.[4] Around the same time, Chrétien was alarmed by a television interview in which U.S. senator Jesse Helms called for an invasion of Iraq.[5] Before long, the American press started reporting on leaked intelligence reports linking Saddam Hussein to al-Qaeda. By January 2002, Kergin was fielding questions from reporters curious if Canada would support an invasion of Iraq.[6]

Over the next few months, it became clear that America was headed for war with Iraq. In August, the clerk of the Privy Council, Alex Himelfarb, sent Chrétien a memorandum stating bluntly, "U.S. action against Iraq to implement regime change is a question of when, not if, using the justification that the Iraqi government is a sponsor of terrorism and a developer of weapons of mass destruction (WMD)." Himelfarb noted the international community was split on the issue. Canadian policy, however, centred on support for the U.N. arms inspectors. Regarding terrorism, Canada would address "the issues of terrorism when clear evidence is available."[7] Both policies suggested a strategy of patience and evidence rather than a rush to war.

Weeks after Himelfarb's warning, Chrétien informed Blair and Bush, separately, of Canada's position on war with Iraq. In September, in Johannesburg, Chrétien told Blair he was uncomfortable with regime change. He warned of the dangers of "getting in to the business of replacing leaders we don't like" without being covered "under the flag of the UN."[8] No country, Chrétien told Blair, could invade Iraq without U.N. authorization. Chrétien did not view military action as simply a continuation of United Nations pressure on Iraq to disarm, but as part of a new American concept of national security that threatened to undermine the international structures Canada had worked to create.[9]

Days after speaking with Blair, Chrétien met with Bush in Detroit. The relationship between the two men was, by all accounts, a friendly one, with good personal chemistry aided by shared interests in baseball and golf.[10] It was strange, however, when the two men met in private for half an hour without the usual retinue of staffers to hear or record their conversation.[11] Later, Chrétien told his officials that he had told Bush he was concerned over the impending invasion of Iraq, and warned that the international community would not accept an invasion of Iraq without credible evidence of weapons of mass destruction. He stressed the importance of the United Nations Security Council to Canada, noting he would require its approval to participate in a war.[12] Chrétien left the meeting highly skeptical of the American evidence that war was necessary.[13]

Chrétien's comments in Detroit came to serve as the speaking points for the Canadian government. Kergin returned to Washington, equipped with the prime minister's position; from now on his standard response to any inquiries on Canada's participation in an invasion would stress the importance of the Security Council. Mel Cappe, Canada's high commissioner to the United Kingdom, told British officials the same thing. There was a certain ambiguity in the position expressed by Chrétien and by the Canadian diplomat. For as Cappe put it to the British, Canada sought agreement among the international community before military action, *preferably* through a Security Council Resolution at the United Nations.[14] Underlying this Canadian position, however, was the prime minister's skepticism of American motives and his worry that American security strategy now emphasized unilateral military intervention.[15]

In the early fall, Bush appeared before the United Nations General Assembly and argued for increased international pressure on Iraq to disarm. A month later, in November 2002, the Security Council passed Resolution 1441, declaring Iraq "in material breach of its obligations" to disarm. The resolution was only agreed upon after intense negotiation, and the negotiation resulted in a contradictory document. It did not directly authorize the use of force, but instead stressed "serious consequences." For those who interpreted this phrase to mean military force, the lack of a time limit resulted in further confusion. In Britain, the ambiguity of 1441 and the looming war caused a rift in the governing Labour caucus and a major crisis for Tony Blair. To assuage his critics and his party, Blair promised to seek a second, less ambiguous, resolution from the Security Council.[16]

The confusion inherent in 1441, and Blair's promise, led to further negotiations in New York. During the negotiations, Chrétien worked the telephones, calling President Vicente Fox of Mexico and President Ricardo Lagos of Chile, both of whose nations were represented on the Security Council. Noticing the stress these men were facing, Chrétien remarked to Minister of Foreign Affairs Bill Graham that although Canada constantly sought a seat on the Security Council, holding a seat was a mixed blessing. At times like this, it would bring enormous pressure like that faced by Mexico and Chile. While free of the Security Council, Canada was able to operate at the United Nations with fewer constraints.

As diplomacy took its meandering course in New York, the United States continued its preparations for war. Members of the Canadian Forces, along with troops from countries who would join the invasion, participated in planning for the invasion at the headquarters of United States Central Command in Florida. But a significant Canadian troop presence in Iraq was a moot point after a January 9, 2003, meeting in Washington between Defence Minister John McCallum and Secretary of Defense Donald Rumsfeld. In the meeting, Rumsfeld made clear he was not seeking Canadian troops for Iraq and preferred Canada to focus on Afghanistan. Neither the Pentagon nor the Office of the Secretary of Defense intimated to the Canadian embassy that they would require Canadian troops in Iraq, or that they were upset when Canada eventually did not send troops.[17] But to suggest, as do political scientist Janice Gross Stein and former chief of staff to the minister of defence, Eugene Lang, that Canada's decision to commit almost two thousand troops to Afghanistan got Canada "off the hook in Iraq" misconstrues the American pressure on Canada in the lead-up to war.[18] There was a strong desire from elements in the Canadian military and Department of National Defence for Canada to participate in the invasion, and they conveyed this to their American counterparts. But it was the White House, not the Pentagon, that sought the Canadian flag and the political cover it granted an invasion.[19] The decision to take a command rotation in Afghanistan alleviated none of the pressure on Canada to publicly support the legitimacy of an invasion of Iraq by committing even a small number of military elements to the invasion.[20]

Immediately following the Rumsfeld-McCallum meeting, McCallum announced that Canada would participate in an invasion of Iraq authorized by the United Nations. If, on the other hand, U.N. authorization was not forthcoming, Canada would still have a choice to make. McCallum's statement put the Canadian position more publicly than Chrétien preferred. The prime minister quickly corrected McCallum, to put the emphasis back on the United Nations, declaring, "On matters of peace and security, the international community must speak and act through the U.N. Security Council."[21] This ambiguous position led to further confusion. The U.S. embassy in Ottawa understood the Canadian position to be a wink and a nod suggesting that Canada would join a coalition even if there were no further United Nations Security Council resolutions.

Why this confusion? And why did Canada insist on such an ambiguous position if it believed so deeply in the role of the United Nations? The answer can be found in the very near past, in 1999, when Canada and its allies in the North Atlantic Treaty Organization launched an air war over Kosovo. The use of force had not been sanctioned by the United Nations because of Chinese and Russian threats to veto any resolution. In 2003, the Canadians were ensuring, through a careful choice of words to the Americans, in press conferences and in the House, that a door be left open for Canadian participation if the Security Council overwhelmingly approved a military action but a Russian or Chinese veto prohibited a resolution.[22] It is by this logic that Chrétien could argue Resolution 1441 did not necessarily need to be augmented by another resolution to authorize an invasion, if everyone could only agree on what it meant. Afterward, the seeming discrepancy between the two situations — Kosovo and Iraq — was a point of criticism made by many, including American ambassador to Canada Paul Cellucci.[23] But as David Anderson, who sat in the Cabinet during both decisions, noted, the "difference was primarily that the international community was simply much more coherent on the Kosovo issue."[24] Both in public statements and in private, Canadian officials never ruled out Canada's participation and support of an invasion, even without a resolution. It was not the technicalities of a resolution that mattered as much as the desire for an international consensus that would give the invasion legitimacy.

By early 2003, it was clear just how incoherent the international community had become. Toward the end of January, Blair called Chrétien to tell him a further resolution was going to pass in the Security Council and that Canada should lend it moral support. Canada's permanent representative to the United Nations, Paul Heinbecker, who was in frequent telephone contact with Chrétien from late January until mid-March, told him Blair was wrong and the British and Americans would not get a second resolution authorizing war. Heinbecker, from New York, told Chrétien, "People here just don't believe they've made the case."[25]

On January 30, Bill Graham met with Colin Powell in Washington, and Powell previewed some of the evidence he would present to the Security Council the following week. In another frank discussion, Graham told Powell that war would "be a terrible problem for the United States and for everybody" and warned that the United States risked appearing as an occupier. Powell disagreed, saying, "This will be all over quickly." He told Graham a resolution was a good thing, but should be achieved before February. Graham got the clear impression Powell and the Americans had already made up their minds.[26] In the press conference that followed, Graham insisted four times that Canada would want any war with Iraq to be sanctioned by the United Nations.[27]

Graham's repeated reference to the United Nations reflected Canadian public thinking on the issue. Two days after Graham's meeting with Powell, an Ipsos Reid poll found 36 percent of Canadians against war altogether, with 46 percent supporting war only with U.N. backing. A mere 10 percent of Canadians supported military action without the backing of the United Nations.[28] Nonetheless, the government was willing, at least publicly, to entertain the idea of supporting an invasion with Security Council approval but without a resolution. For Cappe in London, it seemed that by remaining somewhat ambivalent and ambiguous, the Canadians forced the Americans to take them seriously as a potential partner. This ensured

Canada would be listened to in New York and Washington while negotiations on a further U.N. resolution continued.[29]

On January 27, Hans Blix, chairman of the United Nations' weapons inspection commission, reported to the Council that "Iraq appears not to have come to a genuine acceptance … of the disarmament which was demanded of it." This rebuke had a double-edged effect, spurring the Iraqis to increase co-operation while the United States held up Blix's comments as independent verification of their claims that Saddam would not disarm.[30]

The next week, on February 5, Powell appeared before the Council and presented a number of photos and sound recordings to illustrate the threat posed by Saddam. Powell's presentation, according to Heinbecker, "was a load of crap, the best case that could be pieced together, but evidently full of problems and inconsistent in several cases with what the U.N. had reported from the ground." Photos of a fighter jet spraying poison gas were dated from the war against Iran. Satellite photos purporting to show chemical-weapons sites, later disproved, were "pretty evidently bogus at the time," while accounts of intercepted conversations were so unspecific "they could be taken to mean almost anything." Heinbecker was astonished that this was the best the Americans had to offer, and felt few were persuaded.[31]

Canadian officials had their own reason to question the intelligence presented by Powell. They had access to the same information and had already found it wanting. In autumn 2002, Bush had offered to send intelligence experts to Ottawa to brief the prime minister, and later offered to come and brief Chrétien personally. Chrétien and his advisers agreed that it would be particularly uncomfortable to dispute the president's evidence in person, and decided information should be passed to Canada through regular intelligence-sharing channels.

Eddie Goldenberg recalls that intelligence was not a factor in the Canadian decision on Iraq.[32] Intriguingly, however, it seems that Canadian intelligence officials made a highly successful analysis of the Iraqi weapons program. During the lead-up to the war, the International Assessments Staff (IAS) in the Privy Council Office (PCO) served as the intelligence assessment branch for both Foreign Affairs and the PCO. Through its established links with other intelligence communities, the IAS received large quantities of information on supposed Iraqi weapons programs, including the intelligence behind Tony Blair's claim that Iraq had weapons of mass destruction that could be deployed in forty-five minutes. The Canadians also received intelligence passed along from the Iraqi defector "Curveball," the informant responsible for Colin Powell's claims of mobile weapons-production vehicles. Despite the amount of circumstantial or indirect intelligence reporting that suggested an active WMD program, the lack of any direct intelligence led the IAS to assess repeatedly that there was no evidence Iraq had an active WMD program, or had developed the necessary delivery capacity.[33]

Perhaps one of the most important pieces of intelligence collected by the Canadian government did not concern the working of Saddam Hussein's government, but the Bush administration. In the months before the war, the intelligence liaison officer at the Canadian embassy in Washington received regular briefings from the Central Intelligence Agency but was also made aware of frustrations in the American intelligence community. As a result, the Canadians were aware the CIA was under political pressure to produce information confirming Saddam Hussein's arsenal, and knew a debate over the accuracy of the American intelligence was raging secretly in Washington.[34]

Nonetheless, the Americans had presented their intelligence at the Security Council, and Powell was continuing efforts at the United Nations as Canada wished. Heinbecker, in New York, knew no compromise was possible between the hard positions of yes or no on war. But if the decision-making was elongated in time, with Iraq facing a set timeline and a simple pass-or-fail disarmament test, he thought agreement might be reached at the Security Council. This was the next logical step in a series of resolutions that had increasingly turned up the heat on Iraq. The Canadian plan could have assured the Americans, as Heinbecker later put it, that "the diplomatic process wasn't going to last forever, and the Europeans and the rest of the international community would have the assurance that it wasn't going to be straight off to war."[35] Chrétien backed Heinbecker's plan. In his memoir, he explains that if the negotiators could agree on a six- to eight-week delay, he hoped to have forced American military planners to delay their plans and give "everyone more time to work out a diplomatic solution."[36]

In a bid to support this diplomatic effort, Chrétien told the Chicago Council on Foreign Relations that "if it must come to war, I argue that the world should respond through the United Nations." Chrétien commended Bush for approaching the United Nations in the fall of 2002 and urged the

United States not to give up on the world body. "The long-term interests of the United States," suggested Chrétien, "will be better served by acting through the United Nations than by acting alone."[37] Chrétien followed up his speech with calls to world leaders seeking their support for a compromise position at the United Nations.

On February 19, Heinbecker brought the Canadian compromise position before the Security Council. He suggested the Security Council direct Hans Blix to establish a list of "key remaining disarmament tasks," in order of urgency, and to present the list to Iraq with a deadline for compliance.[38] In the days following Heinbecker's speech, Graham took the floor in the House of Commons to explain Canada was working at the United Nations "to avert war by clarifying the situation."[39] Canada, Graham said, had two objectives: First, by suggesting a resolution with a timeframe, the international community could communicate to Saddam Hussein that his failure to comply could not drag on any further. Second, the Canadian proposition reminded the international community that a U.N. solution was possible and desirable.[40]

Back at the United Nations, on February 24, Heinbecker circulated a discussion paper intended to "close the gap between the radical French position and that of the Americans."[41] The Americans, initially silent on the Canadian proposal, expressed their disapproval when it became obvious it would divert votes from a new American-drafted resolution.[42] The next day the United States, United Kingdom, and Spain introduced a draft resolution stating, "Iraq has failed to take the final opportunity afforded to it in Resolution 1441."[43] The draft was abandoned when it became clear it would not receive the necessary votes in the Security Council.

From Ottawa, Prime Minister Chrétien maintained telephone contact with Lagos and Fox. Both men were under pressure from the United States to join the coalition, but they told Chrétien that they would not participate if Canada refused.[44] Decision time was looming for all nations involved, but Chrétien maintained in the House of Commons that the best means of achieving peace was "working discreetly and effectively, as our ambassador to the United Nations is doing."[45] Heinbecker continued to work the backrooms and corridors of the United Nations, seeking a compromise. In the Security Council, he warned that precipitate action risked undermining both international law and the institution of the Council. Rather than six weeks, Heinbecker shortened the suggested deadline for Iraqi compliance to three weeks. By compromising on a resolution, Heinbecker told the Council, "disarmament of Iraq can be had without a shot being fired."[46]

The Canadian delegation opted not to try to apply direct pressure on the Americans to accept the compromise, for Heinbecker was sure the Americans would ignore a Canadian appeal that advised a compromise. The only chance was through the gathered strength of countries that agreed with Canada. Canada had recently served on the Security Council and was familiar with its politics. The Canadian delegation did generate some momentum for a compromise, helped particularly by the British delegation, frantic to reach a rapprochement between the French and American positions.[47] Besides the British, Heinbecker recalls, there were even "some Americans who hoped for compromise that might avoid a potentially fateful adventure that lacked international sanction."[48]

The Canadian position might have succeeded by two means. If the French had accepted the compromise, the British would also have had to accept and the Americans would have had to commit to the compromise or face war without the support of their closest ally. If Washington had agreed to the compromise, the French would have lost all basis for complaint.[49] Heinbecker believed that the idea was sound, but that the Americans had already made their decision for war, stating, "War was not the final recourse for them." Despite Chrétien's backing, Heinbecker had little expectation of success, but the consequences of failure to reach an agreement were so obvious that a full effort was justified.[50]

The Canadians were disappointed, but not surprised, when White House spokesman Ari Fleischer dismissed the Canadian compromise, and a similar Chilean one, as a "non-starter."[51] The Americans were careful not to appear too ham-handed, however, and did not go far in opposing the Canadian idea publicly. It appeared to Kergin in Washington that the United States had taken a calculated look at the positions in the Security Council and realized the French were too far committed to an anti-war position to agree to a resolution that allowed the possible use of force.[52] A lack of French support eliminated hope for the compromise.[53] It is striking, however, that one of the results of the Canadian compromise position could have resulted in U.N. approval for war. This would have placed Chrétien in a much more difficult political position at home.

Canadians, in the aggregate, were strongly against war in Iraq. There had been large rallies in Canadian cities during the diplomacy at the United Nations. Once again, on March 15, large protests swept provincial capitals, Ottawa, and smaller cities. Over two hundred thousand protesters took to the street in Montreal. In Vancouver, there were ten thousand protesters, five thousand in Toronto, two thousand in London, 1,500 in Ottawa, and hundreds in Edmonton, Winnipeg, and Halifax.[54] In contrast, a few Canadians, including several provincial premiers and business lobbyists, fretted Canadian failure to comply with the United States would adversely affect Canadian trade. Overall, however, neither Kergin in Washington nor Anderson, Graham, or Goldenberg in Ottawa saw serious evidence the Americans would retaliate.

Despite this outpouring of public opinion, the Canadian government never attributed any of its decisions to the demands of public opinion. According to David Anderson, demonstrations are only taken into account by a Cabinet if the demonstrations "confirm an existing position or are a real surprise." When they do confirm a position, they are a political boon to a government.[55] It is for this reason, perhaps, that the Cabinet or the prime minister's office spent little time discussing how their decisions might impact Quebec politics.[56] Had Heinbecker's compromise been achieved at the Security Council, discussions in Ottawa would no doubt have revolved entirely around *la belle province*.

After months of diplomacy, the Americans and British clumsily abandoned the United Nations. On March 15 and 16, while the leaders of Spain, Portugal, Britain, and the United States met in the Azores, the British made a last unsuccessful effort to convince the Security Council to adopt a new resolution authorizing force. Hans Blix would later write that by March 16 his inspection was operating at full strength, and "Iraq seemed determined to give [UNMOVIC (United Nations Monitoring, Verification and Inspection Commission)] prompt access everywhere." That same day, he took a call from a United States diplomat urging the expeditious withdrawal of Blix's inspectors from Iraq.[57] War was imminent.

On March 17, a morning telephone call from the British government put a pointed request to Ottawa.[58] The British call, in fact, put four questions to the government, including whether Canada would provide political or military support for the invasion and if Canada would make its assistance public.[59]

Immediately, Heinbecker was telephoned in New York, and he reported that no U.N. resolution authorizing the use of force would succeed. Chrétien, his foreign policy adviser Claude Laverdure, Goldenberg, and Heinbecker were all opposed to supporting an invasion.[60] In Chrétien's office, Goldenberg insisted the prime minister make his response in the House of Commons before informing Cellucci or any other foreign government. The British and American delegations in Ottawa were informed at noon that the prime minister would provide an answer to the British questions in the House around 2:15 that afternoon. By the time Chrétien spoke, the Cable News Network (CNN), which had been informed that breaking news was about to be made, broadcast Question Period live.[61] Chrétien stood in the House and announced, "If military action proceeds without a new resolution of the Security Council, Canada will not participate." His remarks were met with loud cheers and an ovation from his ministers and backbenchers — all live on American television.[62] Afterward, a Canadian official informed the British and American embassies that Canada appreciated their nations' efforts at the United Nations, and that although the terror of 9/11 was still fresh in the minds of Canadians, Canada would not participate in the invasion of Iraq.

The decision not to inform the Americans ahead of time but to let them hear of it in Chrétien's remarks to the House of Commons created an undiplomatic spectacle in the House later regretted by some. Kergin, who believed the courtesy of a communiqué should have been extended to the United States, says the decision resulted in some unnecessary bad will. The difficulties derived more from a lack of acceptable practice than from the substance of the decision.[63] Later comments from Chrétien and his staffers further distanced Bush from Chrétien. Bush cancelled a state visit planned for May 2003, and at the end of that month, Bush's national security adviser, Condoleezza Rice, called Laverdure to tell him the two leaders' relationship was "irreparably broken."[64]

Chrétien's decision not to participate was hardly the end of the story. One Cabinet member asked her colleagues, "What if [the Americans] find WMDs?" No one could answer her question, and a tense wait followed Chrétien's decision to abstain from the coalition.[65] While the ground assault against Iraq unfolded rapidly with early success, the Canadian as well as French and German governments were uneasy. They continued to privately pressure the British on their claims of the reputed weapons of mass destruction.[66] It would be months before the Canadians had the grim satisfaction of knowing they had made a wise choice.

The war in Iraq left behind a number of shattered reputations and careers of American public servants. The American ambassador to Canada, Paul Cellucci, is surely one. Cellucci had not taken care to cultivate close relationships with a broad cross-section of officials in Ottawa, and isolated himself from senior Canadian political advisers.[67] He seems to have largely ignored the possibility that Canada would not participate in the invasion, and interpreted Canada's ambiguous position without nuance.[68] The American mission in Ottawa, it seems, was too wrapped up in stories of discord within the Liberal Party to realize Chrétien would make the decision virtually alone. Still, it had been clear to some in Washington that Canada would not participate barring Security Council approval, and Bush's chief of staff, Andrew Card, told Chrétien, "You told us right from the beginning what you intended to do.... We should have believed you."[69]

Following the invasion, Kergin directed Canadian consulates to study whether anything had changed in U.S.-Canada business relations. Although some individual consumers made choices designed to spite Canada, including refusal to buy Canadian maple syrup, there was no large-scale punishment meted out and no major contracts lost. The study determined that there was no economic consequence to Canada's decision.[70] In November 2004, Graham gave a speech to the Chicago Council on Foreign Relations, and his audience, during the Q&A afterward, suggested two reasons Canada was insulated from an economic backlash: First, Canada had made its decision without what was perceived as the self-righteous attitude of the French. Second, the American business community had significant investments in Canada and the notion that Americans could punish Canadian businesses without harming themselves was a chimera. It was clear to Graham that economic integration worked in Canada's favour.[71] The economic data confirm that there were no significant changes to Canada's economic position vis-à-vis the United States. In 2003, Canada's merchandise trade balance with the United States was at the lowest point of a decline that had begun in 2001. Following Canada's refusal to join the invasion, the Canadian trade balance actually improved.[72] American foreign direct investment in Canada, which had steadily increased since the 1990s, continued to grow after the Iraq invasion.[73]

The overwhelming difference in the Canadian decision-making process and that of the United States and the United Kingdom was the point at which war became a legitimate instrument of foreign policy. Publicly, the Canadian government continued to suggest that that point had simply not yet arrived, though it admitted such a time might come.

Still, it is possible to see how things might have turned sour for Canada, and quickly, on two fronts. First, what if Canada's United Nations proposals had been accepted, the Iraqis had not complied, and force was used? This would not have changed the fact that there were no weapons of mass destruction in Iraq, and might have had worse consequences for a United Nations that sanctioned an invasion. The domestic political crisis for Chrétien would have been profound, though it is difficult to gauge against the crises that soon ended his premiership. Second is the matter of intelligence analysis and its use in policy. That Canadian intelligence analysis lined up closely with the instincts of the prime minister is much more a matter of coincidence than correlation, let alone causation. What if the prime minister of the day had been more deeply concerned by the possible effects of disagreement with the United States? Might Canada have then ended up in the position of the United Kingdom, the United States, and Australia, whose governments, with the same intelligence, had come to employ it in very different ways?

Nonetheless, these two potential disasters only highlight what was saved by Chrétien's decision. They pale, furthermore, in contrast with the horrific costs in treasure and blood the war could have cost Canadians. Overall, the prime minister's appreciation of the situation, made so early, resulted from what his colleagues describe as an uncanny intuition. It stemmed from his ability to see through the flattery and cajolery of the United States; to understand that the Americans had not proven their case; and largely, as one Cabinet member put it, because "it offended every nerve in his body."[74] Both Graham and Anderson identify the unquantifiable "shrewdness" of Chrétien as the major factor behind his decision.[75] Chrétien anticipated Canadian political opinion on the topic but made his decision long before demonstrators had taken to the streets. He knew instinctively that the American evidence was insufficient to "convince any judge in a rural courthouse" before Canadian intelligence analysts came to the same conclusion.[76]

Of course, the official historical record of the Canadian decision — that which was written down, anyhow — is still sealed tightly in the sepulchre of archives. When it is released, the documents might show this to be the rarest of diplomatic events, when public opinion and a nation's leader, intelligence analysis and crass politicking, moral judgment and expediency were most neatly aligned. But this righteousness did not — and could not — prevent the invasion and the bloody war that followed. This realization surely tempers any sense of satisfaction and raises worrying questions about Canada's place in the major decisions of war and peace in the twenty-first century.

NOTES

1. An earlier version of this paper appeared as "But He Has Nothing On At All: Canada and the Iraq War, 2003," *Canadian Military History* 19, no. 3 (2010): 5–19. I am indebted to the interviewees, cited in this chapter, who agreed to be quoted for this essay.

2. Rick Fawn outlines much of this criticism, and contributes to it himself, in "No Consensus with the Commonwealth, No Consensus with Itself? Canada and the Iraq War," *Round Table: The Commonwealth Journal of International Affairs* 97, no. 397 (2008): 519–33.

3. Michael Kergin (ambassador to the United States, 2000–05), interview with the author, Toronto, April 10, 2008.

4. Greg Fyffe (executive director, international assessment staff, Privy Council Office, 2000–08), interview with the author, Toronto, March 31, 2008.

5. Jean Chrétien, *My Years as Prime Minister* (Toronto: Alfred A. Knopf Canada, 2007), 306.

6. Kergin, interview with the author.

7. Chrétien, *My Years as Prime Minister*, 307.

8. Ibid., 307–08.

9. Eddie Goldenberg, *The Way It Works: Inside Ottawa* (Toronto: McClelland & Stewart, 2007), 289.

10. Chrétien, *My Years as Prime Minister*, 310; Paul Cellucci, *Unquiet Diplomacy* (Toronto: Key Porter Books, 2007), 122; and Goldenberg, *The Way It Works*, 285.

11. Goldenberg, *The Way It Works*, 286–87.

12. Kergin, interview with the author.

13. Goldenberg, *The Way It Works*, 286–87.

14. Mel Cappe (high commissioner to the United Kingdom, 2002–06), interview with the author via telephone, March 14, 2008.

15. Goldenberg, *The Way It Works*, 289.

16. Resolution 1441 (2002), United Nations Security Council, November 8, 2002, www.un.org/depts/unmovic/new/documents/resolutions/s-res-1441.pdf (accessed August 15, 2014); Philip H. Gordon and Jeremy Shapiro, *Allies at War: America, Europe and the Crisis Over Iraq* (Toronto: McGraw-Hill, 2004); and David M. Malone, *The International Struggle Over Iraq: Politics in the UN Security Council 1980–2005* (New York: Oxford University Press, 2007), 196.

17. Michael Kergin, interview with the author. See also Rob McRae, "International Policy Reviews in Perspective," in *Canada Among Nations 2004: Setting Priorities Straight*, ed. Fen Osler Hampson, Norman Hillmer, and David Carment (Montreal: McGill-Queen's University Press, 2005), 63.

18. Janice Gross Stein and Eugene Lang, *The Unexpected War: Canada in Kandahar* (Toronto: Viking Canada, 2007), 71.

19. Bill Graham (minister of foreign affairs, 2002–04), interview with the author, Toronto, February 20, 2008.

20. This should also put the WikiLeaks "scoop" of a purported Canadian promise to aid the invasion of Iraq in perspective. Consider, too, the deep chasm between the headline and the facts reported in this article: Greg Weston, "WESTON: Canada Offered to Aid Iraq Invasion: WikiLeaks," *CBC News*, May 15, 2011.

21. "Liberal Dissent, Confusion Brewing Over Iraq Crisis, Star Reports," *Canadian Press NewsWire*, January 14, 2003. Available online at *Canadian Business & Current Affairs* index (hereafter *CBCA*).

22. Goldenberg, *The Way It Works*, 296.

23. Cellucci, *Unquiet Diplomacy*, 146.

24. David Anderson (minister of the environment, 1999–2004), interview with the author via telephone, March 11, 2008.

25. Paul Heinbecker (ambassador to the United Nations, 2000–04), interview with the author via telephone, March 17, 2008.

26. Graham, interview with the author.

27. Robert Russo, "Powell Briefs Graham on Decisive February 5 Speech at UN on Disarming Iraq," *Canadian Press NewsWire*, January 31, 2003, in *CBCA*.

28. Donald McKenzie, "Ten Percent of Canadians Support Unilateral Strike Against Iraq: Poll," *Canadian Press NewsWire*, February 2, 2003, in *CBCA*.

29. Cappe, interview with the author.

30. Malone, *International Struggle Over Iraq*, 197.

31. Heinbecker, interview with the author.

32. Eddie Goldenberg (senior policy adviser to the prime minister, 1993–2003), interview with the author, Toronto, May 7, 2007.

33. Fyffe, interview with the author.

34. Ibid.

35. Heinbecker, interview with the author.

36. Chrétien, *My Years as Prime Minister*, 313–14.

37. Jean Chrétien, "Notes for an Address by Prime Minister Jean Chrétien to the Chicago Council on Foreign Relations" (speech, Chicago, February 13, 2003), http://epe.lac-bac.gc.ca/100/205/301/prime_minister-ef/jean_chretien/2003-12-08/stagingpm_3a8080/default.asp@language=e&page=newsroom&sub=speeches&doc=chicago.20030213_e.htm (accessed August 15, 2014).

38. Minutes of the 4709th meeting of the United Nations Security Council, February 19, 2003: 28; available at: www.un.org/documents/.

39. Canada, Parliament, House of Commons, *Debates,* vol. 138, February 20, 2003, www.parl.gc.ca/HousePublications/Publication aspx?Language=E&Mode=1&Parl=37&Ses=2&DocId=718653 (accessed August 14, 2014).

40. Ibid., February 21, 2003, www.parl.gc.ca/HousePublications/Publication.aspx?Language=E&Mode=1&Parl=37&Ses=2&DocId=721909 (accessed August 14, 2014).

41. "Text of Canadian Discussion Paper on Iraq That Canada's UN Ambassador Circulated This Week," *Canadian Press NewsWire,* February 27, 2003, in *CBCA.* Quote is Graham's, in Canada, Parliament, House of Commons, *Debates,* vol. 138, February 27, 2003, www.parl.gc.ca/HousePublications/Publication.aspx?Language=E&Mode=1&Parl=37&Ses=2&DocId=740924 (accessed August 14, 2014).

42. Robert Russo, "Wary Bush Says Canadian Proposal on Iraq Gives Saddam Too Much Time," *Canadian Press NewsWire,* February 26, 2003.

43. Malone, *International Struggle Over Iraq,* 198–99.

44. Chrétien, *My Years as Prime Minister,* 313–14.

45. Canada, Parliament, House of Commons, *Debates,* vol. 138, February 25, 2003, www.parl.gc.ca/HousePublications/Publication.aspx?Language=E&Mode=1&Parl=37&Ses=2&DocId=730546 (accessed August 14, 2014).

46. Minutes of the 4717th meeting of the United Nations Security Council, March 11, 2003, 19–20.

47. Malone, *International Struggle Over Iraq,* 199.

48. Heinbecker, interview with the author.

49. Gordon and Shapiro, *Allies at War,* 153.

50. Heinbecker, interview with the author.

51. Gordon and Shapiro, *Allies at War,* 153.

52. Kergin, interview with the author.

53. Malone, *International Struggle Over Iraq,* 199.

54. Arpon Basu, "Some 200,000 People in Montreal Join Countrywide Protests Against War in Iraq," March 15, 2003, and "1,250 Turn Out in Edm, Winnipeg, Vancouver for Vigils to Oppose Iraqi War," March 17, 2003, both in *Canadian Press NewsWire,* in *CBCA.*

55. Anderson, interview with the author.

56. Goldenberg, *The Way It Works,* 297; and Eddie Goldenberg, email message to author, June 2, 2008.

57. Hans Blix, *Disarming Iraq* (New York: Pantheon, 2004), 3–6.

58. Goldenberg, interview with the author.

59. The questions are recounted in Goldenberg, *The Way It Works*, 1.

60. Goldenberg, *The Way It Works*, 2–4.

61. Goldenberg, interview with the author.

62. Canada, Parliament, House of Commons, *Debates,* vol. 138, March 17, 2003, www.parl.gc.ca/HousePublications/Publication.aspx?Pub=Hansard&Mee=71&Language=e&Parl=37&Ses=2 (accessed August 14, 2014).

63. Kergin, interview with the author.

64. Goldenberg, *The Way It Works*, 307.

65. Goldenberg, interview with the author.

66. Peter Stothard, *30 Days: A Month at the Heart of Blair's War* (London: HarperCollins, 2003), 199–207.

67. Goldenberg, interview with the author.

68. This inability to distinguish between a second U.N. Security Council resolution and international consensus — perhaps without a Security Council resolution — is also evident in Rick Fawn, "No Consensus with the Commonwealth, No Consensus with Itself? Canada and the Iraq War," *The Round Table* 97, no. 397 (2008): 519.

69. Chrétien, *My Years as Prime Minister,* 315.

70. Kergin, interview with the author.

71. Graham, interview with the author.

72. Chart 20.2, "Merchandise Trade Balance," in *Canada Year Book: Official Statistical Annual of the Resources, History, Institutions and Social and Economic Conditions of Canada* (Ottawa: Statistics Canada, 2009), 238.

73. Ibid.; and "International Investment Position, Canadian Direct Investment Abroad and Foreign Direct Investment in Canada, by Country, Annual (Dollars)," CANSIM Table 376-0051, excerpt in Department of Foreign Affairs and International Trade, "Foreign Direct Investment Statistics," www.international.gc.ca/economist-economiste/statistics-statistiques/investments-investissements.aspx (accessed July 12, 2010).

74. Anderson, interview with the author. Consider, for example, Chrétien's previous position against war in Iraq in 1991.

75. Graham, interview with the author; and Anderson, interview with the author.

76. Goldenberg, *The Way It Works*, 287.

12

TOUJOURS LA POLITESSE? THE "IMPOLITE NO" ON IRAQ IN HISTORICAL PERSPECTIVE

Kim Richard Nossal

INTRODUCTION

The decision of Jean Chrétien's Liberal government to decline to participate in the coalition of the willing, put together by the U.S. administration
of George W. Bush in March 2003, provides us with an excellent opportunity to assess some of the established verities in Canadian-American
relations about the role of power in the relationship and the consequences
for Canada of saying no to the United States on important strategic issues.

My purpose in this chapter is to question one of the common assumptions in the practice and culture of Canadian-American relations: that
when Canadian governments decide that it is in Canada's interest not to
join the United States in a global national-security initiative in which
Washington has a deep interest, the reaction of the United States will vary
considerably depending on *how* the Canadian government says no. Put
briefly, if the Canadian government says no carefully, politely, and diplomatically, the administration in Washington might not be happy with the
Canadian decision but is unlikely to impose negative costs on Canada or
Canadians by way of retaliation. By contrast, the argument runs, when the
Canadian decision is embraced carelessly, impolitely, or undiplomatically,
the response in the United States is likely to be angrier and more retaliatory.

To assess this argument, I look at two occasions when the Canadian government said no to an American administration on a global security issue that Washington deemed to be important to its interests. The first was the refusal of the Chrétien government to join the coalition of the willing in Iraq in 2003. The second was the refusal of the Progressive Conservative government of Brian Mulroney to accept President Ronald Reagan's invitation to join the Strategic Defense Initiative (SDI) in 1985. As we will see, the SDI decision was widely characterized at the time as a "polite no," and while the Reagan administration was none too happy, there were few significant consequences for Canadian-American relations. By contrast, the decision in 2003 can be characterized as an "impolite no," and the unhappiness of the Bush administration was clear and evident in Washington's response.

In other words, I will show that the conventional wisdom holds in each of these cases. However, when these Canadian refusals are examined in a broader historical perspective, it can be seen that the conventional wisdom holds only for the short term. I will conclude that over the medium and longer term, in those relatively rare cases where the Canadian government chooses to refuse an American request for co-operation on a global security matter, it makes very little difference to the relationship whether the refusal is delivered politely or impolitely.

CHRÉTIEN'S "NO" ON IRAQ

It was clear in the fall of 2002 that the Bush administration was resolved to seek regime change in Iraq. The elimination of the Saddam Hussein regime had been official policy since the Iraq Liberation Act was passed during the administration of Bill Clinton in 1998, and the Republican Party had embraced the "full implementation" of that act's regime-change provisions in its 2000 election platform. The real acceleration, however, occurred in the fall of 2002, beginning with Bush's speech to the United Nations General Assembly on September 12.[1] The momentum for war gathered steam in the weeks thereafter, with the decision of the Security Council to find Iraq in material breach of earlier U.N. resolutions, particularly over the issue of weapons of mass destruction, and the announcement by Bush on November 20 at the NATO summit in Prague that the United States would "lead a coalition of the willing" to disarm Iraq if Saddam Hussein chose not to disarm.[2] It was the search by the United States for political and material support among its allies for its more aggressive policy toward Iraq that posed a considerable challenge to the Chrétien government. For, as the chapters by Timothy Sayle, John English, and Jack Cunningham detail, the Chrétien government's decisions on Iraq were being framed in a domestic context of widespread opposition to the Bush administration's approach to Iraq.

Chrétien had been advised by Alex Himelfarb, the clerk of the Privy Council, as early as August 14, 2002, that "U.S. action against Iraq to implement regime change is a question of when, not if, using the justification that the Iraqi government is a sponsor of terrorism and a developer of weapons of mass destruction." Himelfarb had advised the prime minister that the United States would be seeking allied support "as soon as the end of August."[3]

The initial approach came on September 9, when Chrétien and Bush met in Detroit to announce new security measures at the Ambassador Bridge. In a private meeting that was held without any advisers present, Bush pressed Chrétien for support; for his part, the prime minister told Bush that Canada would participate in military action against Iraq only if the international community — in the form of the United Nations — approved it. And, he suggested to Bush, the international community would need convincing evidence of weapons of mass destruction before giving such approval.[4]

Over the course of the fall, the U.S. government would press, publicly and privately, for Canadian support for a forceful approach to Iraq. For example, on November 14, 2002, the U.S. secretary of state, Colin Powell, met with Canada's foreign affairs minister, Bill Graham, to express the hope that Canada would be part of a "like-minded coalition."[5] The next day, a U.S. *démarche* requested Canadian officers be assigned to assess what contributions Canadian Forces could make to Operation Iraqi Freedom.[6]

The Cabinet took approximately three weeks to consider the U.S. request, eventually approving the travel of officers to Central Command (CENTCOM) headquarters in Tampa, Florida, in early December. This was followed by a briefing to the minister of national defence on December 15, 2002, which contained only the recommendation that the Canadian military continue to hold discussions with its U.S. counterparts on planning.[7] Documents obtained under Access to Information legislation suggest that among the proposals was the offer of six hundred to eight hundred troops, including infantry from the Royal Canadian Regiment and armour from the Royal Canadian Dragoons.[8] However, this proposal did not have the approval of Cabinet, and was probably, according to at least one military source, the result of a mid-level military planner "freelancing."[9]

Although by December 2002, Canadian officers were engaged with their U.S. counterparts at CENTCOM in planning for an invasion of Iraq, the Chrétien government was pursuing a policy of purposeful ambiguity on the issue of what Canada was actually planning to do. On the one hand, government ministers, including the prime minister himself, implied that if there were a Security Council resolution authorizing the use of force, Canada might participate. This was, by most accounts, the decision made in a Cabinet meeting in January 2003.[10]

Thus, when the minister of national defence, John McCallum, was asked by reporters in Washington about Canadian policy following a meeting with Donald Rumsfeld, the U.S. secretary of defense, on January 9, McCallum simply articulated that Cabinet decision. As he put it to reporters, "If ... the Security Council authorizes the use of force, then Canada will definitely be part of that military group." However, if there were no Security Council resolution, or if the situation were what he called "grey or murky," then Canada would decide at that time whether to join a coalition of the willing. As he noted, "We much prefer [a U.N. mandate] but we may do it [contribute militarily] otherwise."[11] This indeed was the government's policy, at least in January 2003, but, as Janice Gross Stein and Eugene Lang note, "no one in the government had articulated the Canadian position quite this clearly before."[12]

McCallum's remarks in Washington sparked considerable criticism in Ottawa, most notably from Liberal backbenchers. Carolyn Parrish (Mississauga Centre) went on record saying, "I can't believe that McCallum is down in Washington farting around like this, making stupid statements," and threatened to quit the Liberal caucus and run as an independent in the next election.[13] The Liberal chair of the House of Commons Standing Committee on Foreign Affairs, Bernard Patry, likewise criticized the minister for going "too far."[14] And, most importantly, Chrétien himself upbraided McCallum publicly, claiming that he was answering a "hypothetical" question "that he ha[d] reflected upon and corrected since that time." McCallum himself backpedalled swiftly: "If there is one thing that I learned last week, it is the danger of answering hypothetical questions and speculation. Of course I don't disagree with the Prime Minister."[15]

On the other hand, the government kept its options open, never entirely closing the door to participation. For example, even when Chrétien was chastising McCallum for his Washington remarks, "he pointedly drew attention to the Kosovo example," when Canada had joined the United States and its NATO allies in using force against Serbia in 1999 without U.N. Security Council authorization.[16] Likewise, when Bush telephoned Chrétien briefly on January 22 seeking Canada's political support for the American position, the prime minister remained ambiguous, noting that Canada would support a war only if the United States and Britain "have great evidence ... that Saddam Hussein ... is not following the instructions of the United Nations." Asked the following day if he were worried about failing to support the United States, Chrétien responded that it would all depend on what the U.N. inspectors searching Iraq for WMDs found: "If I have to say no [to the United States], I will. If I have to say yes, I will. We are an independent country." For his part, Minister of Foreign Affairs Bill Graham was no less ambiguous: when asked what Canada would do if the United States invaded Iraq without U.N. approval, Graham responded, "We are in favour of multilateralism, and of course that eliminates the idea of a unilateral attack."[17]

The unwillingness of the prime minister or the minister of foreign affairs to express clearly what was emerging as Canadian policy (unless there were a U.N. Security Council resolution authorizing the use of force against Iraq, Canada would not be part of a U.S.-led force; there would be no "Kosovo cop-out," as Bill Graham would call it ten years on[18]) left considerable confusion in the minds of those observing Canadian policy. As Joe Clark, leader of the Progressive Conservative Party, put it at the end of January, "No one knows where Canada stands. Our allies don't know, our citizens don't know, [Chrétien's] own government doesn't know."[19] This, however, was clearly the government's purpose. And the degree to which this approach succeeded can best be seen by how the English-language press interpreted the prime minister's remarks on January 22 and 23, 2003. On January 24, the headline in the *Globe and Mail* was "PM to Bush: Hold Off On War." In the *Toronto Star*, the headline was "Chrétien Supports

U.S. Push for War," while the *National Post* headline the following day was "PM's War Message a 'Confused Muddle.'"[20]

However, in February, there was growing hesitation in Cabinet about Iraq, even as Canadian Armed Forces officers were increasing their activities in Tampa and Qatar, joining allied counterparts in planning for an invasion.[21] According to one account, Cabinet was not persuaded by Bush's State of the Union address on January 28, or Colin Powell's presentation to the United Nations on February 5, both of which sought to lay out the American case for forceful action against Iraq; the skepticism of some Canadian officials was further fuelled by a refusal by the United States to share the raw intelligence on which the Bush administration was basing its case for military action.[22]

Thus, in February, there were some changes in Canadian policy. First, the government approved a leadership role for the NATO-led International Security Assistance Force (ISAF) in Kabul.[23] Second, Chrétien sought not only to clarify the government's position on the importance it attached to the legitimizing role of Security Council authorization, but also to see if Canada could broker a compromise at the United Nations. The prime minister gave a speech to the Chicago Council on Foreign Relations on February 13, in which he put the case for the multilateral approach to Iraq. Paying tribute to "the leadership that the United States is showing in forcing Saddam Hussein to abide by the resolutions of the United Nations," Chrétien nonetheless expressed caution about the use of force: "But if it must come to war, I argue that the world should respond through the United Nations. This is the best way to give legitimacy to the use of force in these circumstances." And while he agreed that "we must all be concerned about the proliferation of weapons of mass destruction," Chrétien argued that "the long-term interests of the United States [would] be better served by acting through the United Nations than by acting alone."[24]

This rhetorical recommitment to the centrality of the United Nations was accompanied by an effort to broker a compromise at the United Nations itself. Although Canada was not a member of the Security Council, Canada's permanent representative to the United Nations, Paul Heinbecker, sought to secure approval for a resolution that laid out a set of steps that Iraq would have to take by a clear deadline, with authorization for the use of force in the event of non-compliance.[25] However, it was clear that none of the key protagonists in the deadlock on the Security Council were interested in a compromise. The United States in particular regarded the Canadian intervention as not at all helpful,[26] while a cable from the U.S. embassy in Ottawa dated March 3 dismissed it as "too little, too late."[27]

At the same time, the Canadian military's activities in U.S.-led war planning continued to leave the impression with many U.S. officials that the Canadian position articulated in January still held. Indeed, that same March 3 cable reported that James R. Wright, assistant deputy minister for global and security policy in the Department of Foreign Affairs and International Trade, told the U.S. embassy that Canadian policy remained "unchanged — yes if action is endorsed by the Security Council, 'to be determined' if not." Wright urged patience, promising that the Canadian government would decide quickly once the Security Council had acted.[28]

The decision, in fact, came quickly. On March 16, the United States, Britain, and Spain met in the Azores and brought the diplomatic process to an end. According to Eddie Goldenberg's account,[29] on the morning of March 17, Chrétien's foreign affairs adviser, Claude Laverdure, received a communication that had been sent to Foreign Affairs by the British government asking for a Canadian response to four questions: Would Canada provide political support for military action against Iraq? What military capabilities would Canada contribute? Would Canada make its position public? And what support would Canada provide for humanitarian assistance and reconstruction in Iraq? The Canadians were asked for their response by noon, since Bush was planning to deliver his ultimatum to Iraq that evening.

The shortness of time accelerated the process of decision, which was made by Chrétien himself, in consultation with Laverdure, Goldenberg, and Heinbecker by phone from New York. A draft announcement was prepared. McCallum and Graham were summoned to the prime minister's office, where the proposed announcement was read to them, and they were asked for their views.[30] Then Chrétien went into Question Period, where it was expected that Stephen Harper, the leader of the Opposition, would ask a question about Iraq, giving the prime minister an opportunity to make the announcement.

At 2:15 p.m., Chrétien rose in the House of Commons in response to the expected question by Harper:

Mr. Speaker, I want to set out the position of the Government of Canada. We believe that Iraq must fully abide by the resolution of the United Nations Security Council. We have always made clear that Canada would require the approval of the Security Council if we were to participate in a military campaign.

Over the last few weeks the Security Council has been unable to agree on a new resolution authorizing military action. Canada worked very hard to find a compromise to bridge the gap in the Security Council. Unfortunately, we were not successful. If military action proceeds without a new resolution of the Security Council, Canada will not participate.[31]

There was no effort to further justify the decision. No explanation was offered for the apparent inconsistency between Canadian acknowledgements of the dangers posed by a putative WMD-armed Iraq that would warrant the use of force in the case of Security Council authorization,[32] and the decision to stay out of the coalition purely because of a political process in New York. No explanation was offered for why Canada had been willing to use force against Serbia in 1999 without Security Council authorization, but not against Iraq in 2003. No explanation was offered for why members of the Canadian Armed Forces were serving with American forces that were on their way to Iraq, or why Canada continued to command Task Force 151, a multinational naval task force deployed in the Persian Gulf that was designed initially to support Operation Enduring Freedom, but in the event of military action against Iraq would become "dual-tasked," supporting both Enduring Freedom and Operation Iraqi Freedom.[33] No explanation was offered for why the government persistently claimed to be opposed in principle to regime change, but would explicitly say, as Bill Graham did when war broke out, that "we as a government are supportive of the United States' desire to get rid of Saddam Hussein, to deal with weapons of mass destruction.... We wish our American friends and our British friends Godspeed."[34]

While the substance of the decision was not welcomed by the administration in Washington, the major problem was the way in which it was delivered. As Terry Breese, the director of the Office of Canadian Affairs at the State Department from 2003 to 2006, put it, "It wasn't that they [the Canadians] said no, it was the way they said it." The Canadian decision was delivered to the United States in a particularly undiplomatic way. Chrétien ordered that the deputy minister at Foreign Affairs inform the U.S. embassy and the British High Commission in Ottawa that the prime minister would be making an announcement on Iraq at 2:00 p.m., but there was no advance notice given to anyone of the Canadian decision. It was agreed that Claude Laverdure, Chrétien's foreign policy adviser, would put a call through to Condoleezza Rice, Bush's national security adviser, but only as Chrétien was rising to speak in the Commons. In addition, Foreign Affairs was ordered to organize a meeting at the Lester B. Pearson Building for American and British diplomats for a formal meeting after the announcement. Otherwise, there was to be no prior announcement.

The rationales for this departure from normal diplomatic practice underscored the distance that had developed between the Chrétien government and the Bush administration. To be sure, Chrétien notes in his memoirs that he "wanted to inform Parliament and the Canadian people first." However, it is clear from his memoirs that there were other factors at work as well. He noted, for example, that the request for a decision had not even come from the Americans but the British. "The president hadn't called me, so I didn't think I had to call him with my decision."[35] According to the account by Janice Gross Stein and Eugene Lang, Bill Graham wanted to call his counterpart, Colin Powell, or the U.S. ambassador in Ottawa, Paul Cellucci, but "Goldenberg wasn't having it," arguing that it was inappropriate that the U.S. government be informed before the Canadian people.[36] On the other hand, Graham is also on record as having chosen not to call the American ambassador, because, as he put it, "the ambassador from the United States is quite capable of watching Canadian television."[37]

Second, the announcement in the Commons itself was delivered in a way that was guaranteed to anger the U.S. government, if not ordinary Americans. As Chrétien finished his statement, Liberal MPs, joined by MPs from the New Democratic Party and the Bloc Québécois, jumped up to give the prime minister a thunderously joyous standing ovation. The ovation was so long and so joyous — fully twenty-six seconds — that Deputy Prime Minister John Manley became visibly nervous and began to motion members of the Liberal caucus to sit down and stop applauding.[38] Moreover, the U.S. embassy, which had been informed by Foreign Affairs at noon that there would be an important announcement, had alerted

CNN, so the Commons proceedings was carried live on that network and broadcast on other U.S. networks' national newscasts that evening (where it was juxtaposed with news of Bush's address to the nation announcing the ultimatum delivered to Saddam Hussein).

American reactions to both the announcement and its method of delivery were both swift and negative. Certainly, the evident joy in the faces of most Liberal MPs, who clearly did not share the sensibilities of the deputy prime minister, spoke volumes to American officials (and, it is clear, to ordinary Americans) about Canadian attitudes. Moreover, the absence of any prior communication of the decision rankled. As Brian Bow notes in his study of the linkage politics in Canadian-American relations, an official in Washington pointedly remarked, "How hard would it be to make that call? ... This is a clear case of wanting to make a big hit with domestic audiences, and not caring much about how it would ... have an impact in Washington."[39]

However, there was also considerable anger at the decision itself. Perhaps the most clearly angry official was Paul Cellucci, the U.S. ambassador in Ottawa, who had obviously taken seriously the ambiguous signals he was receiving from the prime minister, members of his Cabinet, and other officials of the possibility that, in the end, Canada would participate in some way.[40] After the decision, Cellucci "tore a strip off" Graham personally,[41] but also let it be known in a series of public speeches that the United States was "disappointed" and "upset" with the Canadian government.[42] Likewise, Michael Kergin, the Canadian ambassador in Washington, acknowledged that he received "stiff comments" from administration officials and "outright contemptuous remarks" from members of Congress.[43] Bush's main response to the decision was to cancel an official visit to Canada in May, nominally on the grounds that the war in Iraq was keeping him too busy. However, the time that he was to have been in Ottawa was instead pointedly allocated to a visit from one of the members of the coalition of the willing, John Howard of Australia.[44] In his memoirs, Chrétien downplays the negative reactions of the administration and, for example, spins the cancellation of a state visit by Bush as a mutual decision.[45] But by the end of May, the Bush-Chrétien relationship was, in the words of Condoleezza Rice, "irreparably broken" (though what precipitated the break was not the Iraq decision, but Chrétien's comments about the U.S. deficit[46]).

MULRONEY'S "NO" ON SDI

The decision of the Progressive Conservative government of Brian Mulroney to refuse the Reagan administration's invitation to join the Strategic Defense Initiative suggests an alternative way to say no to the United States. In March 1983, Reagan proposed a system to protect the United States from attack by strategic nuclear ballistic missiles. The Strategic Defense Initiative, immediately dubbed "Star Wars," after the popular film series of the late 1970s and 1980s, was a research and development program designed to create a defensive shield through the deployment of innovative weapons systems deployed on land and in outer space. As the program began to accelerate through 1984, the administration in Washington was keen to counter the objections of the Soviet Union that SDI violated existing arms-control treaties, and one of the ways it sought to do this was by securing the approval of, and participation in, the program by U.S. allies, which would give SDI greater global legitimacy.

Canadian participation was discussed at the summit meeting between Brian Mulroney and Ronald Reagan in March 1985, and the issue, according to Mulroney, "remained high on the agenda" that spring.[47] The first reaction of the newly elected Progressive Conservative government seemed positive — the defence minister, Erik Nielsen, echoed Reagan's claim that SDI would rid the world of the threat of nuclear weapons, and the prime minister spoke glowingly of the thousands of jobs that Canadian participation in SDI would bring.[48]

However, this initial enthusiasm dissipated after a formal invitation was extended by the U.S. secretary of defense, Caspar Weinberger, to Canada to participate in the program on March 26; and opposition emerged, not only within the public more broadly, but also within the Progressive Conservative caucus. Mulroney decided not only to send a senior public servant, Arthur Kroeger, to Washington to report on the implications of Canadian participation, but also to ask the special parliamentary joint committee that had been created to review Canadian foreign policy to offer advice on the issue. The Special Joint Committee on Canada's International Relations, chaired by Jean-Maurice Simard, a Conservative senator from New Brunswick, and Thomas Hockin, the Conservative MP from London West, spent the summer of 1985 holding public hearings across the country.[49]

As Mulroney admitted in his memoirs, his Cabinet was receiving conflicting advice on the issue. On the one hand, the government was being pushed to say no by public opinion and a strong peace movement. This widespread opposition was well reflected in the report of the Simard-Hockin parliamentary committee that examined the issue in the summer of 1985. In August, the committee reported that more information was needed before it could draw conclusions about SDI, but in the interim it recommended that the government not agree to participate.[50]

On the other hand, there was strong support from some Cabinet ministers. And from Washington, the prime minister was being urged by the Canadian ambassador, Allan Gotlieb, to say yes:

I personally believe that nothing would astound both the Administration and the Congress more than if the Mulroney government would enunciate a negative policy on SDI. It would affect the way the U.S. Government sees Canada — more than any other decision would do. The impact of such a decision would, I believe, infuse virtually every aspect of the Canada-U.S. relationship.[51]

In the end, however, Mulroney decided that his government would reject participation in SDI. The prime minister's own explanation to Gotlieb revealed clearly the government's conflicted preferences. On the one hand, Mulroney believed that SDI research was both necessary and prudent given Soviet capabilities. On the other hand, he was clearly concerned about the depth of opposition in Canada: "The Opposition, the NDP, the media, all the anti-U.S. elements in our society, would make SDI participation by Canada the endless focus of debate, hostility, dissent, and division."[52] The calculation was simple: the continued controversy on the issue would have been more detrimental to the improved climate in Canadian-American relations that Mulroney was trying to foster than a refusal.

The way in which the decision was communicated to the United States government was clearly designed to minimize the negative reaction in Washington. On September 5, Gotlieb was flown to Ottawa to be personally briefed by the prime minister on the importance of conveying to the White House that while Canada supported SDI, the political costs of government participation would be too high.[53] On September 7, the prime minister met with his caucus to inform them of the decision. He then telephoned Reagan at Camp David to tell him that later in the day he would announce Canadian policy on SDI: that Canada believed that SDI was consistent with the Anti-Ballistic Missile Treaty of 1972 and was a prudent initiative given similar initiatives by the Soviet Union; and that there would be no government-to-government participation, although Canadian firms and universities would be free to participate in SDI research if they wished. These decisions were then announced at a press conference.[54]

Mulroney's memoirs make clear that when the two leaders spoke by phone, Reagan was disappointed by the decision.[55] In his examination of Canadian-American relations, Patrick Lennox notes that "Washington was reportedly 'not even upset' by Ottawa's SDI decision," and that "Reagan even thanked Mulroney for the opportunity to work with Canadian firms."[56] But the continuing closeness of the personal relationship between the president and prime minister between the SDI decision in 1985 and the end of Reagan's presidency in 1989 suggests that the negative decision had little long-term impact.

CONCLUSION: WHAT IMPACT POLITENESS?

I have characterized the decision on Iraq as Chrétien's "impolite no"— to contrast it with the common characterization of the Mulroney decision on SDI as a "polite no." But what *political impact* does politeness — or lack of it — have on the Canadian-American relationship?

It is clear that the way in which the "no" on Iraq was delivered aggravated the negative reaction produced by the harm to American interests done by the Canadian decision. Even strong critics of the Bush administration's policy on Iraq, like Paul Heinbecker, concede that the performance in the House of Commons was "circus-like" when it should have been solemn.[57] Likewise, the refusal of the Chrétien government to engage in such standard diplomatic/political niceties as alerting a friendly government whose interests it was about to negatively affect prior to a public announcement was deeply impolite, and almost seemed purposely designed to cause offence. By the same token, it is clear that

the way in which the Mulroney government communicated its decision
to the Reagan administration helped mitigate the negative reactions that
would have been produced by the decision not to lend Canadian legitimacy to the SDI project.

But if we look at the trajectories of the Canadian-American relationship in the years after 1985 and 2003, we would be hard-pressed to see anything but short-term effects. Indeed, in the case of the Strategic Defense
Initiative, there do not even appear to have been short-term negative
effects — other than the perhaps obvious observation that the Mulroney
government's hope that Canadian firms and universities would be able to
participate in SDI research without government-to-government participation proved to be a vain one.

In the case of the "no" on Iraq, the negative consequences of that decision were limited in both time and scope. The widely expressed fears that
the U.S. government would retaliate in ways that would be highly costly
to ordinary Canadians never materialized, though Brian Bow notes that
on some issues, such as the long-running dispute over lumber, the Bush
administration's approach was coloured by the Iraq decision.[58]

Indeed, the findings in this chapter confirm Brian Bow's contention
that in Canadian-American relations, the main form of linkage politics is
what he aptly calls "grudge linkages."[59] While coercive retaliatory linkages
are basically, in his words, "off the table" in relations between Canada and
the United States, the resentments that can be generated by actions on both
sides remain. Issues in the relationship are not "hermetically sealed," and
annoyance at behaviour on one issue can bleed into other issues and affect
how they are processed and resolved.

But because grudges are essentially *personal* psychological construc-
tions — they are formed by individuals, and are inexorably directed at
individuals for perceived wrongs[60] — they tend to be an ephemeral phe-
nomenon in some contexts. To be sure, in contexts where there is low
human mobility, grudges can be long-lived. Consider the prevalence of
grudges in universities, which are generally marked by low mobility among
the professoriate; or consider grudge-holding in some rural communities,
where grudges can sometimes be trans-generational. But in the case of governments, where many officials are highly mobile, grudge-holding tends to
be temporally limited, as individual officials tend not to be in the same

position for long periods of time. There are obviously some exceptions — members of the United States Congress, for example, tend to hold office for an average of ten years — but in most cases, the cast of policy-makers is highly fluid over time.

Such an observation has considerable implications for grudge linkages in the Canadian-American relationship. It suggests that the negative impacts of such cases as the "impolite no" on Iraq will likely be of relatively brief duration as the officials in place during the grudge-generating episode move on. However, by the same token, it predicts that the positive impacts in cases of officials who are committed to pursuing a co-operative relationship that seeks to avoid grudge creation — such as the Mulroney government's "polite no" in 1985 — will be likewise limited. "*Toujours la politesse*" may be wise words to live by, but in the context of international relations, the impact of politeness — or its absence — is likely to be limited.

NOTES

1. George W. Bush, "President's Remarks at the United Nations General Assembly" (speech, New York, September 12, 2002), http://georgewbush-whitehouse. archives.gov/news/releases/2002/09/20020912-2.html (accessed August 15, 2014).

2. Administration of George W. Bush, "The President's News Conference with President Vaclav Havel of the Czech Republic in Prague, Czech Republic" (transcript, November 20, 2002), www.gpo.gov/fdsys/pkg/PPP-2002-book2/pdf/ PPP-2002-book2-doc-pg2097.pdf (accessed August 15, 2014).

3. Quoted in Jean Chrétien, *My Years as Prime Minister* (Toronto: Vintage Canada, 2008), 307. See also Eric J. Lerhe, *Canada-US Military Interoperability: At What Cost Sovereignty?* (Ph.D. thesis, Dalhousie University, 2012), 229.

4. For accounts of this private meeting, see Chrétien, *My Years as Prime Minister,* 308–10; and Eddie Goldenberg, *The Way It Works: Inside Ottawa* (Toronto: Douglas Gibson, 2006), 286–87.

5. Brian Bow, *The Politics of Linkage: Power, Interdependence, and Ideas in Canada-U.S. Relations* (Vancouver: University of British Columbia Press, 2009), 136–37.

6. Canada, Department of National Defence, "Briefing Note for Minister of National Defence on Canadian Access to US Military Planning," November 15, 2002, cited in Lerhe, *Canada-US Military Interoperability*, 238; also Donald Barry, "Chrétien,

Bush, and the War in Iraq," *American Review of Canadian Studies* 35, no. 2 (2005): 220–21.

7. Lerhe, *Canada-US Interoperability*, 240–42.
8. Chris Wattie, "Ottawa Offered to Join Iraq War: Proposal to Send 600–800 Soldiers Dropped Suddenly in Favour of Afghan Plan," *National Post*, November 27, 2003.
9. Lerhe, *Canada-US Interoperability*, 265, ftn. 122.
10. Bow, *Politics of Linkage*, 137; Barry, "Chrétien, Bush, and the War in Iraq," 222. Goldenberg (*The Way It Works*, 291) asserts that at *all* the Cabinet meetings during this period, "there was no support in Cabinet for participating in an American-led war in Iraq without the sanction of the United Nations" — an assertion that is clearly not supported by the historical record: see, for example, Timothy A. Sayle, "But He Has Nothing On At All: Canada and the Iraq War, 2003," *Canadian Military History* 19, no. 4 (2010), esp. 8.
11. Paul Koring, "Canada May Fight Without UN Support," *Globe and Mail*, January 10, 2003.
12. Janice Gross Stein and Eugene Lang, *The Unexpected War: Canada in Kandahar* (Toronto: Viking Canada, 2007), 55.
13. Quoted in Lerhe, *Canada-US Interoperability*, 247.
14. Stein and Lang, *Unexpected War*, 55.
15. Shawn McCarthy and Daniel LeBlanc, "PM Scolds McCallum on Canada's Role in Iraq," *Globe and Mail*, January 16, 2003; Stein and Lang, *Unexpected War*, 56; and Bow, *Politics of Linkage*, 137.
16. Barry, "Chrétien, Bush, and the War in Iraq," 222.
17. Jeff Sallot, "PM to Bush: Hold Off On War," *Globe and Mail*, January 24, 2003.
18. Patrick Graham and Bill Graham, "The Reporter, His Foreign-Minister Father and the War That Consumed Them," *Globe and Mail*, March 16, 2013.
19. Quoted in Rick Fawn, "No Consensus with the Commonwealth, No Consensus with Itself? Canada and the Iraq War," *The Round Table* 97, no. 397 (2008): 521.
20. Sallot, "PM to Bush"; Allan Thompson, "Chrétien Supports U.S. Push for War," *Toronto Star*, January 24, 2003; and Chris Wattie, "PM's War Message a 'Confused Muddle': Is He For or Against? Media Not Sure Where Chrétien Stands," *National Post*, January 25, 2003.
21. See Lerhe, *Canada-US Interoperability*, 250–52.
22. Jeff Sallot, "Proposed Iraq Briefing Had Canada Skeptical," *Globe and Mail*, March 12, 2004. One Canadian official, interviewed by Sallot a year later, claimed that Powell "went to the Security Council and unloaded a tractor-trailer full of mythology."
23. On the February decision to commit troops to ISAF in Kabul, see Stein and Lang, *Unexpected War*, 65–72.
24. Jean Chrétien, "Notes for an Address by Prime Minister Jean Chrétien to the Chicago Council on Foreign Relations" (speech, Chicago, February 13, 2003), http:// epe.lac-bac.gc.ca/100/205/301/prime_minister-ef/jean_chretien/2003-12-08/

stagingpm_3a8080/default.asp@language=e&page=newsroom&sub=speeches&doc=chicago.20030213_e.htm (accessed August 16, 2014); Chrétien, *My Years as Prime Minister,* 311–12; and Goldenberg, *The Way It Works,* 291–95.

25. For details, see Bow, *Linkage Politics,* 138–39; Sayle, "Canada and the Iraq War," 13; and Goldenberg, *The Way It Works,* 295–96. For a blisteringly trenchant critique of what he calls "Canada's unprincipled (hyper-) multilateralism in Iraq," see Frank P. Harvey, *Smoke and Mirrors: Globalized Terrorism and the Illusion of Multilateral Security* (Toronto: University of Toronto Press, 2004), 193–215.

26. Stein and Lang, *Unexpected War,* 74–75.

27. See United States, Ottawa embassy, Cable 03OTTAWA589, "Canadian Political Director on Iraq," March 3, 2003, http://wikileaks.org/cable/2003/03/03OTTAWA589.html (accessed August 16, 2014). Paul Cellucci, the ambassador, noted, "The GoC [Government of Canada] is relishing its chance to encourage consensus at the UNSC [U.N. Security Council], however unlikely that might be. Canada has heard our message, from President Bush on down, that its proposal is too little, too late. But multilateralism is an article of faith in Ottawa...."

28. Cable 03OTTAWA589, "Canadian Political Director on Iraq," March 3, 2003, quoted in Lerhe, *Canada-US Interoperability,* 253.

29. Goldenberg, *The Way It Works,* 1–8.

30. As Stein and Lang note, "It was clear to both men that the question was rhetorical and did not invite a serious discussion about the merits or content of the statement." Ten years on, Graham was to reflect that "the decision was the Prime Minister's. It's like a Shakespearean play: I wasn't the king, but I was one of the Earls": Graham and Graham, "The Reporter, His Foreign-Minister Father and the War."

31. Canada, Parliament, House of Commons, *Debates,* vol. 138, March 17, 2003, www.parl.gc.ca/HousePublications/Publication.aspx?Pub=Hansard&Mee=71&Language=e&Parl=37&Ses=2 (accessed August 16, 2014).

32. After the 2003 invasion and the discovery that there were no weapons of mass destruction, a number of officials sought to distance themselves from the view that prior to the invasion they did not believe there was a WMD threat. For a forceful argument about this historical revisionism, see Frank P. Harvey, *Explaining the Iraq War: Counterfactual Theory, Logic and Evidence* (Cambridge: Cambridge University Press, 2012), esp. 227–30.

33. For a discussion of the dual-tasked nature of the Canadian command of TF 151, see Lerhe, *Canada-US Interoperability,* 282–305. Note that Lerhe shows the degree to which the Stein and Lang narrative on TF 151, in *Unexpected War,* 79–90, is highly contested.

34. Quoted in Harvey, *Smoke and Mirrors,* 195. As Harvey asks, "In the end, what 'principle' was Canada defending?"

35. Chrétien, *My Years as Prime Minister,* 314.

36. Stein and Lang, *Unexpected War,* 76. For Goldenberg's account, see *The Way It*

Works, 3 and 7.

37. Quoted in Fawn, "No Consensus," 525.

38. Video of the announcement available at: www.youtube.com/watch?v=iPVOhva_
    cwI (accessed August 16, 2014); Manley's nervousness begins at 1:37.

39. Bow, *Linkage Politics*, 140.

40. Paul Cellucci, *Unquiet Diplomacy* (Toronto: Key Porter Books, 2005), 131.

41. Stein and Lang, *Unexpected War*, 77.

42. Paul Cellucci, "We Are Family," *Policy Options* (May 2003), 13; and Gloria
    Galloway, "U.S. Rebukes Canada," *Globe and Mail*, March 26, 2003.

43. Sayle, "Canada and the Iraq War," 17; and Sunny Freeman, "Canada's 'No' to Iraq
    War a Defining Moment for Prime Minister, Even 10 Years Later," *Huffington
    Post*, March 19, 2013.

44. Bow, *Linkage Politics*, 142.

45. Chrétien, *My Years as Prime Minister*, 315.

46. Goldenberg, *The Way It Works*, 307.

47. Brian Mulroney, *Memoirs: 1939–1993* (Toronto: McClelland & Stewart, 2007), 350.

48. Adam Bromke and Kim Richard Nossal, "A Turning Point in U.S.-Canadian
    Relations," *Foreign Affairs* 66, no. 1 (1987), 163; and James Rusk, "PM Support on
    Star Wars Pleases US," *Globe and Mail*, February 2, 1985.

49. Nelson Michaud and Kim Richard Nossal, "The Conservative Era in Canadian
    Foreign Policy, 1984–93," in *Diplomatic Departures: The Conservative Era in
    Canadian Foreign Policy, 1984–93*, ed. Michaud and Nossal (Vancouver: UBC
    Press, 2001), 14.

50. Special Joint Committee on Canada's International Relations, *Interim Report
    Pertaining to Bilateral Trade with the United States and Canada's Participation
    in Research on the Strategic Defense Initiative* (Ottawa: Government of Canada,
    August 23, 1985).

51. Quoted in Mulroney, *Memoirs*, 351.

52. Allan Gotlieb, *The Washington Diaries, 1981–1989* (Toronto: McClelland &
    Stewart, 2006), 318.

53. Ibid., 318–19.

54. Mulroney, *Memoirs*, 352; and Jeff Sallot, "Peace Groups Pleased by Rejection of
    Star Wars," *Globe and Mail*, September 9, 1985.

55. Mulroney, *Memoirs*, 352.

56. Patrick Lennox, *At Home and Abroad: The Canada-US Relationship and Canada's
    Place in the World* (Vancouver: UBC Press, 2009), 80.

57. Freeman, "Canada's 'No' to Iraq War."

58. Bow, *Linkage Politics*, 156.

59. Brian Bow, "Rethinking Retaliation in Canada-U.S. Relations," in *An Independent
    Foreign Policy for Canada? Challenges and Choices for the Future*, ed. Brian J. Bow
    and Patrick Lennox (Toronto: University of Toronto Press, 2008), 63–82.

60. On grudge-holding, see Roy F. Baumeister, Julie Juola Exline, and Kristin L.

Sommer, "The Victim Role, Grudge Theory, and Two Dimensions of Forgiveness," in *Dimensions of Forgiveness: Psychological Research & Theological Forgiveness*, ed. Everett L. Worthington, Jr. (Philadelphia: Templeton Foundation Press, 1998), 79–104.

13

THE POLITICS OF DISARMAMENT: CANADA AND THE INVASION OF IRAQ, 2002–03

Jack Cunningham

Reviewing David Stevenson's history of the First World War in the pages of *The New Yorker*, Adam Gopnik observed that the two world wars of the twentieth century taught clear but contradictory lessons: "The first teaches us never to rush into a fight, the second never to back down from a bully."[1] The respective perils of allowing the momentum toward war to become irresistible, and of emboldening an aggressor by persisting in compromise too long were invoked repeatedly in the debate among Canadian politicians in the run-up to the 2003 invasion of Iraq. Speaking in the House of Commons, Brian Pallister of the right-wing Opposition party, the Canadian Alliance, warned, "The threat posed by Saddam Hussein is stronger today than it was three years ago. Why is the government's response weaker?"[2] Not quite a year later, Liberal prime minister Jean Chrétien told the Chicago Council on Foreign Relations that "war must always be the last resort, not only because of the human suffering it causes, but also because of the inevitable unintended consequences."[3]

It is tempting to conclude that for conservatives, the pertinent, if usually tacit, analogy was the Munich Agreement of 1938, while for liberals it was the supposed mad rush to war of August 1914. Such was certainly the tenor of the parliamentary debate, perhaps above all in the six months leading up to the commencement of the invasion in March 2003. The reality, at least as confronted by the Chrétien government, was more complex. During those six months, when the danger of precipitate resort to military action seemed far more pronounced than that of injudicious appeasement, it made sense to stress the one set of hazards over the other, but Canadian policy-makers were aware of both. The Chrétien government was criticized at the time, and has been taken to task since, for the inconsistency of its stance.[4] But while its articulated position was often ambiguous and reactive, its goal was consistent, arguably as far back as the 1998 Operation Desert Fox. That goal was the disarmament of Saddam Hussein, which Canada consistently distinguished from his ouster. Chrétien's government supported multilateral measures designed to ensure the former, and to gather the evidence that would determine if it could be achieved without the latter. Proponents of regime change insisted the two were inseparable, and as they blurred the distinction in the final weeks before war, Canada sought to reinforce it by pressing for a compromise resolution at the United Nations that would provide for the collection of more evidence on the extent of Iraq's disarmament, with war to come if disarmament was not taking place.

The Chrétien government's handling of the impending invasion of Iraq, and its dealings with the administration of George W. Bush more broadly, reflected the prime minister's aversion to either visible intimacy or open conflict in Canadian-American relations. His predecessor, Brian Mulroney, whose rhetoric emphasized bilateral harmony, and who was close to presidents Ronald Reagan and George H.W. Bush, was subjected to strong criticism from the nationalist left for his notional readiness to compromise Canadian interests. Chrétien, on the other hand, pursued low-key and businesslike relations, which irritated both uncritical supporters and vehement critics of American policy, but left other Canadians reasonably content.[5] In the months leading up to the invasion of Iraq, the Chrétien government tried to position itself domestically as centrist, between the extremes of the Canadian Alliance and its sympathizers, who were perceived to share the Bush administration's haste to resort to force, and the left-wing New Democratic Party (NDP) and Quebec sovereigntist Bloc Québécois (BQ), perceived as dogmatically averse to military intervention, the facts of the case notwithstanding. Deputy Prime Minister John Manley neatly encapsulated the thrust of the government's positioning when he said in the House, "We have a party over there that wants us to be opposed to the United States even when it is right. We also have a party that wants to agree with the United States even when it is wrong."[6] The centrist cast of Canadian policy pertained to both ends and means. In terms of means, the government practised what we might call evidence-based policy-making and, particularly after Saddam readmitted United Nations weapons inspectors, paid particular attention to their findings as a guide to appropriate action, rather than following a pre-existing predilection for a given course. As for ends, the goal was always the containment and disarmament of Saddam Hussein, backed by coercive diplomacy as required, but distinct from his overthrow. One guiding assumption was that the weapons inspectors' evidence should be used to construct international consensus and guide policy. Clear evidence of Saddam's compliance would demonstrate that he need not be ousted, and would place an insuperable obstacle in the path of those propounding this course; clear evidence of non-compliance would prove the reverse and provide political legitimacy for resort to invasion. The situation would, of course, be difficult if the evidence were ambiguous, as it turned out to be.

Canadian participation in the first Gulf War, under the Mulroney government, had been controversial in Canada, and Chrétien, then the leader of the Opposition, had seemed to dither over sending troops.[7] It was in the aftermath of hostilities that it became clear that Saddam's weapons of mass destruction (WMDs) programs, particularly his nuclear weapons program, had been further advanced than generally believed. Under U.N. Security Council Resolution 687, weapons inspectors of the United Nations Special Commission (UNSCOM) were empowered to inspect the dismantling of Iraqi WMD facilities and programs, and when the regime obstructed their work in late 1998, Canada supported Operation Desert Fox, a four-day bombing campaign to induce compliance, conducted by the administration of President Bill Clinton and the government of British prime minister Tony Blair. Speaking to the North Atlantic Council in support of Desert Fox, Chrétien's foreign minister, Lloyd Axworthy, highlighted the proliferation of WMDs as a major threat to world security. UNSCOM inspectors were withdrawn from Iraq prior to Desert Fox and not readmitted; from 1999 on, inspection of Iraqi compliance was conducted from outside Iraq's borders, by the U.N. Monitoring, Verification and Inspection Commission (UNMOVIC), and widely regarded as inadequate.[8]

Even before the terrorist attacks on New York and Washington, Chrétien and his associates were put off by the aggressive unilateralism of the George W. Bush administration, manifest in its disavowal of the Kyoto Protocol on global warming, and its announced intention to withdraw from various international agreements.[9] After the attacks, Chrétien responded to the American preoccupation with domestic security by approving new procedures and a ramping up of spending on border security. Canadian Forces were also sent to Afghanistan, to take part in the overthrow of the Taliban regime that had harboured the al-Qaeda terrorists behind 9/11, an operation that had the approval of both the United Nations and the North Atlantic Treaty Organization. But it soon became clear that at least a strong faction within the Bush administration was convinced of the need to deter future terrorist attacks, perhaps involving WMDs, by rogue regimes. In his 2002 State of the Union address, Bush identified Iraq as part of an axis of evil that included Iran and North Korea, and a subsequent commencement address he gave at West Point, as well as a speech by Vice-President Dick Cheney to the United States Naval Academy at Annapolis, denied that Saddam was effectively contained and disarmed. Blair was in essential agreement but recognized the legal and political objections against overthrowing Saddam. Blair favoured wrong-footing him by highlighting his defiance of serial resolutions demanding his disarmament and giving weapons inspections a final chance to succeed, and resorting to Saddam's overthrow only after he had declined to co-operate.

The hawks in Bush's entourage, led by Cheney and Secretary of Defense Donald Rumsfeld, saw little to gain by working through the United Nations, suspecting Saddam would provide only partial co-operation with the weapons inspectors, should he consent to their return. Their fears were that the readmission of inspectors would engender complacency and erode international willingness to confront him, while leaving his WMD capabilities largely intact. In September of 2002, Blair visited Bush at Camp David, the presidential retreat in Maryland, where the advocates of an early resort to Saddam's forcible removal, headed by Cheney, and the proponents of going to the United Nations, led by Blair and Secretary of State Colin Powell, debated the question. As one historian concludes, Bush essentially "split the difference," agreeing to seek Saddam's disarmament through the United Nations, but concluding that, at the end of the day, war to remove him was likely to prove necessary.[10]

In August, the clerk of the Privy Council, Alex Himelfarb, had warned Chrétien that an American-led invasion of Iraq was inevitable, and that the Bush administration would soon be canvassing its allies for support. When the two leaders met in Detroit for a bilateral summit prior to the September session of the U.N. General Assembly, Chrétien told Bush he would not support military action against Iraq without a U.N. resolution, and that he was not yet convinced by the evidence that Saddam had WMDs.[11] Speaking before the General Assembly three days later, Bush made the case for disarming Saddam, pointing to the past resolutions the Iraqi dictator had flouted, claiming that the question of the hour was, "Will the United Nations serve the purpose of its founding or will it be irrelevant?"[12] As Brian Bow has written, this would "turn the tables" — judging the United Nation's relevance by its approval of American actions, rather than judging American actions by the degree to which they could command U.N. support.[13] Chrétien's minister of foreign affairs, Bill Graham, praised Bush's efforts to work through the United Nations and implicitly approved the notion that its handling of Iraq would be a test by which the world body might be legitimately judged, though he stressed the need for disarmament to be achieved multilaterally. He added that "the onus is clearly on Iraq" to readmit the weapons inspectors.[14]

The salient questions were whether Saddam's verifiable disarmament could be accomplished under U.N. auspices and whether this would be an acceptable outcome for the Bush administration. There were early indications that the first might be achievable. Saddam announced the unconditional acceptance of the inspectors' return on September 16, and when there were rumours that he might try to constrain their access to sensitive sites, Graham called for a strong inspections regime and endorsed the assumption that Saddam would not disarm without the threat of force, noting that "the United States came to the United Nations, which is what we asked them to do."[15] There were encouraging signs that the second might be within reach as well. At the August Asia-Pacific Economic Cooperation (APEC) Summit on Sustainable Development, Graham and Colin Powell chatted at the foreign ministers' dinner, and Powell suggested that "if Saddam Hussein co-operates, there won't be an attack" because if such co-operation materialized, "there will have been a 'regime change' or 'change in the regime.'" When Mexican foreign minister Jorge Castañeda asked if it would be possible to stipulate this in the U.N. resolution governing the readmission of the inspectors then under negotiation, Powell replied, "I've carried the hawks so far — don't make it impossible for me."[16]

On November 8, the Security Council unanimously passed Resolution 1441, declaring Saddam "in material breach" of his obligations under previous resolutions, giving him "a final opportunity to comply," and warning of "serious consequences" if he did not.[17] But two weeks later at NATO's Prague summit, Bush was sounding quite unlike Powell, warning that in Saddam's case "containment doesn't work. Neither does [sic] threats of retaliation."[18] In the background, American officials canvassed allies as to their willingness to help in the event of military intervention. At this point the French were inclined to press for an explicit Security Council mandate for any resort to force, and reluctant to respond positively to any U.S. request while the situation in Iraq remained fluid. German chancellor Gerhard Schroeder told reporters that Germany would grant access to its bases and rights of overflight and transit, "but no direct military involvement."[19] Foreign Affairs Minister Bill Graham met his British counterpart, Jack Straw, while exercising in the gym. Straw took the position that British support was "contingent on any intervention being in accordance with international law," which Graham found "a bit disingenuous" and smacking of "the Kosovo cop-out."[20] (This last referred to NATO's bombing of Kosovo in 1999.[21]) So, Britain was now at least open to the possibility of military intervention without explicit U.N. approval.

As for Bush, he was now in a strong position domestically. Prior to the 2002 mid-term elections, he had sought congressional authorization for military action, securing margins of 77 to 23 in the Senate and 296 to 133 in the House of Representatives, with his fellow Republicans lining up behind him, and Democrats anxious to take the issue off the table in order to concentrate on the domestic issues they thought would help them. In fact, Bush's Republicans gained eight seats in the House and two in the Senate. As Canada's ambassador to the United States, Michael Kergin, explained to Graham, this was the first time in more than a hundred years that this had happened to the president's party in the mid-terms, and it was a result of Bush's personal popularity and "the war vote."[22] For the moment, Canada would take part in contingency planning within the framework of Resolution 1441, sending officers to United States Central

Command (CENTCOM) in Tampa, but this was without prejudice to the Canadian decision in the event of war.[23]

As part of the inspections process set out in Resolution 1441, the Iraqi regime was given thirty days to present a declaration on the state of its facilities and programs pertinent to WMDs, after which the inspections process would commence in earnest. The Iraqi declaration was submitted on December 7, and the chief weapons inspector, Hans Blix, briefed the members of the Security Council on its contents on December 19. He pointed out that much of the 1,200-page document was a rehashing of Iraqi declarations from 1996 and 1997, and that the supporting documentation was incomplete. It now seems clear that Saddam's strategy was to co-operate with Resolution 1441 in part, enough to encourage Security Council members like France and Russia to oppose any resort to force as unjustified, and thereby to split the coalition at the United Nations in favour of his disarmament. The report changed the atmosphere, convincing many in Blair's government that Saddam would not be fully compliant, and emboldening the hawks in the Bush administration. Even Powell now stated publicly that Saddam was in material breach, and Cheney urged Bush to announce that the grounds for war now existed. The danger was that the United States might urge military action on a that others would consider insufficient. This could pose problems for Blair, given the importance he attached to U.N. approval, and still more for Chrétien.[24] While the Bush administration lambasted Saddam for insufficient co-operation, planning for an invasion of Iraq went ahead.

When the newly appointed Canadian minister of national defence, John McCallum, went to Washington in early January for a visit with Rumsfeld, he expected the discussion to focus on Iraq. Instead, Rumsfeld urged that Canada take over the lead role in the International Security Assistance Force (ISAF) in Afghanistan, thereby freeing up American troops for Iraq. When McCallum indicated this would leave no Canadian troops for any hypothetical hostilities in Iraq, Rumsfeld took the point.[25] After the meeting, McCallum told reporters that Canada would support military action if authorized by the United Nations but reserve judgment if the United States acted unilaterally. His comments opened the divisions within Liberal ranks between those more and less sympathetic to the case for military action. The chairman of the House defence committee, David

Pratt, defended McCallum's remarks as an accurate statement of the government's position, while a hitherto obscure backbencher, Carolyn Parrish, grabbed headlines by threatening to leave the Liberal caucus and sit as an independent should Canada take part in war without a U.N. mandate. Chrétien chastised McCallum publicly for answering a hypothetical question and made the case for acting through the United Nations, and added the caveat that sometimes, as in Kosovo, circumstances dictated action outside that framework. Indeed, the prime minister misstated the situation in Kosovo, claiming that the NATO action had a degree of U.N. sanction, though "not as clear as some lawyers would have liked." Pressed as to whether Canada might take part in military action without U.N. approval, he replied, "You are just speculating. I'm not speculating."[26] In Kosovo, of course, while there may not have been legal clarity, there was little dispute about the facts; it was clear that ethnic cleansing was taking place.

Much ink has since been spilled over the degree to which Chrétien was insistent on U.N. authorization, or whether he might have acquiesced in action without it, given clear evidence that Saddam was in violation of U.N. resolutions and a sufficiently broad coalition.[27] To ask how much U.N. approval mattered *versus* the evidence of Iraqi violations is in part to oversimplify the question. Both U.N. approval and the assembling of any broad coalition outside the U.N. framework were seen as dependent upon the evidence that the weapons inspections produced. A lack of consensus for invasion or even a Security Council veto based on evidence of Iraqi compliance was one thing, but a veto taken in *defiance* of the evidence was quite another. U.N. authorization was presumptively necessary, but this necessity was contingent on the evidence on Iraqi actions and capabilities and could be waived if that evidence were clear. Hence the consistent importance attached by the Canadian government to ensuring that UNMOVIC had sufficient time to determine with as much certainty as possible if Saddam was in compliance with his obligations, and Chrétien's preservation of the Kosovo option. When Blix made his first report on Iraqi compliance on January 27, he presented a picture that was ambiguous enough to maintain, if not reinforce, the divisions within the Security Council and the wider international community. He stressed the distinction between process and substance. Iraq, he said, had been co-operative on matters of process, particularly concerning access, but less forthcoming on substance, particularly the provision of information. He concluded that on matters of compliance, "presumptions don't solve the problem. Evidence and full transparency may help," and called for more time.[28]

In Canada, the subsequent Cabinet discussions revolved around the lack of clear evidence that Saddam had WMDs, and Washington's consequent failure to convince others of the need to oust Saddam. On January 28, Industry Minister Allan Rock told Cabinet that when he and Minister of International Trade Pierre Pettigrew had attended the recent meeting of the World Economic Forum in Davos they found that Powell, attempting to make the administration's case that Saddam was not in compliance, "didn't persuade people." Indeed, "anti-American sentiment [was] strong there." The Canadian public, he continued, would support a "back-fill" in Afghanistan, but was also rightly unconvinced that Saddam had WMDs and that war was necessary. Manley made the point that the inspectors needed more time to establish whether Saddam had WMDs, "so we insist on compliance." The only supporter of Canadian participation in any American invasion was the minister of state for international financial institutions, Maurizio Bevilacqua, who remarked, "If they go, we have to go — we're married." Transport Minister David Collenette urged his colleagues not to be rattled by press or Opposition criticism that the government's position was unclear. Blair, he suggested, had staked out a very clear position and was now in trouble with the British electorate; straddling the fence was the "right place." Chrétien concluded that Bevilacqua might want to be with the Americans in any invasion but, at least for now, he did not.[29] At a subsequent Cabinet meeting on February 2, Manley, generally reputed to be one of the more right-wing ministers, and highly sympathetic to the Americans, cautioned that regime change in Iraq was "breaking ground and dangerous," only to be tried if the evidence for Saddam's non-compliance were strong. Collenette noted that Canada was in the "Five Eyes" intelligence-sharing arrangement with the United States, United Kingdom, Australia, and New Zealand, and Five Eyes material apparently showed no evidence of Iraqi WMDs: "If we haven't seen it it's not there!"[30] The Canadian ambassador to the United Nations, Paul Heinbecker, was convinced that on the basis of the available evidence, the United States would be unable to secure even a majority in the Security Council for a resolution explicitly authorizing military intervention.[31] Blix noted that Iraqi compliance was still less than total, but he had found no evidence of proscribed weapons programs yet. He was convinced that the combination of containment and robust inspections would eventually reveal any Iraqi non-compliance, but the Bush administration was asking too much in terms of proof that Saddam lacked WMDs: "How do we prove a negative?"[32] As for the intelligence on WMDs that the Bush administration had passed on to him, almost all had been "erroneous or misleading." "No decision on war should be based on so-called intelligence," he concluded.[33]

Much of the debate in Canada, as elsewhere, turned to the question of whether Resolution 1441 provided sufficient authority for an invasion in the event of Iraqi non-compliance, or if a further resolution more explicitly authorizing military intervention was required. Chrétien had not objected, and had apparently agreed, when John Manley said a further resolution was not required as a matter of law, adding, "The inspections will answer that."[34] In other words, Resolution 1441 was accepted as sufficient authority for military intervention, if the inspections provided sufficient justification of Saddam's non-compliance. There was the question of international law, but a separate question of fact as well. That same day in the House of Commons, Canadian Alliance leader Stephen Harper lamented that "we never used to be a spectator" but were now absent from the coalition "prepared to keep the pressure on Saddam to comply with United Nations resolutions, including Resolution 1441." Chrétien replied, "If Saddam Hussein fails to comply with resolution 1441, not only the U.S., but its allies will be there to ensure that weapons of mass destruction are removed from Iraq. That is the resolution. It is very clear." But, he continued, "we must wait for a clear report from the inspectors. Mr. Blix has asked for more time to do his work."[35]

On February 11, Chrétien's Liberals voted down a BQ motion that would have set a further Security Council resolution explicitly authorizing force as a precondition of any deployment of Canadian troops. Chrétien said, "We were among the first to state very clearly that a Security Council resolution was required." In the summer of 2002, "there was a strong possibility of the Americans and the British intervening directly without the Security Council. We have maintained our position, however. There has been a Security Council resolution." When BQ leader Gilles Duceppe charged that voting against the resolution would give the government a blank cheque to go to war, Chrétien said, "Absolutely not.... We hope that Saddam Hussein will provide Mr. Blix with the necessary information so that all this can be settled peacefully. But the United Nations Charter contains rules that must be followed."[36] The question of the evidentiary, as opposed to the legal, basis of action had yet to be resolved, and the latter was a necessary but not sufficient condition of the political legitimacy required for war to be acceptable. While Chrétien does not appear to have ever made an explicit public statement that Resolution 1441 was sufficient authorization for military action, he took pains to keep open the door to military action with only that as authorization, and resisted the Bloc's effort to close it.

At one point it had seemed that Powell's much-anticipated presentation to the Security Council on February 5 would meet the need for the information necessary to judge the facts about Iraqi compliance. A few days earlier, Straw had told Graham that the Blair government preferred to have a further Security Council resolution "for the obvious reasons." This would clearly establish material breach and bring in a larger coalition. He thought that Russia and China could "recognize material breach" and would not exercise the permanent member's veto. European opinion was split, and "Germany oppose[d] war but might support a 2nd resolution. France would not veto." Powell had a good opportunity to persuade the Security Council and the wider world on February 5. Straw believed "that war can still be avoided but only if the pressure is kept on and Saddam 'cracks' [what that means was not spelled out — leaves the country?]."[37] When Powell did appear before the Council, he set out the Bush administration's case that Saddam retained WMDs and had to be forcibly disarmed.[38] But Powell was far less persuasive than Straw had hoped; his presentation was a hash of speculation, rumour, and records of ambiguous conversations, the highlight coming when he held aloft a plastic vial that he said had once contained botulinum toxin. It changed virtually no minds, and Heinbecker was among those convinced that Powell had either been deceived by the hawks in the administration or was parroting a case he knew to be unconvincing.[39]

Chrétien made a last public effort to persuade the Americans to give the U.N. process more time, telling the Chicago Council on Foreign Relations that war should be the last resort and that given sufficient time, the United Nations would still prove up to the task of disarming Saddam.[40] By now, it seemed there was precious little chance of averting war. The German foreign minister, Joschka Fischer, told Graham that from his conversations in NATO he had the impression that the Americans had settled on a given day by which war had to commence. He had asked the Americans, "'What do you need to declare victory?' 'Saddam must be gone.' Not even a Pinochet solution."[41] But by this stage, the debate that mattered was the one in the Security Council.

Bush and his advisers, even Powell, saw no need for a further resolution, but Blair was convinced one was necessary to carry the British public with him and to win a parliamentary vote on going to war. At the end of January, he flew to Washington and prevailed on Bush to seek a resolution. He was unable to persuade the Americans to move back the timetable for hostilities, now tentatively set for March 10. This left Blair very little time to garner support for a resolution, and at a time when the weakness of the evidence of Iraqi non-compliance, and then Powell's damp squib of a Security Council presentation, led British public opinion to turn sharply against participation in an invasion. This became clear on February 15, when London witnessed the largest anti-war rally in its history.[42] Pursuit of a further resolution was hardly eased by Blix's report to the Security Council on February 14, which was largely a litany of progress. Blix reported more than four hundred inspections at more than three hundred sites, without notice and with access almost always granted, and on the ongoing destruction of fifty litres of mustard gas. As for WMDs, he noted, "So far UNMOVIC has not found any such weapons, only a small number of empty chemical munitions, which should have been declared and destroyed." Blix did conclude that where proscribed weapons existed, "they should be presented for destruction," adding, "If they do not exist, credible evidence to that effect should be presented."[43] Yet the thrust of his presentation was that co-operation was improving, that where Iraq had yet to comply there was probably little cause for concern, and that the inspections process was working, leaving no need for war. In the absence of a permanent member's veto, a further resolution required nine votes out of the fifteen on the Security Council. Spain and Bulgaria were on side with London and Washington, and Syria, China, France, Germany, and Russia against. This left the "M6" states (Mexico, Chile, Pakistan, Cameroon, Angola, and Guinea) in the middle: A further resolution would require the support of five.[44]

Canada was not on the Security Council, but Chrétien and Graham decided to establish if there was room for compromise, by asking Heinbecker to present the Council with two questions for clarification: "What specific disarmament tasks remain? And how much time should Iraq have to complete them?"[45] If the former could be identified and deadlines for compliance established, it might still be possible to verify if Saddam were disarmed, so that war could either be averted or at least begun on a proven *casus belli*. Chrétien wanted this to be a low-key exploration of possibilities, lest it elicit open opposition and embarrassing rejection, but on the morning of the twentieth, he and Graham woke up to find that the modest step had been leaked by a "senior Canadian official" in Ottawa, with the *Globe and Mail* headline reading, "PM Aims to Broker Iraq Deal." The article in Canada's newspaper of record quoted the official as saying, "The only way we can bridge this 'bomb now or inspect forever' mentality is to say, 'Let's pick a date far enough in the future so we will know if the Iraqis are following through.'" Another official was quoted as saying that the idea of setting explicit benchmarks and deadlines for Iraqi compliance had been floating around the United Nations for some time, "but Canada is the first to articulate it in the Security Council."[46] As Graham noted, "Our rather useless idea at the UN (which we rather backed into) has now become a 'major Canadian diplomatic initiative,'" which James Wright, the assistant deputy minister for global and security policy in Graham's department, was widely suspected of leaking. Chrétien was "furious at the exaggeration of expectations so my job is to downplay it — but still push it."[47]

Over the days ahead, Chrétien and Graham would talk to their respective counterparts on the phone while Heinbecker canvassed support within the Security Council. Straw, increasingly apprehensive about the prospect of war without a further resolution, warned Graham, "People's patience is running out; we can't get into an [August] '14 syndrome. You can't keep 250 thousand troops on standby forever." If war was to be averted, Saddam had to comply on matters of substance, and the inspectors had to say he was doing so. A second resolution, he added, might not be necessary. At this stage, he added further, "a lot depends on France."[48] On February 24, the United States, Britain, and Spain, backed by Bulgaria, presented a draft resolution declaring Saddam Hussein in "further material breach" of his disarmament obligations and called for an early vote on military action. Chrétien saw it as a "resolution lite" and concluded, "There's nothing we can do — they'll go."[49]

France was strongly opposed, and proposed instead that inspections be extended for a further four months (with the prospect of renewal), which would have taken them to July and the middle of the hot season, when invasion would be almost impossible.[50] While chances for success seemed poor, the Canadians presented a further attempt at a compromise, in the form of an informal memo entitled "Ideas on Bridging the Divide." This noted that "an open-ended inspection process would relieve the pressure on the Iraqis to disarm," while "a truncated inspection process would leave doubt that war was a last resort." The Canadian process sought to put the focus back on disarmament inspections and the collection of evidence as a guide to policy, by calling again for precise benchmarks and deadlines close enough to sustain the pressure on Saddam while providing "sufficient time for judgments to be made whether the Iraqis were co-operating on substance in disarming." The inspectors were to prepare an inventory of disarmament tasks and deadlines, and make weekly reports to the Security Council, followed by a final report on the twenty-eighth. The Council would meet again on the thirty-first. In the event of "substantial Iraqi compliance," monitoring would continue. If the Iraqis were not complying, "all necessary means would be used to force them to disarm." If Iraq persisted in evasion, "the Council reserve[d] the right to act at any point."[51] As a means of gathering the intelligence necessary to make a final judgment on whether Iraq's disarmament could be accomplished short of regime change, the plan had much to commend it. And, as the American journalist Fred Kaplan pointed out, American acceptance would delay military action by an inconsequential two weeks, while allowing the Bush administration the appearance of having tried to meet the doubts of others and thereby providing additional legitimacy for invasion should it prove unavoidable.[52]

There was interest among the M6, who floated the ideas in the proposal, as Heinbecker reported from New York.[53] The Canadian diplomat David Malone, then serving as president of the International Peace Academy in the same city, reported on a conversation with Sergey Lavrov, the Russian ambassador to the United Nations, who criticized the Canadian plan for "setting a date to [sic] close to American desiderata." As Malone pointed out, it was insufficiently appreciated "that we have two extreme positions in the Council, not just the U.S. one." Representatives of other countries, including Mexico's ambassador, Adolfo Aguilar, were remarking on the intense bilateral pressure being applied by Washington.[54] Heinbecker reported that Chilean president Ricardo Lagos had raised a variant of the Canadian plan, providing for a forty-five-day period of inspections rather than a month, with Powell, and "got the brush off."[55] Chances of the Anglo-American resolution passing were undermined further on March 10, when French president Jacques Chirac gave a broadcast in which he denied there were any grounds for war and threatened a veto of any resolution authorizing resort to force. On March 13, the British ambassador to the United Nations, Sir Jeremy Greenstock, presented a British variant of the Canadian plan, built around six benchmarks and with an April 17 deadline; it was rejected by the French foreign minister, Dominique de Villepin, before discussion could even commence. The British continued discussion until March 17, so as to forestall a French resolution against the use of force at all. The Anglo-American resolution was withdrawn on March 17, hours after Blair won the House of Commons vote authorizing resort to war; and that evening Bush gave a broadcast in which he issued an ultimatum to Saddam, who was given forty-eight hours to leave Iraq.[56] In a last effort to make his case for an international audience, Chrétien had appeared on ABC television's *This Week*, said Bush had "won" now that Saddam was surrounded and contained, and warned against the precedent that regime change in Iraq would set. Having kept open the possibility of intervention without U.N. approval *à la* Kosovo in the event of strong evidence and a capricious veto, he now moved to stress the differences between the two cases. In Kosovo, he said, "we went to stop the genocide. There was no change of regime there." The drift of events was clear when Chrétien was followed on the broadcast by Bush's national security adviser, Condoleezza Rice, who insisted that "the problem with the notion of containment is that, first of all, it isn't working."[57]

Early on the morning of the seventeenth, an official at the British embassy in Ottawa called Chrétien's foreign policy adviser, Claude Laverdure, with four questions: Would Canada support the invasion politically? Would it say so publicly? Would it contribute militarily? And would it aid Iraq's reconstruction after hostilities?[58] Graham was exercising in the House of Commons gym when he was pulled off the treadmill by his aide, Dan Costello, to take a telephone call from Chrétien in the office of Elinor Caplan, the minister of citizenship and immigration. Chrétien asked Graham for his response to the four questions. Graham and Costello drafted a statement for Chrétien to read in the House, in which he would announce, "If military action proceeds without a new resolution of the Security Council, Canada will not participate." Chrétien's chief of staff, Eddie Goldenberg, added the statement, "Canada worked very hard to find a compromise to bridge the gap in the Security Council. Unfortunately we were not successful." Canada was insistent that Saddam abide by the disarmament resolutions and would keep its naval vessels in the Persian Gulf as part of the struggle against terrorism.[59] Graham added a further handwritten passage, faxed to Laverdure from Caplan's office, that recognized "the crucial role that the United States and the U.K. have played" in getting Saddam to disarm, and reaffirmed at greater length that Canada remained "committed with our allies to our common cause in the war against terrorism," and would "continue our efforts at their side in Afghanistan."[60]

At this point the government rather lost control of events. Chrétien delivered the first statement in the House in a sitting that aired live on CNN, to raucous cheers and Manley's visible discomfort.[61] He neglected to deliver, or did not receive, Graham's further and more emollient (to American ears, at least) passage, which was delivered in the emergency debate on Iraq later that night, and only by a junior minister, Gar Knutson.[62] One has to assume few Americans were paying attention. Other atmospherics were not conducive to a warm American reception of the Canadian announcement. The initial inquiry about Canada's stance had come from the British, not the Americans, so the response did not follow that channel. Chrétien had directed that the deputy minister of foreign affairs inform the British High Commission and American embassy that a decision was forthcoming, and Laverdure telephoned Rice, but only as Chrétien was making the announcement. Goldenberg persuaded Chrétien that Graham should not call Powell or Cellucci, on the grounds that the Canadian public had to be informed before the Americans; nonetheless, this was a striking departure from the standard niceties of diplomacy.[63] When Chrétien was asked by the NDP's foreign affairs critic, Alexa McDonough, if he would confront Bush directly on the alleged illegality of the war, he replied only that he considered it "my obligation to inform the House of Commons first and the Canadian public" and that the Americans were being informed at lower levels.[64] While not calling Bush directly may have given offence, it at least had the merit of allowing Chrétien to evade the dilemma of either speaking to Bush with unwelcome candour or explaining to his opponents why he had not. Powell telephoned Graham later that afternoon, and each agreed to respect the other's decision, to treat it as legitimate, and to refrain from criticism; the tone, Graham jotted down, was of "respectful regret."[65]

Chrétien and Graham were concerned about narrowing the grounds of disagreement with the United States for the sake of the bilateral relationship and to ease America's return to the U.N. system once hostilities were over. It was in the interests of their partisan opponents to do otherwise. The Canadian Alliance sought to present the gap as very wide indeed, and as the fault of a government that was dogmatically anti-American, while the NDP argued that the Canadian position *should* be hostile to Bush administration actions, but that the Chrétien government was hypocritically combining critical rhetoric with co-operative actions. Harper and his shadow foreign minister, Stockwell Day, lamented Canada's estrangement from its allies in the House, as they would do a few days later in an op-ed for the *Wall Street Journal*.[66] Harper tried to embarrass Chrétien by asking him if Resolution 1441 provided sufficient authority for invasion, as the prime minister's past statements had implied. Chrétien replied that when Bush and Blair had presented their "resolution lite" to the Security Council, they had "superposed [*sic*] this resolution over 1441, and they did not get the authorization from the Security Council."[67] Scholars of international law may debate whether this somewhat Jesuitical interpretation holds water, but as a practical matter Blair was widely viewed as having conceded the necessity for a further resolution, thereby undermining the case for action without one; and the question of any inconsistency regarding this point on Chrétien's part rarely arose.

NDP House leader Bill Blaikie, presumably fearful that the Liberals would steal the NDP's thunder with anti-war voters, criticized Chrétien for seeking a compromise at the United Nations, claiming this would have amounted to "a fig leaf for a war that the United States wanted in any event," and that it was only the failure of that initiative that had led the government to its current position.[68] He then made the point that in the interests of consistency the government should withdraw its naval and other forces in the Persian Gulf. Chrétien replied, somewhat lamely, that Canada had personnel on exchange with British and American forces in the Gulf, but they were not in combat roles.[69] Harper got in a jab along the same lines, noting that the government was opposed to military actions but contributing forces anyway: "What a bizarre position."[70] Of course, Canada could not have withdrawn all its forces from the region without severe damage to relations with Washington; nonetheless, Chrétien, Graham, and McCallum had been concerned enough to spend time and effort seeking letters of instruction for the naval vessels in the Gulf that would not put Canada in the position of a belligerent against Iraq, but would allow it to keep the ships in theatre as the Americans wished.[71] In the evening emergency debate, McDonough asked if the government would lead the charge against Bush's actions at the United Nations before the invasion commenced, and Graham referred to his conversation with Powell that afternoon, saying he had informed his counterpart that despite the current disagreement, "nothing would distract from the respect that we owed each other," and that the day's announcement had laid out the government's position adequately for all to see.[72] With the atmosphere of the announcement obviously less civil than the government had hoped, Graham made a point a few days later of telling the House that "it was the action of the United States and the Americans' promise of the use of force that led Saddam Hussein to recognize that he had the duty to disarm" and that "Saddam Hussein acquired weapons of mass destruction. This is clearly what started this and brought us to where we are."[73]

Other events made it easy for the Bush administration to see the announcement as part of a pattern of hostile comments. At the Prague summit, Chrétien's press secretary had referred to Bush as a "moron" and the prime minister had fired her only after several days' delay, and reluctantly, while the egregious Carolyn Parrish, entering a meeting on February 26, had been caught saying, "Damn Americans, I hate those bastards." Natural Resources Minister Herb Dhaliwal responded to Bush's ultimatum to Saddam by denouncing the president as a "failed statesman." Chrétien did not publicly reprimand Dhaliwal, who rejected private demands from the prime minister that he apologize.[74] Cellucci invited Graham for dinner on the twenty-fourth, and chastised the government for being "politically opportunistic." Rejecting the war while keeping the ships in the Gulf, he went on, "was really insulting." He indicated that Bush would cancel a scheduled visit to Canada, and Elliott Abrams, a White House official whose responsibilities intersected with Dhaliwal's, would not meet with him, "so there's a freeze at the top." Graham found "absolutely no appreciation about [sic] what we are doing at all," and concluded that Cellucci had "gotten shit from Washington because he misled them about our intentions." Cellucci got most of his coverage of Canadian news from the right-leaning Global Television Network and *National Post*, so he had "a false sense of where Canada is."[75] His emphasis on the lack of political support rather than the assistance Canada was providing on the ground indicated that the former was what mattered to Bush. Graham discussed the meeting with Chrétien the next day, and the prime minister philosophically concluded that if Bush's visit was cancelled, that was "his decision." He felt that the government's decision had "defined us as Canadians."[76]

But Cellucci would cause problems later that day, speaking at a luncheon of the Economic Club of Toronto, at which he said the United States would be on hand to help with any threat to Canadian security: "We would be there for Canada, part of our family. That is why so many in the United States are disappointed and upset that Canada is not fully supporting us now," even though the Canadian ships, planes, and personnel in the Gulf would "provide more support indirectly to this war in Iraq than most of the 46 countries that are fully supporting our efforts there."[77] McDonough seized on Cellucci's acknowledgment of the Canadian contribution to ask if Chrétien was flip-flopping on participation after all, and he somewhat lamely responded that the Canadian Forces in the Gulf were performing various missions connected with Afghanistan and the war on terror.[78] The larger problem was the charge that the government had now clearly antagonized the Bush administration and Canadians would pay an economic price. Chrétien was worried that the right-wing press, joining forces with the Canadian Alliance, would create "a huge crisis and destabilize public opinion."[79] Chrétien's critics in the press and politics did manage to make hay with the apparent chill in Canadian-American relations. The historian Jack Granatstein warned of American retaliation in the pages of conservative press baron Conrad Black's *National Post*, remarking, "We all want Canada to be sovereign and able to make its own policies in the world. But we also want to eat regularly."[80] Premiers Ernie Eves of Ontario and Ralph Klein of Alberta echoed these concerns, while Thomas d'Aquino of the Canadian Council of Chief Executives declared he would escort a party of business leaders to Washington to refurbish the tarnished relationship.

Within a week, public approval of the government's conduct of the matter dropped from 66 to 56 percent.[81]

Some Cabinet members were alarmed. Bevilacqua lamented that "all actions have consequences," and that we were "seeing a deterioration" in the bilateral relationship. Chrétien reiterated that Liberal MPs should not make anti-American comments.[82] At a meeting of the Cabinet communications committee, Minister of Agriculture Lyle Vanclief said that Canadians hadn't "changed their minds" about the rightness of the government's underlying position, but were uncomfortable with the ill-advised comments by Dhaliwal and Parrish and the apparent backlash against them. Health Minister Anne McLellan went so far as to say that "Cellucci was right to say that he was disappointed."[83] Chrétien's line in the House was that while Cellucci had been disappointed, "among friends, sometimes we can disagree.... We are an independent country. We have the right to disagree with our neighbours."[84] The government took steps to dispel the impression of hostility left by the atmosphere surrounding its announcement of Canada's position, indicating that in the event Saddam employed proscribed weapons it might reconsider its abstention, passing a resolution expressing the hope for a speedy coalition victory, and reiterating Canada's willingness to help with Iraq's reconstruction. And above all, the expected economic backlash never materialized. Chrétien seems not to have expected much by way of retaliation, given the degree of Canadian-American economic interdependence. Ambassador Kergin had pointed out back in late 2002 that "economic access is distinct from our military co-operation — there's no direct linkage,"[85] and Greg Donaghy, head of the Department of Foreign Affairs and International Trade's historical section, had informed Graham that Lester Pearson's famous Temple University speech criticizing American policy in Vietnam had not led Lyndon Johnson to stop congressional ratification of the Auto Pact.[86] Chrétien himself was worried less about loss of access to the American market than about the danger of the U.S. economy dipping into recession as a result of war, something that "affects us all."[87]

Despite the failure of the Canadian effort to broker a compromise built around disarming Iraq on a basis of clear evidence, and the somewhat uneven handling of the announcement of Canada's decision not to support invasion, there was little lasting damage to the bilateral relationship or the government's domestic standing. That the war was remarkably short and the Bush administration preferred to involve others in reconstruction helped to mitigate American resentment, and the absence of economic retaliation ensured that the initial dip in public support for the Chrétien government's handling of the issue quickly reversed itself. To be sure, bilateral intimacy was slow to return, particularly at the level of symbolism; Bush never did visit Canada until Chrétien had been succeeded by his former finance minister, Paul Martin.[88] As it became clear that there were no WMDs and that the occupation was going to be difficult and bloody, public support for Chrétien's position gradually rose from the 50-percent range to the 80-percent range.[89] In the short term, while the public in both Canada and the United States followed the leads of their respective governments, leading to a short-term divergence of public sentiment, the increasingly evident failure of the Iraq invasion led to a convergence of Canadian and American opinion, with the war widely regarded on both sides of the forty-ninth parallel as a mistake.

One of the great what-ifs of this episode is what would have happened had Bush accepted Chrétien's compromise or a variant thereof, and delayed action by a few more weeks to gather more information. Chrétien could hardly decline to take part in a compromise he had sponsored, at least not without grave embarrassment. It is arguable that this would have posed severe problems for him with the Canadian electorate,[90] but this may be overstated. In both Canada and the United States, undecided opinion broke emphatically in favour of the government's decision once that was made, and it seems reasonable to assume that this would have been the case had the Canadian decision been otherwise.[91] Public opinion in Canada was against war without U.N. sanction, though less emphatically than we tend to think; yet opposition was dramatically more pronounced in Quebec, so Canadian participation would have had consequences for the politics of national unity, with a Quebec provincial election looming and the sovereigntist Parti Québécois making much of its anti-war stance. On the other hand, the Quebec election was held on April 14, so a later deadline would have limited any fallout. And if Canadian participation had been limited to verbal support and the presence in the Persian Gulf that the government maintained anyway, the lack of a sizeable troop commitment and with it any significant casualties, would have placed a low ceiling on the intensity of any public opposition. One seeming anomaly in the relevant polling data is that from 2003 through 2007, the Canadian public was almost evenly divided on whether the United States had done the right thing in invading Iraq and ousting Saddam, even as healthy majorities continued to back Chrétien's decision.[92] This suggests that the electorate distinguished between verbal support and large-scale participation, and would have accepted a Canadian policy based on the former, with only a token presence on the ground, in which case Chrétien was not running unreasonable risks by keeping that possibility open under the right circumstances. The discrepancy may also reflect, in part, the counterproductive nature of Cellucci's address and the other indications of displeasure on the part of the Bush administration. Insofar as these allowed Chrétien to highlight the question of Canada's right to an autonomous decision as much as the merits of the question, they made it easier for those who might have backed Canadian participation in the absence of heavy-handed pressure to support the government's decision. Thus Chrétien's cautious, centrist stance could even command the support of some pro-war Canadians.

NOTES

1. Adam Gopnik, "The Big One," *The New Yorker*, August 23, 2004. That historians generally consider these lessons to be reductive if not downright false is inarguable, but beside the point for the argument at hand.

2. Canada, Parliament, House of Commons, *Debates*, vol. 137, February 20, 2002, www.parl.gc.ca/HousePublications/Publication.aspx?Language=E&Mode=1& Parl=37&Ses=1&DocId=1385044 (accessed August 16, 2014).

3. Jean Chrétien, "Discours du Premier Ministre Canadien, Jean Chrétien, devant le Chicago Council on Foreign Relations, le 13 Fevrier 2003" (speech, Chicago, February 13, 2003), www.voltairenet.org/article9061.html (accessed April 26, 2014).

4. For example, on March 17, 2003, the day Prime Minister Chrétien announced Canada would not be taking part in the invasion, Alliance MP Rahim Jaffer charged, "The government has been the opposite of consistent": Canada, Parliament, House of Commons, *Debates*, vol. 138, March 17, 2003, www.parl.gc.ca/HousePublications/ Publication.aspx?Pub=Hansard&Mee=71&Language=e&Parl=37&Ses=2 (accessed August 16, 2014). For a representative specimen of retrospective criticism, see Andrew Richter, "From Trusted Ally to Suspicious Neighbour: Canada-U.S. Relations in a Changing Global Environment," *American Review of Canadian Studies* 35, no. 3 (2005): 471–502.

5. Reg Whitaker, "The Chrétien Legacy," in *The Chrétien Legacy: Politics and Public Policy in Canada*, ed. Lois Harder and Steve Patten (Montreal and Kingston: McGill-Queen's University Press, 2006), 10.

6. Canada, Parliament, House of Commons, *Debates*, vol. 137, February 19, 2002, www.parl.gc.ca/HousePublications/Publication.aspx?Language=E&Mode=1&Parl=37&Ses=1&DocId=1385037.

7. Kim Richard Nossal, "'Quantum Leaping': The Gulf Debate in Australia and Canada," in *The Gulf War: Critical Perspectives*, ed. Michael McKinley (Sydney: Allen & Unwin, 1994).

8. "Address by the Honourable Lloyd Axworthy Minister of Foreign Affairs to the North Atlantic Council Meeting" (speech, December 8, 1998), www.nato.int/docu/speech/1998/s981208i.htm (accessed April 27, 2014). On UNSCOM and UNMOVIC, see the account by UNSCOM's head, in Richard Butler, *Saddam Defiant: The Threat of Weapons of Mass Destruction and the Crisis of Global Security* (London: Weidenfeld and Nicolson, 2000).

9. Richter, "From Trusted Ally to Suspicious Neighbour," 476.

10. Fredrik Logevall, "Anatomy of an Unnecessary War: The Iraq Invasion," in *The Presidency of George W. Bush: A First Historical Assessment*, ed. Julian E. Zelizer (Princeton, NJ and Oxford: Princeton University Press, 2010), 89–100.

11. Jean Chrétien, *My Years as Prime Minister* (Toronto: Alfred A. Knopf Canada, 2007), 307–09.

12. Bush's address to the General Assembly on September 12, 2002, can be found at: www.theguardian.com/world/2002/sep/12/iraq.usa3 (accessed April 27, 2014).

13. Brian Bow, *The Politics of Linkage: Power, Interdependence, and Ideas in Canada-U.S. Relations* (Vancouver: University of British Columbia Press, 2009), 133.

14. Jeff Sallot, "Ottawa Lauds U.N. Approach," *Globe and Mail*, September 13, 2002.

15. Sheldon Alberts, "No Cheating, Graham Warns Iraq," *National Post*, September 21, 2002.

16. "Some Reflections on Last Nights' [sic] dinner," October 24, 2002, folder APEC Dinner, October 24/02, box G-5, papers of the Honourable Bill Graham, privately held (hereafter BGP; all citations to these papers reflect their organization as of early 2014). The author thanks Mr. Graham for access to these.

17. The text of Resolution 1441 is available at: www.un.org/depts/unmovic/new/documents/resolutions/s-res-1441.pdf (accessed April 27, 2014).

18. Graham handwritten note, "Prague 21.11.02," November 21, 2002, f. November 2002, box B-1, BGP.

19. "Countries [sic] Proposed Responses to the US Demarche," n.d. but clearly circa November 21, 2002, f. November 2002, box B-1, BGP.

20. See note 18 in this chapter.

21. NATO's 1999 bombing of Kosovo to stop ethnic cleansing of Kosovar Albanians by Serb forces took place after a threatened Russian veto prevented Security Council

authorization. The intervention was widely regarded by scholars of international law as illegal but legitimate nonetheless. See, for example, Heike Krieger, ed., *The Kosovo Conflict and International Law: An Analytical Documentation, 1974–1999* (Cambridge: Cambridge University Press, 2012).

22. Graham handwritten note, "Iraq," n.d. but late November 2002, f. November 2002, box B-1, BGP.

23. Graham handwritten note, Draft, "Proposed Approach to Responding to the US Request on Iraq," November 19, 2002, n.s., idem.

24. Anthony Seldon, with Peter Snowdon and Daniel Collings, *Blair Unbound* (London: Simon & Schuster, 2007), 142–43. As Logevall points out, Saddam was the co-author of his own misfortune insofar as he stopped short of dispelling all reasonable suspicion that he had WMDs, presumably wanting to deter regional rivals such as Iran by leaving the impression that he might possess them. He could not do so without adding credibility to American and British charges to the same effect. Logevall, "Anatomy of an Unnecessary War," 111.

25. Janice Gross Stein and Eugene Lang, *The Unexpected War: Canada in Kandahar* (Toronto: Penguin Canada, 2007), 46–51. As Timothy Sayle points out in his contribution to this volume, Stein and Lang err in overlooking the ongoing pressure for Canada to provide at least political approval and a token contribution to the invasion of Iraq.

26. Shawn McCarthy and Daniel LeBlanc, "PM Scolds McCallum on Canada's Role in Iraq," *Globe and Mail*, January 16, 2003.

27. For an analysis that stresses Chrétien's attachment to the United Nations and multilateralism, see Brendon O'Connor and Srdjan Vucetic, "Another Mars-Venus Divide? Why Australia Said 'Yes' and Canada Said 'Non' to Involvement in the 2003 Iraq War," *Australian Journal of International Affairs* 64, no. 5 (2010): 526–48. Bow, *The Politics of Linkage*, 129–37 stresses his willingness to sign on to military action if the case for war was strong and U.N. approval was blocked by a "capricious" French or Russian veto. Timothy Sayle stresses the Kosovo precedent and the absence in the case of Iraq of the international consensus that pertained in the case of Kosovo.

28. See the text of Blix's report to the Security Council on January 27, 2003, at www.un.org/Depts/unmovic/Bx27.htm (accessed April 29, 2014).

29. Graham handwritten note, "Iraq," n.d. but January 28, 2003, f. January 2003, box B-1, BGP.

30. Graham handwritten note, "04.02.03," ibid.

31. Graham handwritten notes on conversation with Heinbecker, written on reverse of "Possible Telephone Call to Dr. ElBaradei, Director General of the IAEA: Talking Points," January 27, 2003, ibid.

32. Graham handwritten notes on conversation with Blix, on reverse of "Possible Telephone Call to Dr. Blix, Chairman of UNMOVIC: Talking Points," January 27, 2003, ibid.

33. Graham handwritten note, "Conv. W. Blix," February 12, 2003, f. February 2003, box B-1, BGP.

34. Blix's report to the Security Council: see note 28 in this chapter.

35. Canada, Parliament, House of Commons, *Debates*, vol. 138, January 28, 2003, www.parl.gc.ca/HousePublications/Publication.aspx?Language=E&Mode=1& Parl=37&Ses=2&DocId=658747 (accessed August 16, 2014).

36. Ibid., February 11, 2003, www.parl.gc.ca/HousePublications/Publication. aspx?Language=E&Mode=1&Parl=37&Ses=2&DocId=692185 (accessed August 16, 2014).

37. Graham's handwritten notes on telephone conversation with Straw and undated note to Chrétien on the same day, f. January 2003, box B-2, BGP.

38. Powell's presentation can be found at: www.theguardian.com/world/2003/feb/05/ iraq.usa (accessed April 28, 2014).

39. Paul Heinbecker, *Getting Back in the Game: A Foreign Policy Playbook for Canada* (Toronto: Key Porter, 2010), 145.

40. Chrétien, "Discours du Premier Ministre Canadien."

41. Graham handwritten note on conversation with Fischer, February 19, 2003, f. February 2003, box B-2(a), BGP. The reference to a "Pinochet solution" presumably pertains to the arrangement by which the Chilean dictator Augusto Pinochet remained as commander-in-chief of the armed forces, and something of a figurehead, for a decade after the 1988 constitutional referendum that inaugurated Chile's transition back to democracy.

42. Seldon et al., *Blair Unbound*, 147–52.

43. Blix's report of February 14, 2003, is available at: www.un.org/depts/unmovic/ new/pages/security_council_briefings.asp#6 (accessed August 17, 2014).

44. Seldon et al., *Blair Unbound*, 157.

45. Note by Graham, n.d., f. February 2003, box B-2(a), BGP.

46. Jeff Sallot, Miro Cernetig, and Barrie McKenna, "PM Aims to Broker Iraq Deal," *Globe and Mail*, February 20, 2003.

47. Graham handwritten note, n.d. but February 20, 2003, f. February 2003, box B-2(a), BGP.

48. Graham handwritten note, February 20, 2003, ibid. Blix noted in his diary at the time that the military buildup could generate a momentum of its own that would make it impossible for Bush *not* to go to war. See Blix, op. cit., 109–10. Logevall echoes this, suggesting that beyond the fifty thousand troops required to induce Saddam's compliance, the buildup and the calendar conspired to limit Bush's freedom of action, making war by March — before the hot season — virtually inevitable. Logevall, "Anatomy of an Unnecessary War," 112.

49. Handwritten note of conversation by Graham, n.d. but February 24, 2003, f. February 2003, box B-2(a), BGP.

50. As pointed out by Fred Kaplan in "Give Saddam Two More Weeks: A Good Idea from the Canadians," *Slate*, February 28, 2003.

51. The text of the memo appears at: www.globalpolicy.org/component/content/article/167/35235.html (accessed April 30, 2014).

52. Kaplan, "Give Saddam Two More Weeks."

53. Graham handwritten note, "Conv. w. Heinbecker," March 13, 2003, f. March 2003, box B-2(a), BGP.

54. Fax from Jim Wright to Dan Costello, relaying email from Malone to Heinbecker, Glyn Berry, and Jim Wright, f. March 2003, box B-2(a), BGP.

55. Graham handwritten note, March 12, 2003, ibid.

56. Seldon et al., *Blair Unbound*, 164–71.

57. Stephen Thorne, "No Need for Iraq War, Bush Has Already Won, Chrétien Tells US News Program," *Vancouver Sun*, March 9, 2003. Milosevic was ultimately ousted in an election he unwisely called, but had been indicted for war crimes and crimes against humanity before the International Criminal Tribunal for the former Yugoslavia. Surely regime change was part of what the NATO powers sought.

58. Graham handwritten note, March 16, 2003, f. March 2003, box B-2(a), BGP. The salient passage was apparently added on March 17.

59. Graham handwritten note, March 17, 2003, and typewritten copy of Chrétien's statement as read, with marginalia, ibid. Graham does not appear in the account of this episode by Chrétien and only in passing in that by Goldenberg. See Chrétien, *My Years as Prime Minister*, 314, and Eddie Goldenberg, *The Way It Works: Inside Ottawa* (Toronto: McClelland & Stewart, 2006), 1–5. Goldenberg's account is detailed, but he depicts himself and Laverdure as crafting Chrétien's statement.

60. Graham fax to Laverdure from Caplan's office, March 17, 2003, f. March 2003, box B-2(a), BGP.

61. Canada, Parliament, House of Commons, *Debates*, vol. 138, March 17, 2003. On Manley's discomfiture and the atmosphere of the occasion generally, see Kim Nossal's contribution to this volume.

62. Ibid.

63. See Nossal's contribution to this volume.

64. Canada, Parliament, House of Commons, *Debates*, vol. 138, March 17, 2003.

65. Graham note, "Powell," March 17, 2003, f. March 2003, box B-2(a), BGP.

66. See, for example, Day's comments in Canada, Parliament, House of Commons, *Debates*, vol. 138, March 17, 2003. The op-ed is Stephen Harper and Stockwell Day, "Canadians Stand with You," *Wall Street Journal*, March 28, 2003. Harper and Day drew a sharp distinction between the government's position and that of the Canadian public, saying, "Canadians will be overwhelmingly with us" in their support of the invasion. This was not, to put it mildly, what the relevant polling data suggested.

67. Canada, Parliament, House of Commons, *Debates*, vol. 138, March 17, 2003.

68. Ibid.

69. Ibid.
70. Ibid.
71. See Graham's handwritten notes on conversations with Chrétien and McCallum, March 12, 2003, f. March 2003, box B-2(a), BGP.
72. Canada, Parliament, House of Commons, *Debates*, vol. 138, March 17, 2003.
73. Ibid., March 20, 2003, www.parl.gc.ca/HousePublications/Publication. aspx?Language=E&Mode=1&Parl=37&Ses=2&DocId=771117 (accessed August 16, 2014).
74. Lawrence Martin, *Iron Man: The Defiant Reign of Jean Chrétien* (Toronto: Viking Canada, 2003), 402–03, and 412–13.
75. Graham handwritten note, "Reflections on Conv. w. Cellucci," March 24, 2003, f. March 2003, box B-2(a), BGP. Cellucci also suggested Powell was angered by Canadian efforts to broker a compromise solution at the United Nations. But, as one of Graham's aides jotted down, Powell "told you himself that he understood what you were trying to do," n.s., n.d., but circa March 25, 2003, ibid.
76. Graham handwritten notes, "Conv. w. PM," March 25, 2003, ibid.
77. Paul Cellucci, "We Are Family" (transcript of Cellucci's remarks to the Economic Club of Toronto, March 25, 2003), *Policy Options*, May 2003, 11–13.
78. Canada, Parliament, House of Commons, *Debates*, vol. 138, March 26, 2003, www.parl.gc.ca/HousePublications/Publication.aspx?Language=E&Mode=1&Parl=37&Ses=2&DocId=790100 (accessed August 16, 2014).
79. Graham's undated handwritten notes on Cabinet meeting, March 26, 2003, f. March 2003, box B-2(a), BGP.
80. J.L. Granatstein, "The Empire Strikes Back," *National Post*, March 26, 2003.
81. Donald Barry, "Chrétien, Bush, and the War in Iraq," *American Review of Canadian Studies* 35, no. 2 (2005): 230.
82. See note 79 in this chapter.
83. Graham handwritten notes on meeting of Cabinet communications committee, March 31, 2003, f. March 2003, box B-2(a), BGP.
84. Canada, Parliament, House of Commons, *Debates*, vol. 138, March 26, 2003.
85. See note 22 in this chapter.
86. Note, "From Greg Donaghy at the History Section of the Dept," n.d. and n.s., but late March 2003, f. March 2003, box B-2(a), BGP. Both Barry's article and Kim Nossal's contribution to this volume stress the lack of American retaliation.
87. Graham handwritten note, "Cabinet," apparently February 25, 2003, f. February 2003, ibid.
88. Barry, "Chrétien, Bush, and the War in Iraq," 233.
89. Marc J. O'Reilly and Richard Vengroff, "Canada," in *Public Opinion and International Intervention: Lessons from the Iraq War*, ed. Richard Sobel, Peter Furia, and Bethany Barratt (Washington: Potomac Books, 2012), 225.
90. As argued by Sayle in his contribution to this volume.
91. Barry raises this as a possibility, though he is apparently not persuaded.

92. O'Reilly and Vengroff, "Canada," 226–27. Popular opposition to participation was not dramatically greater in Canada than in Australia, which did take part. See O'Connor and Vucetic, "Another Mars-Venus Divide," 534.

14

AUSTRALIAN PUBLIC OPINION TOWARD THE IRAQ WAR

Ian McAllister

Since the end of the Second World War, defence has only rarely become a political issue in Australia. In part, this reflects the absence of any major physical threat to Australia since white settlement; the only occasion when there was any serious risk of invasion occurred when the Japanese invaded New Guinea in 1942. In part, too, it reflects the fact that Australia has been able to rely on powerful allies to protect it. Prior to the Second World War this role was filled by the colonial power, Great Britain, and during and after the Second World War, by the United States. As a consequence, the public has had few firm views on defence policy and how it should be conducted, nor has it possessed much knowledge about the strategic options available. This situation was sustained by an informal bipartisan consensus within the political elite to exclude defence from everyday political discussion.[1]

The two exceptions to this pattern are the Vietnam War and the Iraq War. Australia first committed combat troops to Vietnam in 1965, in support of the United States, with a phased withdrawal taking place between 1970 and 1973. In the early stages of the war, public opinion was generally supportive of Australia's participation, seeing Vietnam as part of a "domino" pattern, whereby successive Southeast Asian countries would fall under communist rule. However, by the late 1960s, with victory a diminishing prospect, public opinion was more evenly divided and shaped by partisanship.[2] The Liberal-National coalition argued for continued involvement in the war, while the opposition Labor Party advocated withdrawal. The military commitment in Vietnam was an issue in the 1969 election, but more particularly in the 1972 election, which brought Labor to office after twenty-three years in opposition.

Australia's involvement in the Iraq War has been at least as divisive as Vietnam. While Australia's participation in the 1990–91 Gulf War was widely supported by the public and had bipartisan support,[3] the military commitment to the 2003 Iraq War has been intensely controversial.[4] While the Liberal-National coalition government supported participation alongside the United States, the Labor opposition withheld support for the invasion of Iraq in the absence of a U.N. mandate. Initially, the war attracted a narrow majority of the public in support, but intense and emotional conflict within the political elite soon made it a partisan issue. Partisan divisions, coupled with a realization that the insurgency would prevent the Allies from executing a quick withdrawal, weakened the public's resolve, and by mid-2004 a majority favoured withdrawing the troops.

This chapter examines public opinion toward the 2003 Iraq War and Australia's subsequent military involvement in the country. While there is much less survey data than is available in, for example, the United States, a variety of commercial polls have been conducted, as well as the more in-depth and academic 2004 and 2007 Australian Election Study (AES) surveys.[5] The analyses that follow are based on these commercial and academic surveys. The chapter proceeds as follows. The first section provides an overview of the general context of public opinion on defence over an extended period. The second section examines public opinion on the war itself, while the third section deals with partisan differences over the war. The fourth section tests four hypotheses to explain public opinion on the war, while the conclusion seeks to explain public opinion toward the Iraq War within a comparative context.

DEFENCE, THREATS, AND THE U.S. ALLIANCE

Although Australian military forces have been involved in six operations since the end of the Second World War in 1945 — the Korean

War (1950–53), the Malaya Emergency (1950–60), the Indonesian Confrontation (1963–66), the Vietnam War (1962–72), the Gulf War (1990–91), and the Iraq War (2003)[6] — none has represented a direct threat to Australia's security. Moreover, with the exception of the Vietnam War, relatively small numbers of military personnel were involved. The Australian population has, therefore, not been faced with a direct challenge to the country's territorial integrity since the Second World War, and there are relatively few Australians currently alive who harbour any direct memory of the pre-1945 period and the threat posed by the Japanese. The absence of any direct threat for over half a century undoubtedly has had a significant impact on how the public views potential future threats within the region.

The most effective way to place public opinion on defence in context is to examine long-term trends in opinions. Fortunately, three questions have been asked consistently in a range of surveys over an extended period of time: priorities for defence spending; perceptions of security threats to Australia; and support for the security treaty between Australia, New Zealand, and the United States (ANZUS).[7] While no single question provides a succinct answer as to how the public views defence in Australia, taken together these three survey questions convey a general sense of how the public approaches the issue, how opinions have changed in response to major events, and the broad trajectory of opinions.

The public's perception of the countries that may represent a security threat to Australia is perhaps the central driver of overall opinions toward defence. If the people see a serious security threat to Australia, they will be more likely to see defence as important, to take an interest in defence policy, and to place a greater value on international alliances. In the late 1960s and early 1970s, around half the population believed there was a security threat to Australia.[8] Following the effective end of Australia's involvement in the Vietnam War in 1972 and the formal end to the war in 1975, perceptions of a threat declined to 43 percent in 1976. Figure 14.1 picks up the trend and shows that in 1980, following the Soviet invasion of Afghanistan in December 1979, the proportion seeing a threat to Australia increased significantly to 63 percent.

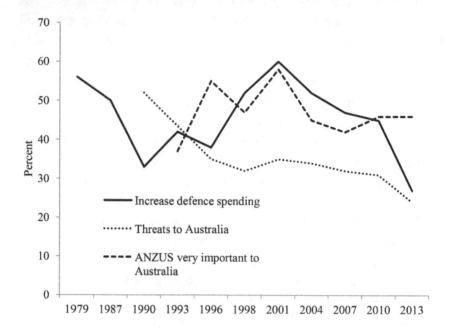

Figure 14.1: Public Opinion Toward Defence, Threats, and ANZUS, 1979–2013

1979–2010: "Do you think the government should spend more or less on defence?"

2013: "Please say whether there should be more or less public expenditure in each of the following areas. Remember [that] if you say 'more' it could require a tax increase, and if you say 'less' it could require a reduction in those services ... defence."

"Threats to Australia" is the percentage of respondents who mentioned at least one country as "very likely" to represent a security threat.

"How important do you think the Australian alliance with the United States under the ANZUS Treaty is for protecting Australia's security?"

Note: Question wordings before 1993 vary slightly.

Sources: McAllister and Makkai (1992); 1979 Australian National Political Attitudes Survey; 1987–2013 Australian Election Study surveys.

Since 1980, the numbers seeing a potential threat to Australia exhibit an almost linear decline, to about half the population by 1990 and one-third by 1998.[9] The 9/11 attacks in the United States in 2001 and the East Timor crisis in 1999–2000 caused only a small increase in threat perceptions before they resumed their downward trend in the late 2000s. The most recent survey, conducted after the 2013 election, shows the lowest proportion ever recorded who see a potential threat to Australia, at just 24 percent of the population.

The trend suggests that the two major events of the postwar years, the collapse of communism and end of the Cold War in 1990, and the 9/11 attacks, have had little impact on the public's sense that a security threat exists to the country.

The second long-term trend in public opinion is whether the public believes more or less money should be spent on defence. Measuring the appropriate level of funding that the public wants for defence is, of course, difficult, particularly if it is divorced from the other trade-offs that may be involved; more government funding for defence might mean, for example, less funding for the environment and so on. Nevertheless, while asking people to opt for more or less funding for defence without any explicit trade-off has limited utility, measuring the trend across an extended period does tell us much about the relative standing of defence in the eyes of the public.

Following the Soviet invasion of Afghanistan, Cold War concerns came to the fore, and in 1980 just over half of the survey respondents wanted more money spent on defence. That proportion gradually decreased through the 1980s, declining to one in three by 1990. Support for defence again rose after the 1990–91 Gulf War, once more reaching Cold War levels in 2000 and 2001 after the East Timor crisis and the 9/11 attacks. Since 2000, support for defence spending has declined consistently with each survey, most recently standing at 27 percent in 2013. This is less than half the proportion in 2001, and by far the lowest proportion during the period for which survey data is available.

Since it was signed in 1951, the ANZUS Treaty has been the cornerstone of Australia's defence policy and, for the United States, one of its most important defence arrangements in the Asia-Pacific region.[10] Starting in 1993, the first survey for which data are available, the proportion of survey respondents who see the ANZUS alliance as "very important" closely tracks the trend in the proportion who want more spending on defence. The trend peaks in 2001, following the 9/11 attacks, when 58 percent viewed the alliance as being "very important." It is notable that even though a historically low proportion in 2013 saw a possible threat to Australia, support for the alliance remained at a high level. How the public views the international environment is therefore only weakly related to views of the ANZUS Treaty.

These broad trends, traced in opinion surveys over four decades, suggest that the end of the Cold War represented a pivotal event for the public's views of defence and security. While there was a declining sense among the public of any security threat to Australia, in the decade leading up to 2001 and the 9/11 attacks, support for defence and the ANZUS alliance actually increased. Clearly, the public viewed threats other than the traditional ones from a nation-state as being salient. That view was cemented by the 9/11 attacks and the 2002 Bali bombings, which served to redefine the concept of a security threat in terms of terrorism. As the next section outlines, this has implications for the public's views of the Iraq War and the association between the war and the threat of terrorism.

PUBLIC OPINION ON THE IRAQ WAR

Following the 9/11 attacks and the subsequent invasion of Afghanistan, it was evident that an invasion of Iraq and the removal of the Saddam Hussein regime was the next foreign policy objective for the United States. However, gathering public consent for the use of military force against Iraq presented major problems for the U.S. government and its major allies, Britain and Australia. Iraq had not overtly threatened any of the three countries, and the war was not endorsed by the United Nations. The justification for the invasion was the belief that Iraq was developing weapons of mass destruction (WMDs), which could be used by terrorists and rogue states. In Britain and Australia, a complementary argument used to justify the use of force against Iraq was the need to support a major ally in a time of war.[11]

Even in the immediate aftermath of the Iraq War, the Australian public viewed it as a relatively unimportant issue, at least in comparison to other issues. For example, in the 2004 AES, respondents were asked, using a closed-question format, which of twelve issues they considered to be the most important in the election. Just 4 percent mentioned the Iraq War, making it the eighth most important issue out of the twelve, just ahead of refugees and asylum seekers (3 percent), and behind terrorism (5 percent). By contrast, 29 percent mentioned health as the most important issue in the election campaign, and 16 percent taxation. In the 2007 AES, just 2 percent mentioned the Iraq War as the most important issue in that election. The lack of saliency of an issue generally means that the public is not well educated on the policy options. In that circumstance, much depends on how the question is asked in a survey, and on the context of the question.

Asking the public questions about Iraq outside the context of an election campaign or using an open, as opposed to closed, question format does not produce any different responses. The Morgan Gallup poll asks survey respondents an open question about the most important issues facing the country. In three surveys conducted between November 2005 and May 2008, just 2 percent nominated the Iraq War as the most important issue, and in the surveys conducted after 2008 the same figure has been 1 percent or less.[12] The low profile of Iraq compared to respondents' other concerns — certainly in relation to everyday issues such as health, education, and taxation — means that citizens are relatively uninformed about the issue, and that has implications for both the depth that a survey can go in asking questions on the topic and for the robustness of the results.

Notwithstanding the public's general lack of interest in Iraq as a political issue, the lead-up to the war produced considerable publicity as the military forces gathered in the Gulf. In a speech to the United Nations General Assembly in September 2002, U.S. president George W. Bush characterized the Iraqi regime led by Saddam Hussein as a "grave and gathering danger." Following a U.N. resolution in November, weapons inspectors began searching for WMDs, but by January 2003 none had been found and the chief weapons inspector, Hans Blix, indicated that the Iraqi authorities had not been fully co-operative. These events were widely reported in Australia, and while the government had not yet made any decision on participation in a future invasion of Iraq, the media, as elsewhere, bracketed Iraq with the threat from international terrorism.[13]

During the military preparations for the invasion of Iraq, those favouring involvement with the United States in the war were in a minority. Figure 14.2 shows that in September 2002, for example, just after Bush delivered his speech to the United Nations, 36 percent favoured involvement in the war, while 53 percent opposed it. Just 11 percent had no opinion, a relatively small proportion; this indicates that the vast majority of respondents had formed an opinion on the issue. As war became seemingly more inevitable, the proportion opposing it gradually declined. In a poll conducted just as the attack on Iraq began, opinion was evenly balanced, with 45 percent in favour and 47 percent against. In two subsequent polls conducted in the days after the invasion, when the coalition forces were clearly in the ascendancy, those in favour reached a majority for the first time.

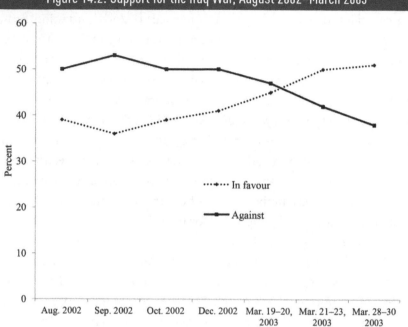

Figure 14.2: Support for the Iraq War, August 2002–March 2003

August–December 2002: "Thinking now about Australia's involvement in possible US-led military action against Iraq with the objective of deposing Saddam Hussein. Are you personally in favour or against Australian forces being part of any US-led military action against Iraq?"

March 2003: "Thinking now about Iraq and Australia's involvement in military action against Iraq. Are you personally in favour or against Australian troops being involved in military action against Iraq?"

Source: Newspoll.

One reason for the change in public opinion was a consequence of extensive government publicity about the reasons behind Australia's military involvement in the war. For example, the prime minister, John Howard, gave a two-hour televised address to the National Press Club on March 13, 2003, in which he argued that the world risked terrorists obtaining WMDs from Iraq.[14] In part, too, the change in public opinion was a classic example of the "rally round the flag" effect first advanced by the political scientist John Mueller.[15] In Mueller's model, U.S. presidents can expect surges in short-term public support during periods of international crisis or war. Mueller's three preconditions for this to occur are that the crisis is international; directly involves the president; and is "specific, dramatic, and sharply focussed."[16] The

Australian case certainly fits this model, not least through Howard's close personal association with the decision to commit troops to the conflict.

A vexed issue for Australia was the role of the United Nations. Liberal policy was to seek a U.N. mandate for military action, but still to proceed to war if that endorsement was not forthcoming. The policy of the Labor opposition was to oppose any participation in the war in the absence of a U.N. mandate. Table 14.1 shows that the public clearly preferred involvement in the war with U.N. support rather than without it.[17] In February 2003, for example, 57 percent supported military involvement if U.N. endorsement was forthcoming; without U.N. endorsement, public support for the war was just 18 percent. Moreover, the strength of opposition to the war without a U.N. mandate was considerable; 58 percent said that they would be "strongly against" military action without U.N. endorsement. This pattern is replicated in a subsequent survey using the same question conducted one month later.

TABLE 14.1: Support for Military Action with and without U.N. Endorsement, 2003				
	With U.N. support		Without U.N. support	
	Feb. 03	Mar. '03	Feb. 03	Mar. 03
Strongly favour	23	27	8	9
Somewhat favour	34	29	10	13
(Total favour)	(57)	(56)	(18)	(22)
Somewhat against	11	11	18	16
Strongly against	28	26	58	55
(Total against)	(39)	(37)	(76)	(71)
Uncommitted	4	7	6	7
Total	100	100	100	100
N of respondents	1,200	1,220	1,769	1,873

"Thinking now about Iraq and Australia's involvement in military action against Iraq. Are you personally in favour or against Australian troops being involved in military action against Iraq if the United Nations supported such action? And if the United Nations did not support military action, are you personally in favour or against Australian troops being involved in military action against Iraq?"

Note: Fieldwork for the February survey was done January 31 to February 2; for the March survey, February 28 to March 2.

Source: Newspoll.

Initially, then, public opinion was narrowly in favour of involvement in the war, but it quickly began to dissipate. As the insurgency gained ground and it became clear that an Australian military presence would be required for the foreseeable future, public support for the war faded. Figure 14.3 shows that in February 2004, almost one year since the invasion and ten months since President Bush had declared "mission accomplished," opinion was evenly divided on whether or not it was worth going to war. Since then, the proportion believing that it was not worth going to war increased significantly. By 2007, the proportion believing that it was worth going to war had more than halved to 22 percent, while 74 percent believed that it was not worth going to war. This is a substantial change in opinion over the space of just three years, and indicates the extent of the public's disillusionment with the way the aftermath of the war was handled.

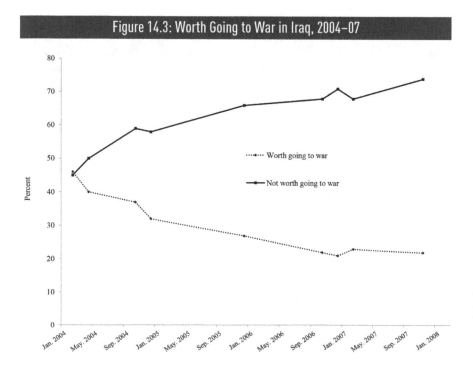

Figure 14.3: Worth Going to War in Iraq, 2004–07

Newspoll: "Overall, do you think it was worth going to war in Iraq or not?"

AES (October 2004, November 2007): "Taking everything into account, do you think the war in Iraq has been worth the cost or not?"

Sources: Newspoll; Australian Election Studies, 2004, 2007.

Finally, did the public think it had been misled over the reasons for the war? And did the public believe that the war had reduced the threat of terrorism, as the government claimed it would do? The issue of how far the public believed it had been misled over the stated reasons for the war was a potent one, given the failure to find any evidence of WMDs following the cessation of hostilities. Table 14.2 shows that in both July 2003 and in February 2004 a majority of the public felt that it had been misled over Iraq's possession of WMDs. In 2003, slightly more believed that they had been "knowingly misled;" by early 2004, opinions were more charitable to the government, and more people thought that they had been "unknowingly misled."

Table 14.2: The Accuracy of Information and the Threat of Terrorism							
	Public information			**Threat of terrorism**			
	Jul. 2003	Feb. 2004		Mar. 2004	Sept. 2004	Oct. 2004	Dec. 2006
Knowingly misled	36	26	**More likely**	65	66	56	64
Unknowingly misled	31	36	**No difference**	30	31	41	31
Did not mislead	25	26	**Less likely**	1	1	2	2
Uncommitted	8	12	**Uncommitted**	4	2	1	3
Total	100	100		100	100	100	100
N of respondents	1,200	1,220		1,200	1,769	1,873	1,200

Newspoll: "Thinking now about Iraq. In the lead-up to the war in Iraq, do you think the Howard government knowingly misled the Australian public about whether Iraq had weapons of mass destruction, unknowingly misled the Australian public, or did not mislead the Australian public?"

AES (2004): "Thinking now about the potential for terrorism in Australia. Do you personally think Australia's involvement in the Iraqi war has made a terrorist attack in Australia more likely, less likely, or has it made no difference?"

Sources: Newspoll; 2004 Australian Election Study.

Whether the Iraq War had reduced the threat of terrorism was also a sensitive issue for the government, since one of the stated aims was to remove the possibility that Iraq could become a haven for terrorists and give them access to WMDs.[18] The head of the Australian Federal Police, Mick Keelty, had been publicly rebuked by the prime minister when he suggested that the March 2004 Madrid train bombings, which killed 191 people, might be linked to Spain's involvement in Iraq. Keelty was forced to clarify his statement, claiming that his initial remarks were taken out of context.[19] However, the second part of Table 14.2 shows that the public largely endorsed Keelty's view. Between March 2004 and December 2006, around two in every three respondents thought that the Iraq War had made a terrorist attack more likely, with the partial exception of the October 2004 poll. In March 2004, for example, at the time of Keelty's statement, just 1 percent thought that the war had made a terrorist attack less likely.

Three conclusions can be drawn from this brief overview of public opinion on the Iraq War between mid-2002 and late 2007. First, public opinion was generally opposed to the war until it had commenced, at which point the "rally round the flag" effect took hold. However, after about a year, public opinion began to move against the war, and by late 2007 around three in every four respondents believed that it had not been worth going to war — a major turnaround in opinion. Second, the narrow majority that had existed in support for the war when it began rested on insecure foundations; just several months after the war had been won, a majority believed that they had been misled about the reasons for the war. More tellingly, a large majority believed that Australia was at greater risk of terrorism as a result of involvement in the war, undermining one of the government's key arguments for going to war in the first place. Third, public opinion in support of the war very much hinged on U.N. endorsement. This was especially important for Labor supporters: in March 2003, just 11 percent supported involvement in the war without U.N. endorsement, but that figure increased to 52 percent in the event that U.N. endorsement was forthcoming. The next section examines the partisan basis to opinions about the war.

PARTISAN DIFFERENCES ON THE WAR

On complex policy issues, or on ones that involve a major decision such as involvement in a war, the public generally takes its cue from the political elite. If there is elite consensus in support of an action or on one side of an argument, then the public will usually follow the elite's lead. For example, a majority of both Liberal-National and Labor supporters supported the invasion of Afghanistan in October 2001, reflecting bipartisan elite support for the policy.[20] However, if the elite is divided, then this will be reflected in a divided public. The 1999 republic referendum in Australia is a classic example of elite division generating public opposition to a complex constitutional change. The move to a republic had attracted majority support in the years immediately leading up to the referendum, but elite divisions effectively caused that public support to dissipate.[21]

The Iraq War was a similarly complex issue, this time involving the most fundamental of all political decisions — the decision to go to war. From the outset, there was a strong partisan element to the debate. The Liberal-National government led by John Howard committed troops to the war, arguing that Iraq had flouted U.N. resolutions to disarm, that WMDs manufactured in Iraq could fall into the hands of other states, and that "no nation is more important to our long-term security than" the United States.[22] By contrast, the Labor opposition opposed involvement in the war, arguing that diplomatic efforts had not yet been exhausted and the United Nations had not authorized military action. As the Labor leader, Simon Crean, put it, "no troops should be sent to war without a UN mandate."[23] These differences were brought into sharp relief when Howard and Crean saw off the troops departing for Iraq in January 2003, and Crean stated, "I don't believe that you should be going,"[24] while Howard said, "It may be that this vessel and the deployment here are involved in wider operations" and hoped that no one would be harmed as a result.[25]

These deep differences between the major parties, in policy but also in tone and emotional intensity, were not lost on the public. Using the 2004 Australian Election Study survey, the first part of Table 14.3 shows that 61 percent of Liberal-National voters in the election considered that the Iraq War had been worth the cost, compared to just 16 percent of Labor voters.

Almost four in ten Liberal-National voters thought that the war had not been worth the cost, more than double the same figure for Labor voters. These are major partisan divisions, representing a difference of 45 percentage points. To place them in context, in the same election the partisan difference on the need for stricter laws to regulate trade unions was 43 percentage points; on the redistribution of wealth, 24 percentage points; and on private versus public schooling, 18 percentage points. In other words, while Iraq did not rank highly as an election issue in 2004, the public was more likely to follow its partisanship on Iraq than on on any other issue in the election.

Table 14.3: Iraq War Worth the Cost, Candidates and Voters, 2004			
	Liberal–National	Labor	Green
	(Voters)		
Worth the cost	61	16	9
Not worth the cost	39	84	91
Total	100	100	100
N	783	587	130
	(Election candidates)		
Worth the cost	90	6	1
Not worth the cost	10	94	99
Total	100	100	100
N of respondents	79	87	121

"Taking everything into account, do you think the war in Iraq has been worth the cost or not?"
Sources: 2004 Australian Election Study and Australian Candidate Study surveys.

The second part of Table 14.3 shows the same results for candidates in the election and provides a potent explanation for the differences observed among the public. Among Liberal-National candidates, 90 percent viewed Iraq as worth the cost, compared to just 6 percent of Labor candidates. This equates to an 84–percentage-point difference between the candidates of the two major parties. Voters may well have been following the partisan cues provided to them by the political elite, and this could substantially account for public opinion toward the war. This hypothesis is tested in the next section.

The longer-term trends in partisan differences in the war suggest that the most substantial changes were in attitudes among Liberal-National supporters. Figure 14.4 shows the commercial survey data presented earlier, disaggregated by voting intention. In 2004, as we saw in Table 14.3, around six in every ten Liberal-National voters thought that the war was worth the cost. The trend in Figure 14.4 shows that this declined almost linearly over a three-year period, dropping to 35 percent in late 2006, increasing slightly to 44 percent in February 2007, and dropping again to 42 percent in November 2007. This was the period in which there was a surge in U.S. troop numbers, and it may have appeared that an end to the war was in sight. By contrast, Labor support for the war, low to begin with, declined at a generally slower rate, to about one in every ten Labor voters in 2007.

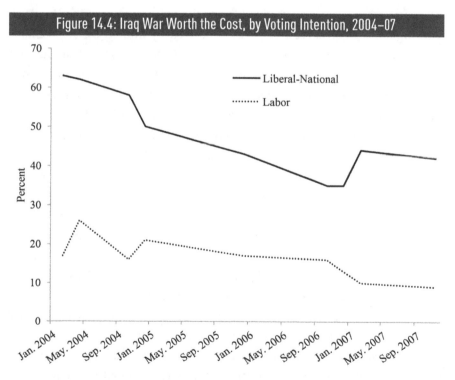

Figure 14.4: Iraq War Worth the Cost, by Voting Intention, 2004–07

Newspoll: "Overall, do you think it was worth going to war in Iraq or not?"
AES (October 2004, November 2007): "Taking everything into account, do you think the war in Iraq has been worth the cost or not?"

Sources: Newspoll; Australian Election Studies, 2004, 2007.

There was, then, a strong partisan element to the debate over the Iraq War, with individuals taking their cues from the views expressed by their own side of politics. Liberals, at least initially, strongly supported the war, while Labor supporters opposed it. Elite division effectively meant that it was unlikely there would be a consistent majority of the public in favour of military involvement. This sets Iraq apart from the other two major overseas military involvements of the postwar years, the Korean and Vietnam wars. A majority of the public supported participation in the Korean War throughout the 1950–53 period.[26] Participation in the Vietnam War became highly contentious by the late 1960s, but initial military involvement was based on a bipartisan consensus between the major parties.

EXPLAINING PUBLIC OPINION ON THE IRAQ WAR

There are four major explanations for public opinion toward the Iraq War, although any rigorous test of them is necessarily limited by the available data. This section uses the 2004 and 2007 AES surveys to test the four explanations. These two surveys provide more depth and continuity than is available in the commercial surveys, but they are obviously less contemporaneous with the beginning of the war in March 2003 and the immediate aftermath. Nevertheless, the surveys provide an important insight into what motivated the public's views of the war in 2004 and 2007, and have the added advantage of enabling us to gain a perspective on how opinions changed in the three-year period between the two elections.

The first hypothesis is that public opinion toward the war was influenced by views of the U.S. alliance. One of the reasons advanced by John Howard for participation in the war was the need to bolster the ANZUS alliance. Brendon O'Connor and Srdjan Vucetic also see the desire to secure U.S. loyalty as the key element in the government's decision.[27] Opinions on the U.S. alliance are measured by two questions: support for the ANZUS alliance itself, and trust in the United States to come to Australia's defence if it were ever attacked.

The second hypothesis sees public opinion being driven by potential security threats from other countries and by views about participation in the "war on terror." It is measured by the number of potential threats that respondents perceive from other countries and by support or opposition to participation in the U.S.-led "war on terror."

The third hypothesis is Mueller's "rally round the flag" effect. Once the war had commenced, this hypothesis predicts that the public would have felt the need to show its support for the military and for the operation the military is involved in, regardless of its earlier views about the justification for the war. This is measured by attitudes toward defence spending and whether defence is viewed as being stronger now than it was ten years earlier.

TABLE 14.4: Explaining Public Opinion toward the Iraq War, 2004 and 2007				
	2004		2007	
	b	beta	b	beta
U.S. Alliance				
Supports ANZUS	.15*	.11*	.10*	.08*
Trusts U.S. to defend Australia	.25*	.19*	.12*	.11*
Threats				
Threats from other countries	.04	.04	-.02	-.02
Supports participation in "War on Terror'	.15*	.14*	.18*	.21*
"Rally round the flag"				
Increase defence spending	.11*	.10*	.07	.07
Defence stronger than 10 years ago	.03	.02	.03	.03
Partisanship				
Coalition partisan	.32*	.13*	.13	.06
Howard rating	.09*	.29*	.09*	.35*
Latham/Rudd rating	-.05*	-.13*	-.04*	-.11*
Constant	.19		.51	
Adj R-squared	.61		.52	
N of respondents	1728		1840	

* statistically significant at p<.01, two-tailed.

Ordinary least squares regression equations showing partial (b) and standardized (beta) coefficients predicting the probability of supporting the Iraq War. For variables, scoring, and means, see the appendix table.

Sources: 2004, 2007 Australian Election Study surveys.

The final hypothesis relates to partisan divisions over the war and, more particularly, to the role of Howard's leadership and his close personal association with the decision to go to war. This is measured by the direction of respondents' partisanship and by their rating of Howard (in both 2004 and 2007) and of the two Labor leaders who contested the election, Mark Latham in 2004 and Kevin Rudd in 2007.

To test the four hypotheses, a regression equation was calculated for 2004 and 2007, using an exactly comparable set of variables.[28] Table 14.4 shows two figures: a partial (b) coefficient, which shows the change in the dependent variable caused by a unit change in an independent variable; and a standardized (beta) coefficient, which shows the relative weight of the particular variable within the equation. Since the variables within both equations are scored in the exactly same way, the partial coefficients are particularly valuable for comparing differences between 2004 and 2007, and the standardized coefficients for evaluating effects within the survey in question.

The results show one unequivocal finding: the strong and consistent effect of Howard's leadership on opinions toward the war. In both equations, Howard's rating is by far the most important variable; in 2004, for example, the standardized coefficient of 0.29 is similar to both measures of the U.S. alliance combined (.11 + .19 = .30). The strength of the leadership effect is also the same in both years, with a partial coefficient of 0.09. By contrast, views of the Labor leader in the particular election are of much lesser importance — usually about one-third as important.[29] Partisanship is about one-third as important as Howard's leadership in 2004 but fails to reach statistical significance in 2007. These results confirm the very strong association between John Howard in his role as prime minister and the decision to participate in the Iraq War.

The hypothesis that the public's views about the war were guided by a desire to consolidate links with the United States is also strongly supported by the survey evidence. The effect is strongest in 2004; by 2007 the impact of views about the alliance are about half as important but nevertheless remain statistically significant. There is also support for the threats hypothesis, although not in the context of security threats from other countries; what mattered to the public was views about the "war on terror." Indeed, between 2004 and 2007 the impact of views about the "war on terror" actually increased slightly. Finally, there is virtually no support for the hypothesis that there was a "rally round the flag" effect, at least measured by the public's views of defence spending and defence preparedness.

These results underscore the significance of leadership and, more specifically, Howard's period as prime minister, in shaping public opinion toward the Iraq War. This leadership effect remains even when partisanship is taken into account, suggesting that the decision to go to war was associated more with the personality of John Howard than with his political view of the world. This finding accords with Howard's personal association with the issue; he was in Washington when the 9/11 attacks took place and, based on this experience, invoked the ANZUS Treaty for the first time in its history. Howard also personally defended the decision to invade Iraq and took ultimate responsibility for it, even enduring a highly personal campaign from a former party colleague in 2004 aimed at ousting him from his seat.[30]

CONCLUSION

In order to engage in war, democracies require the tacit consent of their citizens. As the political scientists Dan Reiter and Allan Stam put it, "democracies win wars because of the offshoots of public consent and leaders' accountability to the voters."[31] While gaining the consent of the public for military action may appear burdensome, it also has the effect of ensuring that democratic leaders are wary of engaging in risky or hastily-planned conflicts. A leader who led her country into an ill-planned war that resulted in defeat could expect to be punished in the subsequent election. For example, British defeat in the Suez Crisis directly led to the resignation of the U.K. prime minister, Anthony Eden, while arguably the Vietnam War was an issue in Lyndon Johnson's decision not to contest the 1968 presidential election.

The requirement of popular support for war means that most of the major postwar conflicts that the main allies in the Iraq War — Australia, Britain, and the United States — have been involved in have attracted bipartisan support. In Britain, the Falklands conflict enjoyed overwhelming public support, and rescued Margaret Thatcher from almost certain defeat in the 1983 general election.[32] In the United States, the involvements in Korea, Vietnam, and Iraq all enjoyed majority public support, at least in their early stages. The Australian experience is more equivocal: Vietnam rapidly became a partisan and electoral issue, while, as we have seen, the Iraq War attracted majority support only when it commenced, and then only for a short period. Moreover, attitudes to the war deeply divided citizens along partisan lines.

The results presented here have confirmed the strong association between leadership and views of the Iraq War observed in other studies,[33] in this case centred on the personality of the prime minister, John Howard. While the decision to go to war in a parliamentary system is a collective one, in all important respects the public directly associated the decision with Howard, and accountability rested with him. A secondary consideration for citizens who supported the war was the desire to maintain the defence alliance with the United States. This is perhaps the most consistent justification for the war, since the surveys show that the public clearly did not believe that the major goal of the exercise — reducing the threat of terrorism — had been achieved.

The dynamics of Australian public opinion on Iraq, measured by a range of surveys over an extended period, suggest that citizens make rational calculations about the likelihood of success or failure and about the potential benefits if the goals are achieved: "public opinion about war is shaped by the same attitudes and orientations that shape domestic politics."[34] In this context, the Australian public saw the threat of terrorism from WMDs and the goal of supporting the United States as sufficient justifications for war; when WMDs could not be found, the sole justification for war was to maintain the U.S. alliance. Adding in trenchant Labor opposition to the war meant that majority support rapidly faded away.

NOTES

1.   In contrast to the United States and many European countries, there is relatively little research in Australia examining public opinion and its role in defence and foreign policy. However, see Ian McAllister, *Attitude Matters: Public Opinion Towards Defence and Security* (Canberra, ACT: Australian Strategic Policy Institute, 2005); Ian McAllister and Toni Makkai, "Changing Australian Opinion on Defence: Trends, Patterns, and Explanations," *Small Wars and Insurgencies* 2,

no. 3 (1992): 195–235; Ian McAllister and John Ravenhill, "Australian Attitudes Towards Closer Engagement with Asia," *Pacific Review* 11 (1998): 119–41; and Derek McDougall and Kingsley Edney, "Howard's Way? Public Opinion as an Influence on Australia's Engagement with Asia, 1996–2007," *Australian Journal of International Affairs* 64, no. 2 (2010): 205–24.

2. Murray Goot and Rodney Tiffen, "Public Opinion and the Politics of the Polls," in *Australia's Vietnam: Australia in the Second Indo-China War*, ed. Peter King (Sydney: Allen & Unwin, 1983).

3. Murray Goot, "Public Opinion and the Democratic Deficit," *Australian Humanities Review* (2003), https://web.archive.org/web/20080501220724/http://www.lib.latrobe.edu.au/AHR/archive/Issue-May-2003/goot.html (accessed August 15, 2014).

4. For accounts and interpretations, see, for example, Lloyd Cox and Brendon O'Connor, "Australia, the US, and the Vietnam and Iraq Wars: 'Hound Dog, not Lapdog,'" *Australian Journal of Political Science* 47, no. 2 (2012): 173–87; Goot, "Public Opinion and the Democratic Deficit"; Brendon O'Connor, "Perspectives on Australian Foreign Policy, 2003," *Australian Journal of International Affairs* 58, no. 2 (2004): 207–20.

5. The Australian Election Study survey is a national, post-election self-completion survey with the sample drawn randomly from the electoral register. All of the data are publicly available from the Australian Social Science Data Archive at the Australian National University (see http://assda.anu.edu.au/). The 2004 survey sampled 1,769 respondents with a response rate of 44.5 percent; the 2007 had a sample of 1,873 respondents and a response rate of 40.2 percent. Details of the commercial Newspoll surveys used in the analyses can be found at: www.newspoll.com.au. These surveys, conducted by telephone, typically have a sample of around one thousand respondents based on a random sample of the national adult population.

6. East Timor is excluded because it was a peacekeeping operation, not a military operation involving offensive military activity.

7. The surveys also consistently ask about trust in the United States to come to Australia's aid in the event of an attack. However, this question is strongly correlated with support for ANZUS, so in the interest of parsimony the latter question is used here. Both questions are used in the multivariate analyses in Table 14.4.

8. McAllister and Makkai, "Changing Australian Opinion," Figure 2.

9. There was a spike in threat perceptions during the first Gulf War in 1990–91, when more than half of the population thought there was a potential security threat. See Rachel Gibson and Ian McAllister, "Defence, Security and the Iraq War," in *Australian Social Attitudes 2: Citizenship, Work and Aspirations*, ed. David Denemark, Gabrielle Meagher, Shaun Wilson, Mark Western, and Timothy Phillips (Sydney: University of NSW Press, 2007), Figure 2.1. See also Murray Goot, "The Polls," in *Australia's Gulf War*, ed. Murray Goot and Rodney Tiffen (Melbourne: Melbourne University Press, 1992). This does now show up in the trend in Figure 14.1 since the spike occurred between the 1990 and 1993 Australian Election Study surveys.

10. See O'Connor, "Perspectives on Australian Foreign Policy, 2003"; and William Tow and Henry Albinski, "ANZUS — Alive and Well After Fifty Years," *Australian Journal of Politics and History* 48, no. 2 (2002): 153–73.

11. See Douglas C. Foyle, "Leading the Public to War? The Influence of American Public Opinion on the Bush Administration's Decision to Go To War in Iraq," *International Journal of Public Opinion Research* 16, no. 3 (2004): 269–94; Steven Kull, Clay Ramsay and Evan Lewis, "Misperceptions, the Media and the Iraq War," *Political Science Quarterly* 118, no. 4 (2004): 569–98; and Erik Voeten and Paul R. Brewer, "Public Opinion, the War in Iraq, and Presidential Accountability," *Journal of Conflict Resolution* 50, no. 5 (2006): 809–30.

12. See Morgan poll (www.roymorgan.com). The ANU poll (www.anu.edu.au/anupoll) also uses an open-question format for the most important issue and shows similar findings to the Morgan polls.

13. See Kull, Ramsay, and Lewis, "Misperceptions, the Media and the Iraq War;" and chapter 4 in Robert M. Entman, *Projections of Power: Framing News, Public Opinion and US Foreign Policy* (Chicago: University of Chicago Press, 2004).

14. John Howard's address to the National Press Club (speech, March 13, 2003), http://parlinfo.aph.gov.au/parlInfo/search/display/display.w3p;query=Id%3A%22media%2Fpressrel%2FPDS86%22 (accessed August 15, 2014).

15. John E. Mueller, *War, Presidents and Public Opinion* (New York: John Wiley & Sons, 1973).

16. Ibid., 21.

17. This pattern is similar to U.S. public opinion. See Kull, Ramsay, and Lewis, "Misperceptions, the Media and the Iraq War," 569.

18. "If Iraq is not effectively disarmed not only could she use chemical and biological weapons against her own people again, other rogue states would be encouraged to copy her, [and] the spread of those weapons would multiply the likelihood that terrorists would lay their hands on them." John Howard's address to the National Press Club, March 13, 2003.

19. Catherine McGrath, "Mick Keelty Pressured to Retract Terror Threat Comments," ABC, www.abc.net.au/am/content/2004/s1067491.htm (accessed August 15, 2014).

20. A Newspoll survey conducted in October 2001 found that 78 percent of Liberal-National supporters and 62 percent of Labor supporters supported Australian military involvement in the war. See www.newspoll.com.au.

21. See Ian McAllister, "Elections Without Cues: The 1999 Australian Republic Referendum," *Australian Journal of Political Science* 36, no. 2 (2001): 247–69. Other examples include morality issues, such as same-sex marriage.

22. Howard's address to the National Press Club, March 13, 2003; address by Simon Crean to Parliament on Iraq (speech, February 5, 2003), www.smh.com.au/articles/2003/02/04/1044318605090.html (accessed August 15, 2014).

23. "You Should Not Be Going: Crean to Troops," *Australianpolitics.com*, January 23, 2003, http://australianpolitics.com/news/2003/01/03-01-23a.shtml (accessed August 15, 2014).

24. Ibid.

25. "Howard Farewells HMAS Kanimbla," *Australianpolitics.com*, January 23, 2003, http://australianpolitics.com/news/2003/01/03-01-23.shtml (accessed August 15, 2014).

26. McAllister and Makkai, "Changing Australian Opinion," 203.

27. Brendon O'Connor and Srdjan Vucetic, "Another Mars-Venus Divide? Why Australia Said 'Yes' and Canada Said 'Non' to Involvement in the 2003 Iraq War," *Australian Journal of International Affairs* 64, no. 5 (2010): 526–48.

28. Earlier analyses used a range of socio-economic status variables as controls, such as gender, age, birthplace, education, and income, but these added little to the substantive results and were excluded on the grounds of parsimony.

29. Simon Crean, who was Labor leader from November 2001 to December 2003, was closely associated with Labor opposition to the war. His successor, Mark Latham, was also opposed to the war without U.N. endorsement, but he was less personally associated with Labor's decision.

30. The campaign used the slogan "Not Happy, John." Howard was opposed in his seat of Bennelong by a former Liberal Party president, John Valder, who became a trenchant critic of Liberal policy on Iraq, claiming Bush, Blair, and Howard were war criminals. See Michelle Grattan, "Not Happy, John: Angry Outsiders Take On Howard," *The Age*, July 28, 2004, www.theage.com.au/articles/2004/07/27/1090693960472.html (accessed August 15, 2014).

31. Dan Reiter and Allan C. Stam, *Democracies at War* (Princeton, NJ: Princeton University Press, 2002), 4; see also Adam J. Berinsky, *In Time of War: Understanding American Public Opinion from World War II to Iraq* (Chicago: University of Chicago Press, 2009).

32. Harold D. Clarke, William Mishler, and Paul Whiteley, "Recapturing the Falklands: Models of Conservative Popularity, 1979–83," *British Journal of Political Science* 20, no. 1 (2000): 63–81.

33. See, for example, Voeten and Brewer, "Public Opinion, the War in Iraq."

34. Berinsky, *In Time of War*, 2.

APPENDIX

AUSTRALIAN ELECTION STUDY SURVEYS

Variables, Scoring, and Means, 2004 and 2007				
			Means	
Variable	**Question**	**Scoring**	**2004**	**2007**
Approves of Iraq War	Now we want to ask you about the current war in Iraq. Do you approve or disapprove of the way John Howard handled the war in Iraq?	4=approve strongly, 3=approve, 2=disapprove, 1=disapprove strongly	2.40	2.27
Supports ANZUS	How important do you think the Australian alliance with the United States under the ANZUS Treaty is for protecting Australia's security?	4=very important, 3=fairly important, 2=not very important, 1=not at all important	3.26	3.22
Trusts U.S. to defend Australia	If Australia's security were threatened by some other country, how much trust do you feel Australia can have in the United States to come to Australia's defence?	4=great deal, 3=fair amount, 2=not very much, 1=none at all	3.02	3.01

Threats from other countries	In your opinion, are any of the following countries likely to pose a threat to Australia's security? ... Japan, United States, China, Vietnam, Malaysia, Indonesia.	Cumulative number of "very likely" mentions	.52	.52
Supports participation in "war on terror"	Please say whether you strongly agree, agree, disagree, or strongly disagree with each of the following statements.... Australia should provide military assistance for the war on terrorism?	5=strongly agree, 4=agree, 3=neither, 2=disagree, 1=strongly disagree	3.03	3.36
Increase defence spending	Do you think that the government should spend more or spend less on defence?	5=more much more, 4=spend some more, 3=about right, 2=spend less, 1=spend a lot less	2.54	3.46
Defence stronger than 10 years ago	Please say whether you strongly agree, agree, disagree, or strongly disagree with . . . the following [statement].... Australia's defence is stronger now than it was 10 years ago.	5=strongly agree, 4=agree, 3=neither, 2=disagree, 1=strongly disagree	3.47	3.49
Coalition partisan	Generally speaking, do you usually think of yourself as Liberal, Labor, National, or what?	1=Liberal or National, 0.5=minor party, none, 0=Labor	.44	.49
Leader ratings	Using a scale from 0 to 10, please show how much you like or dislike the party leaders. If you don't know much about them, you should give them a rating of 5.... John Howard.	0 to 10 scale	5.68	5.10
	... (2004) Mark Latham ... (2007) Kevin Rudd		5.04	6.31

ACKNOWLEDGEMENTS

By definition, a collective volume is the work of many hands. This is perhaps even more the case when, like with this one, it has its roots in a conference — one organized by two institutions, located on different continents on opposite sides of the equator. The 2013 conference in Canberra, from which this book sprang, could not have materialized without the administrative and logistical support of the Asia-Pacific College of Diplomacy at the Australian National University. We thank that institution and its then-director, William Maley, as well as the Bill Graham Centre for Contemporary International History at the University of Toronto, which provided helpful assistance on the Canadian side.

During the subsequent process of turning what was presented at that conference into a book, Srinjoy Bose provided much-appreciated research assistance. At the Graham Centre, John English was a source of well-judged advice.

Dominic Farrell of Dundurn Press and Natalie Meditsky ably edited the manuscript, while Elena Vardon performed an initial copy-edit and prepared the index.

We are grateful to all of our contributors for their hard work and patience in revising their conference papers. A distinctive feature of this collection is the presence of former policy-makers in its pages, and for that we thank the Right Honourable John Howard and the Right Honourable Jean Chrétien for permission to publish their remarks, as well as the Right

Honourable Malcolm Fraser, the Honourable Bill Graham, Paul Barratt, and moderator Melissa Conley Tyler for permission to reproduce the transcript of the memorable forum in which they took part.

Malcolm Fraser merits a special mention. He died during the later stages of this manuscript's preparation, and it is a source of keen regret to us that he has been deprived of the opportunity to read the end product. We vividly recall his energy, seriousness, and mordant wit at the Canberra conference, qualities he displayed over a long and noteworthy career that left its mark on contemporary Australia and the Commonwealth of Nations. It is with abiding respect that we dedicate this book to his memory.

CONTRIBUTORS

Paul Barratt is a former senior Australian public servant, and was secretary of the Department of Defence from 1998 to 1999. He is currently deputy chairman of the Co-operative Research Centre for Advanced Composite Structures and chairman of Australia 21.

John Blaxland is a senior fellow at the Strategic and Defence Studies Centre, the Australian National University. He also served as chief staff officer for Joint Intelligence Operations (J2) at Headquarters Joint Operations Command, and Australian defence attaché to Thailand and Burma. His publications include *Strategic Cousins* (2006).

The Right Honourable Jean Chrétien was prime minister of Canada from 1993 to 2003.

Roger Coate is Paul D. Coverdell Professor of Public Policy at Georgia College and State University, and distinguished professor emeritus of political science and former director of the Richard L. Walker Institute of International Studies at the University of South Carolina. He has published widely on international organizations and global governance.

Melissa Conley Tyler is national executive director of the Australian Institute of International Affairs.

Jack Cunningham is program coordinator at the Bill Graham Centre for Contemporary International History, in Trinity College and the Munk School of Global Affairs, at the University of Toronto.

John English is director of the Bill Graham Centre for Contemporary International History, and a former member of Parliament. His works of Canadian diplomatic and political history include biographies of Lester Pearson and Pierre Trudeau.

The Honourable Bill Graham is a former member of the Canadian Parliament, where he was chair of the Standing Committee on Foreign Affairs and International Trade; minister of foreign affairs; minister of national defence; and leader of the Opposition. He is now chancellor of Trinity College in the University of Toronto.

The Right Honourable John Howard was prime minister of Australia from 1996 to 2007.

William Maley is foundation director, Asia-Pacific College of Diplomacy, the Australian National University. His publications include *Rescuing Afghanistan* (2006) and *The Afghanistan Wars* (2009).

Ian McAllister is a distinguished professor of political science at the Australian National University. His publications include *The Australian Voter* (2011).

Kim Richard Nossal is director of the School of Policy Studies, Queen's University, Kingston, Ontario. His publications include *The Politics of Canadian Foreign Policy* (1997) and *The Patterns of World Politics* (1998).

Charles Sampford is director of the Institute for Ethics, Governance, and the Law, at Griffith University, in Australia. He is also a barrister and has published widely on the international rule of law.

Timothy Andrews Sayle is a postdoctoral fellow at Southern Methodist University's Centre for Presidential History. His doctoral dissertation in history, defended at Temple University, focused on NATO and transatlantic relations during the Cold War.

Ramesh Thakur is director of the Centre for Nuclear Non-Proliferation and Disarmament in the Crawford School of Public Policy, the Australian National University. A former United Nations assistant secretary-general, he is the editor-in-chief of *Global Governance*. His publications include *Nuclear Weapons and International Security: Collected Essays* (2015).

Hugh White is professor of strategic studies at the School of International, Political, and Strategic Studies, Australian National University. He has also been a senior official in the Australian Department of Defence and an adviser to Defence Minister Kim Beazley and Prime Minister Bob Hawke.

INDEX

Also in the Contemporary Canadian Issues Series

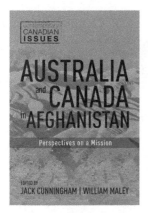

Australia and Canada in Afghanistan: Perspectives on a Mission

Edited by Jack Cunningham and William Maley

Afghanistan is a long way from both Canada and Australia, but from 2001, fate conspired to bring the three countries together. Following the attacks of September 11, 2001, Australia and Canada joined the U.S. and other Western allies in attacking al-Qaeda bases in Afghanistan.

Operation Enduring Freedom began on October 4, 2001, but this was only the beginning of a much longer engagement in Afghanistan for both Canada and Australia, with a legacy much more ambiguous than the initial campaign had promised.

Australia and Canada in Afghanistan: Perspectives on a Mission offers twelve essays from distinguished experts and decision-makers involved in the war. Wide-ranging in scope, their work offers fresh analyses of the Afghan War and on Australia's and Canada's contributions to it.

Jack Cunningham is the program coordinator of the Bill Graham Centre for Contemporary International History at the University of Toronto. He lives in Toronto.

William Maley is Professor of Diplomacy at the Asia-Pacific College of Diplomacy, Australian National University. He is an expert in Afghan politics, refugee issues, and modern diplomacy. He is a member of the Order of Australia and a Fellow of the Academy of the Social Sciences in Australia. He lives in Canberra, Australia.

Available at your favourite bookseller

 DUNDURN

VISIT US AT
Dundurn.com
@dundurnpress
Facebook.com/dundurnpress
Pinterest.com/dundurnpress